Longniddry Legacy

A HISTORY OF
LONGNIDDRY GOLF CLUB

1921-1996

CONTENTS

Page No.

DEDICATION

Apart from the Captain and Vice-Captain, there are normally nine Directors on the Board of Longniddry Golf Club.

This book is dedicated to those unsung Directors who have worked so hard and selflessly down the years for the benefit of Longniddry Golf Club and its members. Typical of them are the late Johnny Munro and Billie McNeill.

They all deserve our enduring respect and gratitude.

Published by Longniddry Golf Club Ltd.
Links Road, Longniddry EH32 0NL.
Printed in East Lothian by D&J Croal Ltd.
Designed and Illustrated by F. Ramos.
Film compilation by Origin Reprographics.
ISBN 0 9535366 0 2

FOREWORD

by the Right Honourable Earl of Wemyss and March, K.T., LL.D., D.UNIV., J.P.

President, Longniddry Golf Club Ltd.

Though not a golfer I am very proud to have been asked to contribute this foreword to the story of Longniddry Golf Course and Club.

I used to play a lot of golf; mainly on Kilspindie, often on Longniddry, occasionally on Gullane; and then in South Africa, where we had long wooden bars to scrape the "greens" a bit level before we putted. But I gave it up for the war, and have only played three times since, not in Scotland.

But surely few Golf Courses give one such natural beauty as Longniddry does, with its distant views of land and sea, its glorious green grass, and the fine trees, particularly the many Scots Pines. These are the remains of Boglehill Wood, whose very name reminds us of the Bogles and other evil spirits, and the witches and warlocks, that used to infest this area, as well as Tranent, North Berwick and elsewhere in the district, to the extent that King Jamie the Saxt himself was impelled to take a lively and personal interest.

And moreover I have, from time to time, had quite a lot to do with the Club and the running of it. I think my best memory (which is referred to in the text for the year 1954 in Chapter VI) was when we, the Estate, set the Club up again as an independent entity. James Rogers, the Factor, and I were worried that our "Proprietary" Club always lost money, and the Estate had to pay up. So we insisted, against some considerable opposition from senior men on the Committee, in making them become a proper Club with full financial responsibility. And so they did, in the early days of 1956.

Almost immediately the County Council said they wished to lay a sewer across the Golf Course. Consternation! But we said that they, the Golf Club, could keep whatever money came as compensation. This gave some comfort; and even more when it turned out that, through receiving this compensation, they actually made a profit of over £70. And before then I joined Mackenzie Ross in laying out new holes for an altered Golf Course, after war time cultivation of the east end had ceased. He had a marvellous pair of legs: every pace they took was exactly one yard, so he measured as he walked.

I congratulate the writers of this history and feel sure that it will be much enjoyed by members and others.

Wemyss

Author's Note

Having light-heartedly agreed in persuasive company to undertake a history of Longniddry Golf Club, I gradually came to recognise the magnitude of the task. As a 1964 incomer I had very little knowledge of Longniddry or its Golf Course outside my own period and my own circle. The process of research has been all the more fascinating and absorbing in consequence.

In thought at least, I have been transported world-wide, as I followed the fortunes of Longniddry Golf Club members. I have found connections with Oklahoma, India, Norway, Kenya and the Sudan. On the playing side I discovered that Longniddry has housed an Open Champion, a British Boys Champion and a British Girls Champion, at least three Walker Cup players and two Scottish Ladies Amateur Champions. A notable symmetry testifies to the quality of the Club's players: At the outset the membership included a Scottish Ladies Champion and a Walker Cup player in Charlotte Stevenson and W B Torrance. It is remarkable that Hilary Monaghan and Raymond Russell justify the same boast 75 years later.

During my researches I have been privileged to have had talks and interviews with many helpful and patient people. These are gratefully acknowledged and all (hopefully) listed elsewhere. Throughout I have had generous support and encouragement from all sides and particularly from Tom Porteous whose original concept the history was and who had already gathered useful information. Included in the acknowledgments list are three persons who deserve special mention: these are, Club member designer and illustrator 'Chico' Ramos and his friend Dave Hall, a graphic artist. The third is reprographics designer and Club member Douglas McIntyre. Together they have created this most attractive and professional presentation of the narrative.

Unfortunately the club records are incomplete. I found myself lacking detailed information about the early years, whilst near to overwhelmed with the more recent material. The overall length of the text has troubled me. I had been advised to shorten it and felt that I should do so. I found however in attempting this that the sense of change through the years and the compilation of a reasonably comprehensive record of events were both damaged by abbreviation. In the end I decided to leave the text, lengthy as it is, in the interests of the historical record.

Each Chapter has been designed as a 'stand alone'. For this reason occasional repetitions may be found. There may also be errors and omissions, and if so I apologise; I have tried to cross check my information.

Aerial view of
Longniddry and its Golf
Course taken about
1966 by Club Member
Stanley Hunter.

It will be understood that there can be conflicting recollections of events.

Over the years Longniddry Golf Club has been to me a constant source of pleasure and regeneration. To be found there are all the delights of our wonderful native game and a social environment of ready comradeship and good humour. I hope that members will derive enjoyment from this account of the Club and will find pleasant memories revived.

Let us hope that the quality of our unique golf course and the social harmony of our membership can be sustained long into the future.

Alastair M Mackechnie, May 1998.

Vice Presidents and Captains
Jubilee Year 1996

Right:
Vice President,
Tom Porteous

Far right:
Lady Vice President,
Kath Rose

Right:
Jubilee Captain, Gordon
Bonnington

Far right:
Jubilee Lady Captain,
Susan Bell

INTRODUCTION

*I*n 1972, Peter Dobereiner, reporting in the 'Observer', described Longniddry as a lovely course with a real sting in the tail and a jewel of a fifth hole. The occasion was the Pringle World Seniors Championship when Slammin' Sam Snead beat Britain's Ken Bousfield for the title over 36 holes.

Although the Longniddry Club was inaugurated in 1921, golf has been played in the vicinity for many centuries. King James V used to visit Gosford for golf and archery. (This was just 100 years after his great grandfather, James II had ruled that 'golf and futbal be utterly criet doun'.) James V was called 'the gaberlunzie king'. He was light-hearted, popular and licentious with as great a reputation as a lecher as his better-known contemporary Henry VIII.

The following extract from an article by Ian Stuart carried in 'Scotland's Magazine' published by the Scottish Tourist Board in January 1975 gives a brief account of Longniddry Golf Course and its history.

'Longniddry lies near the western end of that chain of great links bordering the Lothian shore from Dunbar in the East to Prestonpans in the West. A comparatively young course by the standards of those parts, it tends to be overshadowed by Muirfield and Gullane, but it has a history longer than theirs and those who know it regard it with affection. Which is hardly surprising, for it provides fine golf in a delightful setting.

The road from Aberlady runs by Gosford House and the sands of Gosford Bay until a lane turns off by the sixth green and leads inland. The old village where John Knox is said to have been a tutor is almost submerged under a tide of modern houses, but in the 14th century this was part of the Luffness lands held by Edward III of England and later by the Red Douglases.

Probably no one knows when golf was first played there, but only a mile or two down the road is Seton Castle, built in the 18th century to replace the palace that was a favourite refuge of Mary, Queen of Scots. Much has been written about her playing golf "over fields of Seton" within a few days of Darnley's murder in 1567. The report was almost certainly started by her enemies, but it suggests that golf must have been played there by the mid-16th century.

Two hundred years later, when the seat of the Earls of Wemyss and March was at Amisfield House just outside Haddington, there was already a

The satirist David Lyndsay whom King James V tolerated, cynically observed that the real attraction at Gosford was three local ladies surnamed Weir, Sandilands, and Oliphant. Lyndsay's advice to his Monarch was as follows:

"Sow not your seed in Sandylands

Spend not your strength in Weir

And ride not on an Elephant

For spoiling o' your gear"

1

golfing tradition in the family, and the 7th Earl made a practice of riding over to Gosford to play on the links. Eventually he bought land there to be nearer the golf and appointed Robert Adam , then engaged on Seton Castle, to design a mansion to replace the smaller house that stood on it.

Work was begun in 1790, but the Earl never lived at Gosford, maintaining that the stone made it too damp. Adam died in 1792 before the house was finished and the 8th Earl had part of the completed work dismantled. Later there was a plan to demolish the rest, but it came to nothing, and in 1870 the 10th Earl decided to finish the mansion as his ancestor and Adam had intended.

He appointed an architect named Young to supervise the work. Little known at the time, in later years (sic) Young was to design Glasgow's Municipal Buildings. At Gosford he resisted the Victorian passion for 'improvements' and remained true to Adam's concept. The house was finally completed in 1891, just over a hundred years after it was begun.

Perhaps the Earls of Victorian and Edwardian days did not inherit their ancestor's enthusiasm for golf, or perhaps they played the game somewhere else. Whatever the reason, the Longniddry Golf Club was not formed until 1921. At first there were plans for a course near the house, but in the end a site farther off , though still on the estate, was chosen and the Earl engaged H.S. Colt to design an 18-hole course there. One of the great golf architects, Colt laid out the High Course at Moor Park about the same time.

Since then alterations have been made to Longniddry in which James Braid and Mackenzie Ross, the man responsible for restoring Turnberry after the war, had a hand, but the course remains much as Colt planned it. The Clubhouse was built of stone salvaged from a house on the Amisfield estate.

In 1956 the club, which until then had been administered as part of the Gosford Estate, was handed over to the members with the Earl as President. In recent years the club became the first in the area to permit golf on Sundays.

Although the course is short by modern standards, measuring 6,301 yards from the medal tees, a number of championships and major tournaments have been played here, including the Pringle of Scotland Seniors in 1970 and 1972, the British Senior Women's and the first Carling Caledonian tournament in 1961 when Tom Haliburton and Bernard Hunt both broke *the existing course record with rounds of 64, but lost the event to Christy O'Connor.*

The prettiest part of Longniddry is where the fifth fairway turns left between fine trees and the green is perched high between bunkers and woodland. After the short sixth the next four holes lie across the lane.

These four holes go straight out and back, but across the road again at the eleventh the character of the course changes and it becomes more open and sandy. After the tricky short thirteenth there is a long par four with two small burns crossing the fairway and the sixteenth, modelled on the Road Hole at St Andrews. So back to the eighteenth green below the clubhouse.'

Mr Stuart's 1975 article is a very fair thumb-nail sketch of Longniddry Golf Course and its background. A few editorial remarks are appropriate:

Some changes have taken place since 1975. Gordon Durward is long gone, but fondly remembered and his protègè the friendly John Gray presides in his place. On the course some of the valued trees have fallen, casualties in the battle against Dutch Elm disease – their young replacements not yet dominant.

The Earl of Wemyss has pointed out that William Young designed Glasgow City Chambers *before* he was chosen for Gosford by the tenth Earl for that reason among others. Lord Wemyss also advises that although the family moved into Gosford for Christmas 1890 the Roman date on the arch in the Marble Hall reads 1891 (MDCCCXCI) which gives a better balance to the lettering than MDCCCXC would have done.

Finally it has been established that it was the 15th and not the 16th green which had originally been modelled on the Road Hole at the Old Course.

The following chapters attempt to give a description of Longniddry Golf Club as it is now and as it was originally, together with an account of its origins and developments up to the end of 1996.

Originally three holes at Longniddry were on the seaward side of the road, one of which, according to Gordon Durward (professional at the Club for 23 years), was 'a grand short hole'. At that time the course must have been nearer a true links than it is today; nowadays the first ten holes are almost parkland in character. It is this effect of playing golf in a sylvan setting that is one of the charms of the course.

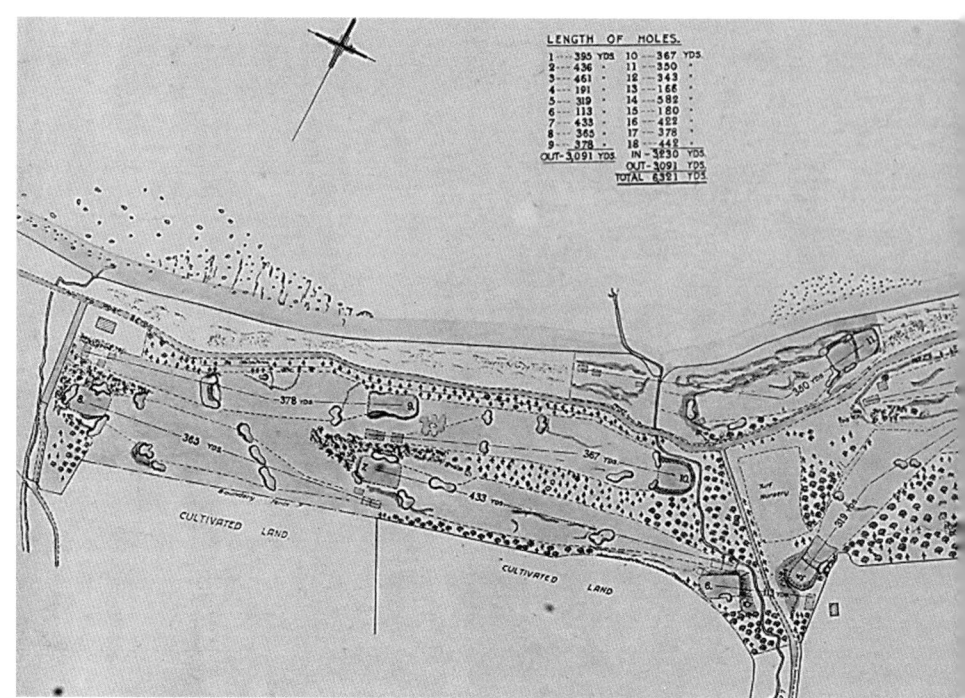

A.F. Simpson's 1930 drawing of the original Golf Course.

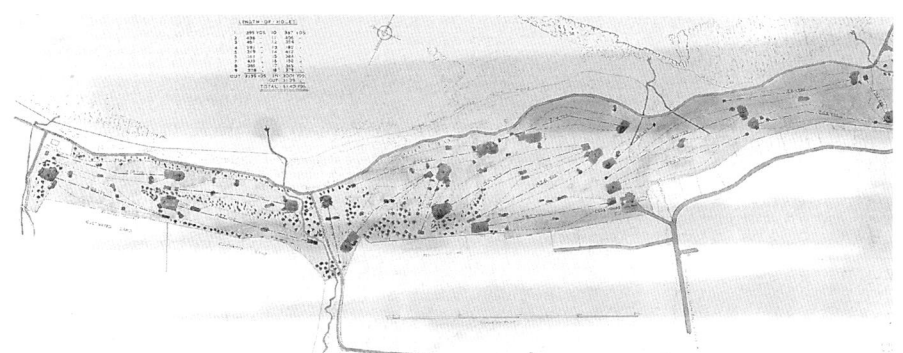

P. Mackenzie Ross's 1946 drawing of the reconstructed Course.

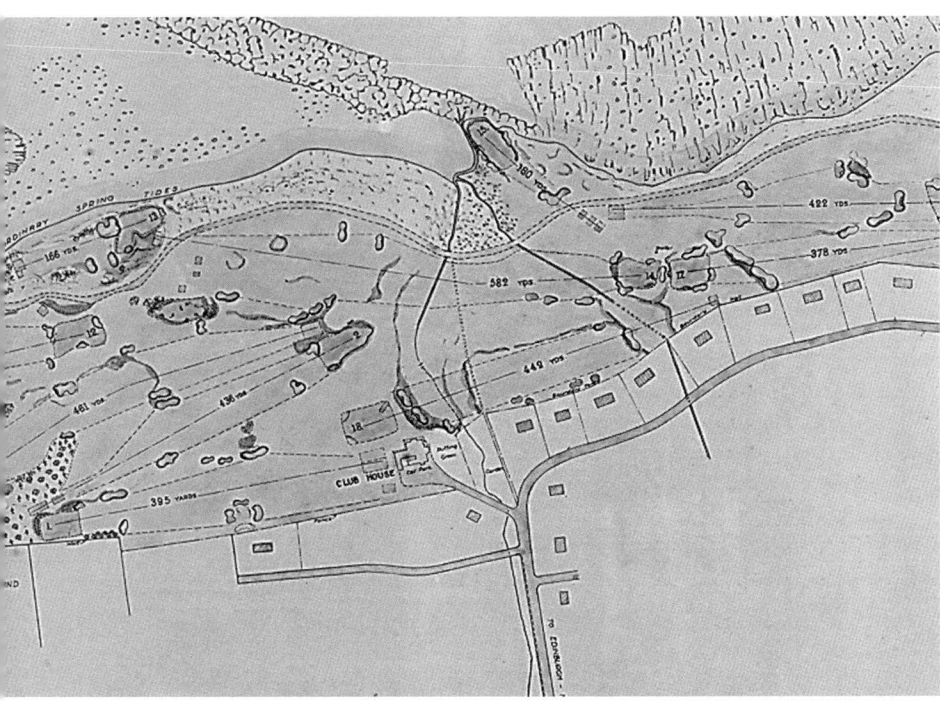

CHAPTER I
LONGNIDDRY GOLF COURSE AND
GREENKEEPING STAFF PAST AND PRESENT

Writing in 1988, Robert Price, a Welsh geologist domiciled in Scotland said in his book, *'Scotland's Golf Courses'* *"The Longniddry Golf Course is rather different from the other links courses in East Lothian. Although it sits on a sand-covered raised beach, and is backed by a fossil cliff line of the post-glacial sea (formed about 6000 years ago) there are sections of the course which are of a parkland character with some fine Scots Pines and various deciduous trees."*

The original Longniddry Course was designed by Harry Colt. For over 20 years he had been a leading golf course architect. The first course which he designed was Rye, described by Robert Green in his Illustrated History as 'a superb English links on the Sussex coast'. Green continues on Colt's career:

"His expertise on the use of sandhills there (Rye) was so well appreciated that he was able to quit his reluctant vocation, the law, to realise his ambition to become a golf course architect. He accepted the position of Secretary at the newly opened Sunningdale Club in 1901 .... Colt was a master. He later designed Swinley Forest, Stoke Poges, St. George's Hill, both courses at Wentworth and the New Course at Sunningdale. The fact

In 1975 Christie O'Connor was talking to Captain Dan Abbot after winning the British Seniors Competition.
"The trouble is",
said Captain Abbot, "we have no par 5s."
"No" said Christie "but you've a lot of very good four and seven eighths".

that he was chosen to lay out the Eden Course at St. Andrews is an indication of the esteem in which he was held. He did other admirable work too, including the extensive revision of both courses at Royal Portrush and the building of le Touquet in France, Kennemer in Holland, Falkenstein at Hamburg and Puerta de Hierro at Madrid."

The earliest drawing of the Longniddry course to hand is dated 1930 and signed A F Simpson, who was Club Captain in 1936 and Club Champion on three occasions. It appears to depict the holes as they were first laid out, but there are some small discrepancies when compared with an earlier description of the course published in 1928. Probably these simply reflect a remeasurement at some time. Generally a few yards have been added to some holes: the giant 14th increasing from 576 yards in 1928 to 582 in 1930 for example; but the change in the last is more substantial: from 334 in 1928 to 442 yards in Simpson's drawing. Today it is measured at 433.

During the war, the entire course east of the right of way across the present 14th and 18th fairways was ploughed up for food production. The original Board Minute declared an intention of somehow preserving the greens in this section, but this evidently proved impractical. The outcome can be seen by comparing the respective positions of the 14th and 17th greens. The pre-war plan shows them aligned east/west, whereas nowadays the greens are side by side, on a north/south axis.

A feature of the original course was the large-sized greens. Three were two-tiered. This green design is rarely used nowadays but a surviving example (now that it has been restored) is Longniddry's 5th.

With the eastern part of the course under cultivation only 15 holes were played. The first five of these were in accordance with Simpson's drawing as were the seventh to the thirteenth inclusive. The sixth had already been changed in 1933 and the fourteenth was shortened from its 582 yards by the construction of a new green which sat in the depression on the fairway between the first burn (The Cadger) and the right of way. The 15th hole was played to the present 18th green from a tee about 150 yards away which can still be seen on the north side of the 18th fairway.

After the war a significant reconstruction of the course was carried out by Mr Mackenzie Ross and his design remains substantially unchanged. Philip Mackenzie Ross had been apprentice to golf course architect Tom Simpson. He joined forces with Cecil Hutchison and among other projects, resurrected Turnberry after the war. His drawing dated 1946 shows the amended course plan and contains a few intriguing items. For example, the 2nd hole is shown as 436 yards whereas it has always been at about its present length: 410 yards in 1928, and 416 yards now, whilst the 12th hole is given as 354 yards against its present measure of 381.

Dick Burge, Club Champion in 1993 has said: *"There isn't a poor hole on the course. They are all good"* They are worth considering individually:

The hole is named after Longniddry's highly regarded professional Gordon Durward OBE. The green is said to have been twice driven by founder member George Mitchell. There is no record of anyone else approaching this feat and there has been speculation as to the circumstances. One thing is certain, and that is that the length of the hole has not varied significantly since opening day. Today's figure with all the authority of modern technology declares 398 yards as in 1928. What has changed is the addition of the small pot bunker beside the green at 7 o'clock. This was added at Gordon Durward's suggestion for two reasons: firstly it would tend to direct shots away from the gardens lining the fairway and secondly it would block a slope-assisted slightly easier route into the green. It is said that Gordon experimented for some hours by throwing golf balls towards the green before deciding exactly where the bunker should be.

From the first fairway wonderful views over the Firth of Forth are seen on the right, whilst the left-hand side is lined with notable and attractive houses. Immediately off the tee to the left stands 'Namara'. In the 50's its name was 'Dormie' and it was occupied by the then Club Secretary 'Lawrie' Lawrence. Subsequently for a time its owner was Ronnie Clutterbuck who laid out in the garden a most impressive model railway system.

Clashfarquar (previously "Blackness") is the next house in the row. It is so arranged that it has windows which survey the prospect across the course to the west, and others which stare in a supervisory fashion at the Clubhouse and first tee. This was the home for many years of Dr. Ian Forbes, a most successful and dedicated Director and later Captain of the Club.

The next dwelling 'Hestan' was once the home of 'Babs' Thomson of Scottish Brewers. 'Babs' was Lady Captain 1964/65. The house is now occupied by Club Members Tom and Nanette Jarron. The eastern neighbour to 'Hestan', is 'Brockhouse Green' and beside it is the mansion built for Stuart Forsyth head of R.W.Forsyth, an important Scottish retailer, in the 1920's. Stuart Forsyth, was the first full Captain of the Club. The house was originally called 'Jock's Lodge.' Nowadays it comprises three dwellings: Rosemount, Claremount and Norwood. The ground to the west of the house on which the recently built Glenholme stands, was originally a paddock for a pony belonging to Stuart's young nephew.

Returning to the Golf Course proper, it is an encouraging thought to players who have started badly that Max Faulkner's record-equalling round of 64 in 1970 began with a six at this hole.

1ST HOLE

DURWARD
398 yards – Par4

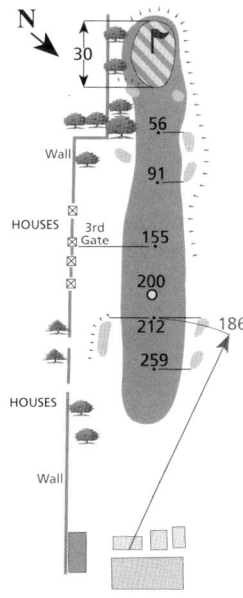

Diagrams by courtesy of Birdie Golf Productions

2ND HOLE

FAIRWAYS
416 yards Par 4

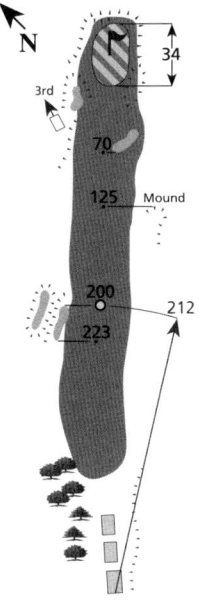

The 2nd hole turns back eastwards to the elevated green 416 yards away, or 410 by 1928 reckoning. The drive is from a high tee to a fairway parallel to the first, but perhaps 20 feet below it. Presumably the sloping rough between the first and second fairways conceals the beginning of the fossil cliff mentioned by Mr Price.

From the tee this hole looks straightforward and benign. A broad fairway, a wide green, only 3 bunkers in sight........ On reflection though, these bunkers are well-placed. A lateral one on the left 200-odd yards from the green complemented by a transverse companion on the right at 70 yards. The third trap, a deep greenside pot bunker at 7 o'clock is balanced at the right hand corner of the green by a protecting mound. The surface of the green itself is just faintly convex in parts with a little six foot high precipice on either side so that a ball running at an angle to the long axis is induced ever so gently to topple over the edge. Not that the shot down the centre line is so straightforward. At 34 yards the green is one of the longest on the course. It is at this point, contemplating the approach shot, that players remember that they should have checked the position of the flag from the first tee. This thought is followed by the realisation that a similar opportunity with respect to the 3rd green was passed up on the 2nd tee.

The story is told that on one occasion balls from the second and third tees collided in flight somewhere over the second fairway.

3RD HOLE

PENTLANDS
416 yards Par 4

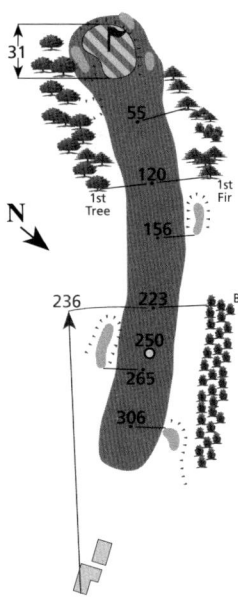

There are no arguments about this hole – all versions give the length as 461 yards. Measuring 443 yards for the ladies, it is the longest hole on the course for both sexes. The profile descends from the ridge of the 2nd green in a long westward slope with the line to the hole curving steadily to the left. From the tee, five peaks of the Pentland Hills can be seen on the western horizon. From left to right they are Carnethy, Turnhouse, Castle Law, Caerketton and Allermuir.

The fairway looks wide enough, but the average male player taking too direct a line can find that the ball has been thrown sideways by the camber of the ground into the deep bunker on the left. For the ladies, on the other hand, the right hand bunker is a greater hazard as the ground off the tee curves to the right and the ball hit apparently straight down the centre line scurries across to the trap like a rabbit to its burrow. Beyond this bunker is a solid wall of sea buckthorn. This has caught even the best of us. Sam Snead, playing for position perhaps, in the morning round of the 1972 World Seniors Championship drove into the buckthorn and lost his ball.

The 3rd green nowadays is pretty straightforward, but not so long ago it contained a depression at the 8 o'clock position which often diverted the ball into the waiting left hand greenside bunker. Interestingly both the 1930 and 1946 drawings show a sand bunker about 100 yards from the green on the left-hand side of the fairway just at the end of the trees. True enough a bunker did exist there until the early 50's. There is still a grassy mound which marks its position. There is also a mysterious depression on the left-hand side of the fairway on the approach to the green, about 20 yards out, but this is not recorded as having been a bunker at any time.

The dominant feature from the elevated 4th tee is Largo Law the high point of the ridge on the horizon across the Firth. Lower Largo, the fishing village which can just be made out on the waterfront below the Law was the home of Alexander Selkirk (the original Robinson Crusoe). Before that, Largo housed the Scottish High Admiral Andrew Wood who kept the Firth of Forth clear of English marauders for King James IV

Dropping the eye to the golf course, the 4th green below is just under 200 yards away. The line of the hole is north west from the high tee in the trees to the well-guarded green, normally through a fierce westerly crosswind. Comparing the present hole with the old photographs it is noticeable that although most of the trees on the right of the green seem to have survived, the single oak tree on the left beside the 5th tee is the only one remaining of a line of four originals. Between the bunker and the 5th tee, three young laburnums are struggling to establish themselves as replacements. The other change has been the lengthening of the hole a distance of 8 yards by taking the men's medal tee further back against the wall of Dr Bill Pollock's garden. One of the concerns over the years has been whether players should be asked to delay their tee shots until the 5th tee is clear. No action has been taken, since on competition days there is already sufficient delay at this hole. A protective netting has been tried but proved unsuccessful.

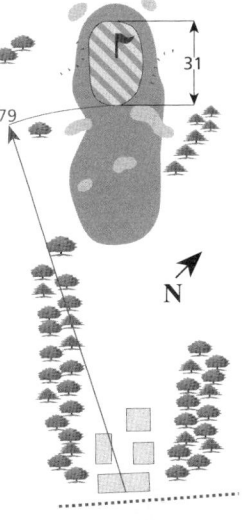

4TH HOLE

LARGO
199 yards Par 3

1920's photograph of the 4th hole from the tee.

5TH HOLE

CADELL'S NEUK
314 yards Par 4

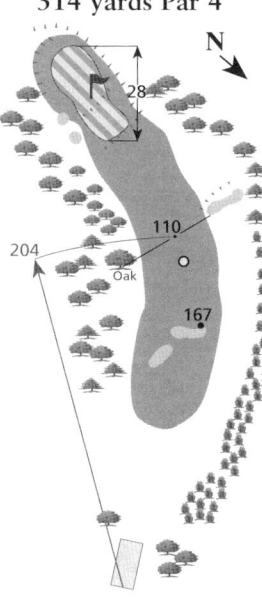

The 5th has been said to be the best hole on the course and has been praised by both Peter Alliss and Peter Dobereiner. A left hand dog-leg, 314 yards long, the hole demands a carefully placed drive and second shot avoiding bunkers and encroaching trees to an uphill elevated two-tier green. For the ladies the combination of a threatening large rose bush off right and a conspiracy of cross bunkers 100 yards away make the tee shot particularly formidable. The very long and brave player, can – in the right conditions – cut the corner. Abe Mitchell, in 1923, having casually asked where the green was, put his drive over the trees onto its lower tier. The green is cunningly protected with bunkers on the front left, a severe nearly vertical slope on the right, and behind, a diabolical little depression curving round the top to catch the over-strong shot.

The making of this green was one of the most expensive operations in the construction of the course. In recent years its original two-tier nature (abandoned in 1937) has been restored, increasing considerably the difficulty of the hole.

Overlooking the green is a substantial house with distinctive curvilinear gables. It was designed by Sir Frank Mears. The Cadell sisters, after whom the hole is named, are thought to have taken up residence in the late 20's. The ladies kept Chinese pheasants and for many years they maintained a Gentian nursery at the south of the house and often displayed rock plants at the Royal Horticultural Society in London. The Cadell family was long connected with the district and was at the forefront of the Scottish industrial revolution, collaborating with such as James Watt and James Murdoch in the development of gasmaking, iron and steelfounding etc.

1920's photograph of the 5th fairway and green under construction

The famous Scottish painter, Francis Campbell Cadell (1883-1937) was a member of the family. Perhaps the most distinguished was Colonel Thomas Cadell, reported to be the only holder of the VC in East Lothian. He won the award for conspicuous gallantry as a young Lieutenant of 21 at the siege of Delhi during the Indian mutiny. He died in 1919 at the age of 83. His son Sir Patrick Cadell followed the family tradition of service in India.

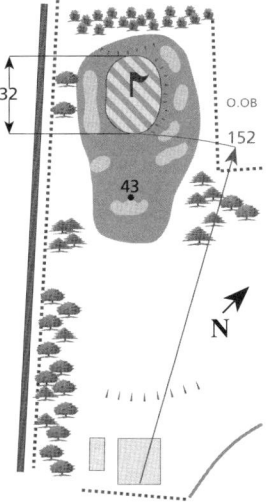

Originally the sixth hole was played westwards over the 'Dean Road' and Canty Burn from the existing high tee above the 5th green. (Presumably this is the top of Mr Price's fossil cliff). The green was at the same level as the tee, across the road 113 yards away. "A niblick shot"according to British Girls Champion Nancy Jupp. In 1933, possibly in reaction to a fatal accident elsewhere on the course, the line of the hole was altered by 90° to run northwards to the present low-level green.

The columns of the Haddingtonshire Courier record that John McCredie, Club Captain in 1937, achieved a remarkable and unrepeatable record at this hole. John was an Edinburgh car sales executive. Playing the original hole across the road in March 1933 in a fourball match he got a hole in one. Although not certain, it is highly likely that this was the last ace scored at the old hole. Two months later John, in the Longniddry Open, playing the new hole parallel to the road got another ace. It must also be extremely likely that this was the first hole in one at the new hole.

The transition from the old to the new hole seems to have been protracted. The ladies Minutes in September 1934 record a request that the flag be left in the old hole (which was still the LGU hole) when the new one was in temporary use at weekends. The request was refused. For many years the men's medal tee for the later 'Dean' hole was on the west side of the little plateau against the fence above the road. In recent years it has been moved across towards the garden wall and further back, so that the shot is now played over the 5th green – a distance of 168 yards to a very well-bunkered (7 of them) target.

Attractive features of the hole are the tight group of six magnificent Scots Pines on the left hand side of the fairway, and the spectacular views, particularly on a summer sunset, through the trees to Fife.

7TH HOLE

GORSE RIDGE
430 yards Par 4

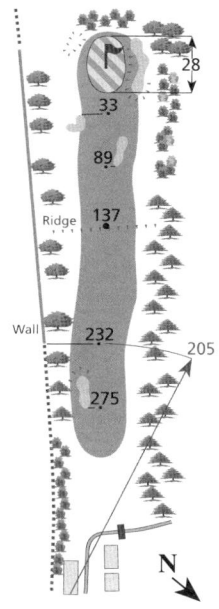

At 430 yards for the men and 420 for the ladies, 'Gorse Ridge' may not be the longest hole on the course, but with stroke index 1 for both, it is certainly one of the most formidable.

The path from the 6th green to the 7th tee crosses the 'Dean Road' on to the western section of the course. The men's and ladies' tees are separated by the Canty burn which winds between them and turns, in a gully, across the front of the ladies' tee. The path crosses the burn on an attractive bridge erected in 1990 on behalf of C. Sheila Mackay in memory of her uncle Joseph Mitchell. He had been the Edinburgh City Water Engineer and a 'weel-kent' member of the club for 41 years. Joseph was also a member of Murrayfield and he played Longniddry chiefly at weekends.

Until recently the men's back tee was dominated by a beautiful overhanging elm, now sadly gone, as are most of the elms on the course. Unseen on the south side of the men's tee, and above it, the depression of the original 6th green still exists, as does the old 7th tee. The name of the hole is taken of course, from the gorse bushes chiefly on the right approaching the green and from the cross fairway ridge 137 yards out. A century ago the 'ridge' was the track for horse-drawn carts which would collect coal from the surface drift mine which existed in the field to the south. (Under the corresponding bunker at the 10th hole, foundations of what may have been a weighbridge office, have been found.)

Trees line both sides of the 7th fairway: mostly deciduous on the left and Scots Pines on the right. The gap in the pines caused by the January storm of 1968 can still be seen filled at present by fast growing disposable Cypresses with young Scots Pines, the long term replacements, slowly maturing between them.

One of the features of the seventh hole is the cleverly-placed lateral bunker in the centre of the fairway 90 yards from the green. It, and its evil companion on the left of the fairway 30 yards out, pose a serious threat to those who have taken the soft-option, right-hand route to the green. The player who is long and brave enough to drive over the left-hand side of the threatening transverse bunker 160 yards from the tee, finds an open line clear of trouble for his second shot to the green.

The 8th hole is named after the family which fought so hard for Scottish independence down the centuries. One member, it is said, while acting as governor of Berwick saw the English hang two of his sons before his eyes rather than surrender the town to the enemy. The Setons were among the most loyal supporters of that early lady golfer Mary Queen of Scots. Perhaps the "fields of Seton" on which she is said to have played just after her husband's murder, included Longniddry's 8th.

The hole is 367 yards long and demands a well-placed long-carrying drive over two transverse echeloned fairway bunkers. These are deep bunkers and tenancy usually costs a shot. Not always though. Some years ago, George Bonnar put his ball on to the green with a 6 iron from the right hand one. The chief validation for this story is that it is told by Ron Herkes, his still slightly incredulous opponent. In the past there was a third bunker in this group on the left hand side. Mercifully this was changed to a grass bunker by a soft hearted greenkeeper some years ago on the request of the ladies and to the relief of many anonymous men. Beyond these cross bunkers the fairway is one of the most lush on the course suggesting a different underlying soil.Those members who played in the 50's can still recall the smell of the pigs who grazed in the field on the left. Apparently the play of the hole was significantly faster in consequence. Proliferation of mushrooms occurred at one time down the left hand side near the fence . A successful second shot westward either over one of the guarding bunkers, or through the throat between them to the tree-ringed green, is one of the most satisfying of the round.

8TH HOLE

SETON
367 yards Par 4

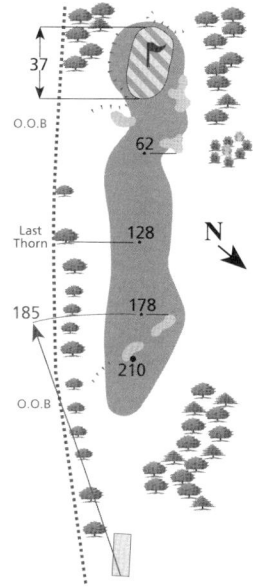

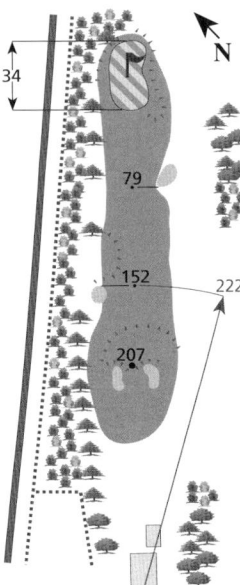

The 9th hole, turns back eastward 374 yards to an elevated green sitting close to the left-hand boundary fence. The drive from the tee of the ninth hole is required to carry over a central mound flanked on either side by deep bunkers. In Simpson's drawing, these are shown joined as a single massive cross-fairway hazard. The hole tends to be played as a slight dog-leg because a ball hit left of centre can be thrown sideways towards the line of buckthorn. The roots of the buckthorn are restrained by corrugated iron sheets inserted parallel to the fence to a depth of about ten feet below ground. The gorse bushes from which the hole takes its name are to be seen in season as a mass of bright yellow beyond the ridge on the right. The green at 34 yards is one of the longest on the course protected at the front right by a 10 foot-high mound. The left-hand approach was at one time dominated by a magnificent Scots Pine. Unfortunately, it fell in one of the winter storms about 20 years ago.

A remarkable match-play coincidence occurred at this hole in two club championships 18 years apart. In 1965 Alex Harvey met Lawrie Reilly (that predatory international centre forward) in the semi-final and the match went to the 27th hole where Alex won. He went on to win the final against Peter Burt. In 1983 Alex and Lawrie met again in the semi-final. Once again the match went to the 27th hole; the result was the same with Lawrie defeated once more. This time Alex went on to beat Ken Archibald in the final. Lawrie was not completely denied however, because between these two occasions in 1970 he won the championship himself.

Alongside the 9th teeing ground there are some dwellings which are of interest. The most easterly is the most recent, constructed during 1994/95. The Club chose not to oppose the planning proposal for this house on the understanding that none of the trees existing at the site were to be damaged. The two older buildings comprise what is now a bungalow and a semi-detached villa. They were both built by Richard Baillie's construction firm in the 1920's for the use of his family. Richard's choice of location was criticised by his mother who always considered that the bottom of Lyars Road would have been a more sensible site. The bungalow is now the home of Victor and Mary Elliott, but it was originally a tea room and confectioners. In the 1920's it consisted of a large dining room presumably with kitchen and toilets. It was called 'The Seton Dean Tea Gardens' although to the family it was known as 'the big tea room'. It was run by Richard Baillie's mother Margaret and her youngest daughter, also Margaret (Mary Elliott's mother) who married a William Broadfoot from Glasgow.

The tea room enjoyed wonderful prospects over the Firth to Fife and a handy location en route to Gosford and North Berwick. For those privileged enough to own a motor car in those days it would have been a popular eating place. There must have been a number of elegant and affluent customers. Some of the Astor family were said to be among the clientele for example together with Balfours and Lyttletons. In the late 30's the tea room was reduced in size when the building was modified to provide a shop and living accommodation for Margaret Broadfoot and her family. The smaller tea room still prospered though. Mary Elliot particularly remembers among the many customers the 'Bookmaker Group' who played at the Golf Course; ladies in elegant expensive coats and frocks and the well dressed men stepping out of impressive and powerful cars. On hot summer days Margaret Broadfoot would take a table outside to the edge of the Golf Course and sell refreshments to the players. Billie Reekie was Club Captain during 1972/73. His playing membership began in 1947 and was still going strong half a century on. He remembers the quiet Sunday mornings on the course in the late forties. With Peter Thomson (Club Champion Steven's father) he would arrive at the 9th tee. They would leave their clubs and step over the fence into the Broadfoot garden. There the tables were laid out to resemble toadstools and the two resting golfers would sit at one and be served with one bottle of lemonade and two glasses. They would resume their game half-an-hour later without difficulty, so quiet was the course in those days. Helping in the tea room would be Mrs Nimmo and her two daughters from Chesterhall. Mary Elliot also recalls that at that time the key to the water hydrant at the eighth was held by the Broadfoots and confesses under gentle questioning to childhood mischiefs such as turning on the water unauthorised or performing handstands on the eighth green.

Richard Baillie was a man of many talents. The eldest of eleven children, he trained as a stone mason, and established himself as a builder of quality

SETON DEAN TEA GARDENS
At 9th Hole of Longniddry Lovely Golf Course.

The advertisement for the Seton Dean Tea Gardens

1967 Club Champion finalists Tom Kemp (left) and David Baillie. They are flanked by Vice Captain Dr Ian Forbes on the left and Captain Joe Sykes on the right.

homes. Many of the older dwellings in Longniddry particularly those lining the Golf Course were built by his company. He also built in Haddington both private and local authority homes. His firm were not confined to housing, they were also involved in reservoir construction. The Hope Reservoir was one of Richard Baillie's. So was the Lady Bower reservoir in Derbyshire opened by His Majesty George VI. Richard Baillie was also an accomplished amateur sculptor and painter both in oils and water colour. Some of his paintings were hung in the Royal Academy. The Baillie family provided the 1967 Club Champion in Richard's grandson David Baillie (Eva's son).

10TH HOLE

FIRS
364 yards Par 4

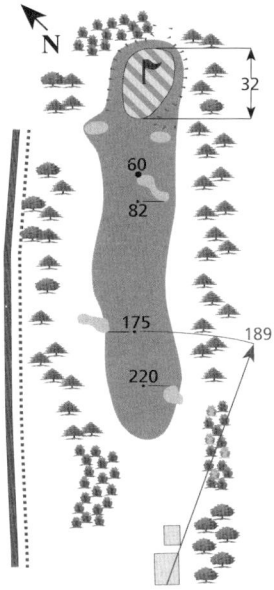

The first hole in the inward half, continues eastward down an avenue of trees 364 yards to a green set in a small tree-backed amphitheatre. Old photographs, kindly presented to the club by the Earl of Wemyss, show substantial ponds in front of the teeing ground. These were deliberately drained off. A filled drain runs the full length of the hole with an outlet into the Canty Burn behind the green.

It is in the vicinity of this green that a circle of Bronze Age standing stones was said to be positioned. They would probably be aligned on some dominant landmark on the horizon, possibly Arthur's Seat to give indication of important dates of the farming calendar. One of the stones was inadvertently unearthed in 1995 during the excavations required for the new irrigation system. It may well have been around these stones that certain dark goings on took place in 1608. A woman, Beigis Tod of Longniddry, was brought to trial for witchcraft. She was accused of meeting the devil at "Deane Fute of Langnydrie" The poor soul was sentenced to be strangled and burnt at the stake on the Castle Hill of Edinburgh according to local historian David Robertson.

Looking down the 10th hole from the tee before the drainage was installed.

An early view of
the approach
to the 10th green.

The original 11th hole lay entirely on the North side of the shore road. It is shown on Simpson's drawing as being 350 yards long. The old tee can still be distinguished west of the burn at the edge of the public car park at the bottom of the Dean. Nancy Jupp describes the hole as a tantalising short par four played over a bunker to a sunken fairway which then dog-legged left to a two-tiered green. There were plenty of sand dunes to the left to catch the wayward tee shot.

It was at this old 11th hole that the tragic accident occurred on 21st July 1929, when Christine Dickson Lawrie was killed by a golf ball. She had been sitting in a bunker knitting, some say, when she was struck. The seriousness of her injury does not seem to have been apparent as she went home on the bus. She died later that day. The hole continued in use until after the War, but things became increasingly difficult. It was found impossible to keep the public off this part of the course and early morning golfers would be faced with the sight of campers' tents pitched on the line of their shots. Players in former years coming off the 10th green towards the main road would find parked there Mr Clark's ice-cream van doing a roaring trade. It would be in position from May to September. Nancy claims that she could make a slider costing a penny last until the 15th green.

The present 11th hole, 'Bents' was originally the 12th, and at 333 yards is substantially unchanged : Simpson measures it as 10 yards longer. The tee stands quite high with a depression in front of it which seems to be steadily deepening with the years. The hole continues eastwards along the side of the buckthorn from which the occasional Scots Pine protrudes. Until recently there was a bunker across the fairway 160 yards from the tee. In 1994 because of the proximity of the hole to the 4th green and 5th tee, at this point, it was decided to fill the bunker and replace it with a smaller one on the right hand side of the fairway. Intriguingly in the 1946 Mackenzie Ross drawing, the hole is presented as 406 yards long. The tee is shown set well back towards the greenkeepers' sheds. Conversation with members who

11TH HOLE
BENTS
350 yards Par 4

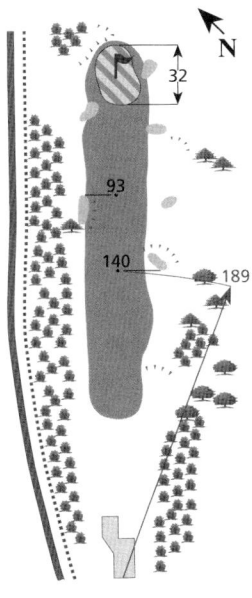

remember the course immediately post-war suggests that the hole was never 406 yards. It seems that the Mackenzie Ross drawing depicts an intention which was never implemented.

Past Captain Peter Lowe tells the story of a remarkable exchange of shots at this hole. It was a knock out match in the Club Championship: Fraser A Hall was playing Duncan Allan. Fraser (a Scottish Universities Champion) drove first, a really long ball which found the green. Duncan duffed his drive down to the left. At that stage Fraser could be forgiven for feeling that he had won this hole, at least. Not so, for Duncan holed his second shot to win the hole. Another notable occasion was in August 1982 when Graeme Mackay holed his tee shot. Magnificent though the stroke was, it was a bit less than as described in the press report which misprinted the distance as 388 yards.

12TH HOLE

COOT'S POND
381 yards Par 4

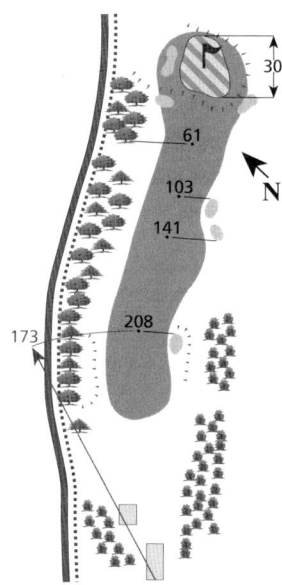

Today's 12th hole dog-legs to the right to a well-guarded elevated green which slopes down from right to left. The length of the hole measured down the centre is 381 yards, and at the angle of the dog-leg there is a substantial mound 140 yards from the green. The hole is named 'Coots' Pond' because the buckthorn on the right of the men's tee conceals a depression which in the past was usually waterlogged, and often inhabited by a family of Coots. The odd chick would pop out of the whins occasionally to inspect the tee shots and then pop back in again. The pond is dried up, except in unusually wet weather nowadays. It is some years since spectating coots have been seen.

The length of the hole given by Mackenzie Ross is 354 yards, and the drawing shows it as a straight line from tee to green. This was the arrangement of the hole when George Taylor drove the green in the 1950s. No doubt others can claim to have done the same. It appears that the additional length and the curvature were obtained by moving the tee back towards the 11th green. Much more recently Willie Weston got into trouble when, having already driven the 11th green, he proceeded to drive the 12th. An irate lady putting on the green at the time, subsequently reported Willie to the committee. Punishment not recorded.

The depression on the left of the fairway was called 'Cowslip Dell'. As well as cowslips, marsh orchids are to be found here. The conifer trees which shield the hole from the road are comparatively recent, having been planted about 25 years ago. Some players recommend a line to the hole down the left of the central mound giving the opportunity to play the second shot against the slope of the green. However longer hitters may prefer to attack from the right flank. This was the Dai Rees approach in 1975. He played down the right, and then stroked an exquisite little hanging shot on to the right-hand shoulder of the green and down to the pin.

The length of the hole for the ladies is 289 yards. For a number of years their back tee was against the fence, at a tight corner of the shore road. Nowadays this is a fast twisting thoroughfare which seems to induce Grand Prix ambitions. The ladies became accustomed to addressing their ball conscious of the loom of madly driven vehicles screaming down the road directly towards them. When, eventually, a car failed to take the corner (fortunately at night) and finished through the fence, it was considered prudent to move the ladies' tee across in front of the men's.

The pre-war 13th hole, had alternative tees on either side of the shore road. The length of the hole was 166 yards running eastwards to a green roughly opposite the present 12th tee on the north side of the road. Nancy Jupp recalls that there was a high mound which descended into the green on the right. Very often the mound had to be putted over to reach the pin.

Today's 13th hole runs back south-westwards across the right of way then over Cadger's Burn and up a short steep ascent to the green 174 yards away. The tee is set beside the road, sheltered from the east by densely growing aspen trees which flicker and shimmer in the wind. The tee shot has several hazards to negotiate : the copse of sycamore trees at the foot of the slope on the left, a stunted but determined hawthorn tree on the right, and a longitudinal bunker blocking the centre of the fairway. There are no other bunkers on the hole, but it is further protected by grass mounds on the right and left edges of the green which itself slopes down ferociously from south-west to north-east. When the 13th has been completed the player finds himself back in the vicinity of the Clubhouse. In bad weather the warm refuge and refreshment which are on offer there sometimes prove too strong a temptation for the tired and weary, or for those who are just having a bad day.

13TH HOLE
RIGHT O' WAY
174 yards Par 3

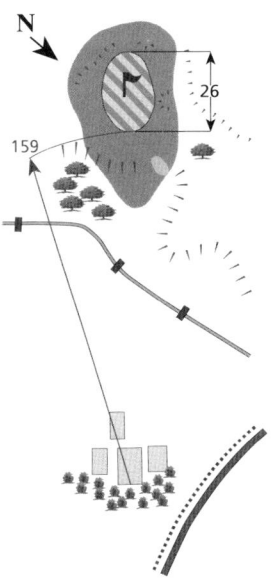

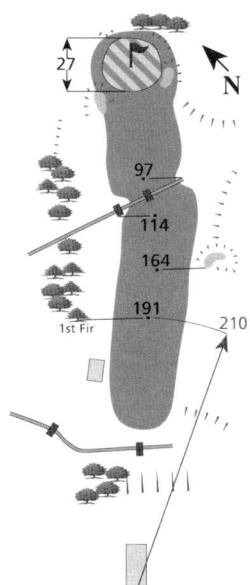

The old 14th hole shown on the Simpson drawing was a formidable 582 yards long. It ran south-eastwards from a tee deep in the dunes, level with the present 12th tee. (It seems likely that the mound on the left of the present 11th green was one of the old 14th tees). The line of the hole crossed over the road, the Cadger Burn and then the Braids Burn to arrive – eventually – in the vicinity of the present 14th green. The hole was designated a bogey six and George Mitchell was one of the few if not the only one, ever to have got home in two shots – circumstances not specified! Particular features alongside the fairway are the spring cowslips, small briar roses and marsh orchids. Larks nested here for many years, until sadly seen off by magpies.

The present hole at 403 yards is difficult enough, particularly for the high handicapper when the east wind blows. Nevertheless Bill Thomson Captain of the club (1994/95) has witnessed a drive from a young competitor in an open competition carry a ball over the green. The weather conditions were exceptionally favourable it should be said.

On the left from the 14th tee the prospect is worth pausing for: to the northwest are the two stately Lomond peaks and then scanning eastwards, Largo Law and Elie Point can be made out. Nearer at hand across the promontory of Fernie Ness the shapes of the two midget submarines said to be Japanese are just visible at low tide in Aberlady Bay. They were scuttled there at the end of the war and used as target practice by the Navy for a time.

The tee stands high, facing the sheltering woods round Gosford House for which the hole is named, and overlooked by the clubhouse a matter of 60 yards away across the 18th green. The line of the tee is slightly skew to the angle of the hole. The clump of sycamore trees below on the left, and the transverse gully of the Cadger burn in front of the tee, severely punish a miss-hit drive, and leave Braids burn, 150 yards away, still to be negotiated. The fairway of the hole between the burns slopes down from right to left. A bunker is situated in the right rough 180 yards from the tee to catch the faded drive. This part of the course was the site of the Longniddry football pitch and was known as Cowslip Field. The little group of young conifers projecting from the main body of foliage on the left was funded in memory of Jack Swinton by his Wednesday club friends. Jack, a newsagent, was a founder member of the Wednesday Club which was established by local shopkeepers to play golf on their weekly half-day.

Presuming a safe drive finishing nicely short of the obliquely running Braids Burn the second shot is played to a green sloping up from west to east and protected by a combination of bunkers and grass hillocks.

The original 15th hole was a short one – 180 yards, but reputed at the time to be one of the best in Scotland. The tee shot was played northwards from the vicinity of the present ladies 15th tee out over the road to a green set at an angle to the line of play and perched on the sea-lashed Boglehill promontory. It is said that when a strong east wind was blowing the golfers on this old 15th hole were in danger of being swept off the green. It is also said that one of the Whitcombe brothers competing in a professional competition found himself playing back and forward across the green to the extent of 10 disastrous shots. On the other hand on August 7th 1931 young Charles Tawse is recorded as having holed in one a distance of 157 yards. Boglehill was the original home of Longniddry's Bathgate family. Thomas N. Bathgate born there in 1872 founded Bathgate's Dance Band. He had 5 sons and a daughter. The fourth son Andrew who died in 1995 brought the Scout Piping Championship to East Lothian two years in succession and became a famed international band leader himself.

The present 15th hole continues eastwards along the side of the shore road 425 yards to an elevated green. The length of the 15th hole shown by Mackenzie Ross is 384 yards. For nearly 25 years after the war the hole was played from the current ladies' medal tee against the road. This had the advantage that tee shots were played away from the line of the road. It also explains the position of the bunker at the right-hand side of the fairway, 147 yards out. The present medal tee was constructed about 1970 using infill contributed by Hart Builders and adding 40 yards to the hole. The bunker at the left hand side of the green is worth noting. Although perhaps modified through time it was originally designed on the basis of the famous sand trap at the green of the Road Hole of the Old Course at St. Andrews.

15TH HOLE

FERNIE NESS
180 yards Par 3

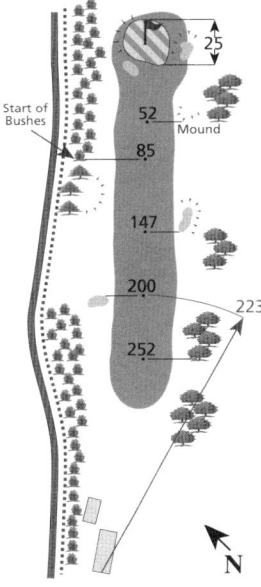

Start of Bushes

25

52

85

Mound

147

200

223

252

N

Below left: Crossing the burn at the shore from the old 11th tee.

Above right: Putting on the original 15th green at Boglehill

The name of the hole 'Fernie Ness' is from the little grass-covered peninsula which projects out to sea on the left. At one time a village existed here and according to records of the Johnston family it was "destroyed" sometime before 1794. Descendant Archie Johnston, himself a fisherman says that originally the Fernie Ness folk fished in shallow-bottomed boats which could be drawn up on the beach. When they changed to larger vessels it was necessary to have a proper harbour and the families moved to Port Seton. There remained at Fernie Ness or was later built, a Toll House which survived until the 1920's.

It was at Fernie Ness that a tragic accident occurred on 27th April 1943. The little peninsula was used as a practice firing range at that time. Aircraft towing target drogues behind them would manoeuvre convincingly off the Fernie Ness Point. Obviously there was a need to simulate true combat conditions. The accident happened when a Chesapeake plane dived at high speed. There was miscalculation or malfunction because the plane flew into a bus at the site and twelve Naval personnel and one civilian lost their lives. Marjory Douglas who at the time lived at Inchmahome made the emergency phone call to alert the authorities to the tragedy.

16TH HOLE

THRUSH'S MEAD
145 yards Par 3

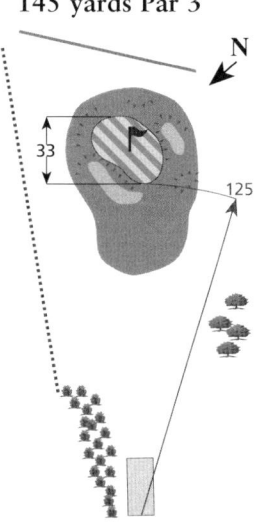

The original 16th hole was similar in position and alignment to the existing 15th. It was 422 yards long. At 145 yards, the present 16th is played from a tee in the extreme north-east corner of the course. Behind the tee is a device which is used to check power station fallout. The terrain between tee and green is virtually featureless, so that distance is difficult to judge. The upward sloping green is aligned skew to the hole and its edges diverge from the entry throat in a combination of bunkers and grass hillocks.

The low-lying house immediately to the left of the tee is 'Evergreen', built for Alistair Harkess in the 1970's. Nowadays it is owned by Club members Bill and Mavis Fenton. Older and more prominent just beyond the tee, gable end on to the course, is 'Inchmahome'. This house was owned in the thirties and perhaps earlier by J. K. Stewart who was Comptroller of Stamps and Taxes for Scotland. In 1938 the Douglases took possession and lived there for many years. Nowadays the owners are club members Jim and Anne Sutherland.

The houses around the 16th green are also worth noting: The hole takes its name from the one with the dormer windows behind the 17th medal tee, 'Thrush's Mead'. (Interestingly, recent inspection of title deeds in the Club's possession, show the name as 'Thrashes Mead') The dwelling is owned nowadays by Club member Jim Bowsher and his wife Joyce, but in the 1940's its occupant was a Professor Guthrie whose recreation was archery. There were no fences in those days and there was open ground between 'Thrush's Mead' and 'Inchmahome'. Marjory Douglas remembers watching with irritated apprehension, the Professor's arrows soaring high above what would become the 16th fairway and plunging into the ground dangerously close to her washing.

The two newer dwellings which now stand between 'Inchmahome' and

'Thrush's Mead' gaze over the course towards the far Forth Bridges. From north to south they are 'Four Winds' and 'Doric View'. They were designed and built in the 1960's by local builder and Club member George Taylor. The low-level bungalow on the other side of 'Thrush's Mead' was designed by Sir Basil Spence of Coventry Cathedral and Glasgow Airport fame, whilst the next, 'Ravelston', behind the green, is a two-in-one dwelling which was built for Professor Passmore. The Professor, a slight and wiry figure, continued to be a keen and persistent golfer well into his eighties and beyond. One of his sons, Charles, an excellent player, was a member of the Longniddry team which won the Winter League in 1978. 'Ravelston's' western neighbour, 'Brulin', with the bright red roof tiles, was the home for many years of the well-liked Doctor Pat and Marjory Gracie, both members. Pat Gracie is now sadly lost to us but he is remembered as a most conscientious and caring GP as well as a highly competitive and high-spirited golfer and cricketer.

Stone cysts, subsequently identified as belonging to a stone-age burial site, were uncovered in this area during the construction of the hole. Beyond the houses to the east of the course Lyars road runs north/south connecting the Shore Road with the main thoroughfare through Longniddry Village. Some say that many of the dead from the Battle of Prestonpans in 1745 were laid out here and that it was from this grisly circumstance that the road got its name. Others are doubtful and point out that it seems an unnecessarily long way from the battlefield to bring the bodies.

17TH HOLE
ARTHUR'S SEAT
434 yards Par 4

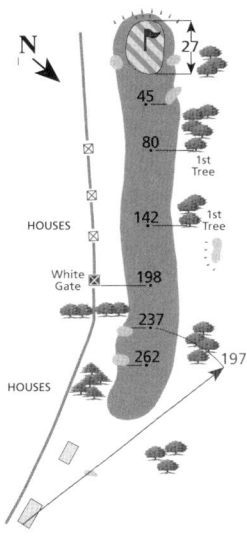

With the 17th hole the player begins to appreciate Dobereiner's 'sting in the tail' remark as he turns westward to face into the sun and prevailing wind. Across the bay the extinct volcano Arthur's Seat broods over Edinburgh.

For the men, today's 17th hole begins from a medal tee in the extreme Southeast corner of the course against the garden wall of 'Thrush's Mead'. From this tee the hole plays as a long dog-leg 434 yards usually into the wind. The ideal shot should be hit on the line of Arthur's Seat for which the hole is named. For the longer hitters there is the additional problem that the ball on landing, may well be pitched to the right by the slope of the fairway into either the rough or one of the little copses of trees. There are in total six of these small plantations. One of them stands behind the 17th green whilst the other five separate the 15th and 17th fairways. They were planted in the 1960's when Bob Anderson was Greens Convenor. It had been decided that some feature was necessary to define and separate the two fairways. Bob, in his thorough way, consulted the Curator of the Edinburgh Botanic Gardens as to the most appropriate flora. He recalls that the original intention was that rarer and more delicate plants such as Hornbeam should be arranged toward the centre of the copses, with hardier and less exotic temporary growths deployed on the perimeter to give protection. In the event, difficulty was experienced in getting the plantations established, and it was chiefly the commoner trees such as Aspen and Rowan which survived.

A consideration for the club is the proximity of the houses adjoining the course to the south of this hole, particularly at the point of the dogleg. Some precautionary measures have been taken in recent years. One of the earliest steps was the erection of a section of protective fence above the garden gate of 'Harmony', the contented-looking house with green woodwork and latticed windows which dozes beside the ladies tee. For some years in the 60's, the house was owned by the popular pair Ian McAdam and his wife Fiona. Later, a projecting copse of trees was encouraged to grow on the left at the corner of the dog leg, and two shallow bunkers were created alongside at the left hand edge of the fairway. A new men's forward tee was introduced in the mid-80's on the east side of the 16th green, thus straightening the hole for the men on non-medal occasions. When played from this new forward tee, the line and length is restored to that of the original 17th hole shown by Simpson as 378 yards in length.

The attractive house with the latticed windows and blue shutters just before the corner is 'Pantiles'. The next dwelling 'Shalimar', is said to have been the first house constructed under the Earl of Wemyss' 1920 Golf Course scheme. It was built for J. C. Rose when he came from St. Andrews to take charge of a branch of the Royal Bank of Scotland in the 1920's. Mr Rose became Captain of the Club in 1938/39. His daughter Kath, now Lady Vice-President, recalls as a young girl, a golf ball coming through the bathroom window while her sister Betty was in her bath. Immediately beyond 'Shalimar' is 'Sharona', owned by Club members Peter and Moira Moodie. Originally this house, then called the 'Sheiling', was occupied by 'Madame and Mr Tensfeldt' who were the proprietors of a 'Unique Ladies Hairdressing Establishment' at 137 Princes Street. Later, the house was owned by James Reid, an art collector, now departed, whose paintings included a Turner original, it is said.

 The prominent dwelling immediately east of 'Sharona' was built by Jim Sutherland in the early 1970's. For obvious reasons, after glance at its roof, it is called 'Greenmantle'. In 1976 Jim and Anne Sutherland donated the handsome Greenmantle Trophy for the Family Foursomes Competition to the Club.

The dark-roofed cottage snuggling beyond 'Greenmantle' is 'Kindrochet'. This is where long-standing Club member Maise Walls lives. She moved there in the 30's with her three young sons.

Although the hole is called 'Hame', and the clubhouse seems quite near at hand down the fairway on the left, there are 433 troublesome yards still to be negotiated, usually into the sun, and often against the wind.

'Hame' is shown on Simpsons 1930 drawing as being originally 442 yards long. On restoration after the war, the Mackenzie Ross drawing gives it as 379 yards, apparently using the present day ladies' tee. Since the hole now measures 433 yards, it must have been restored to the original design.

Seven attractive houses line the hole. Overlooking the tee is an extensive double bungalow 'Ballytrim' owned by Colin Wiseman and his wife Rosemarie. The original house before enlargement belonged to the Harrowers for many years. The next dwelling is 'Forrest Lodge' which sits astride the depression of Braid's Burn. It was built for Ronnie and Fiona Yule in the 1960's. Above the burn is 'Camperdown' and then the red-roofed 'Linkslea' a really beautiful bungalow owned by Jim MacLean and his wife Margaret. Jim is a popular Edinburgh lawyer, but the gentle purity of his speech betrays his Highland origin. Previous owners were called McLeod. They kept two parakeets. The birds regularly sat at the window it is said and watched the players pass up the 18th hole. Continuing down the fairway the ivy covered square built house beside 'Linkslea' is called 'The Geans'. It was owned by Alex Lowe for many years but now belongs to Linda and Tony Conroy, both members of the Golf Club. Linda suggests, and the Scots Concise Dictionary confirms, that the meaning of 'Geans' is 'wild cherries'. There are indeed several old cherry trees in the garden. The penultimate house, 'Eldin' an attractive red-roofed villa, was previously the home of Mrs J J (Annice) Latta, Lady Captain 1980. Nowadays it belongs to banker Norman Lang and his wife Jean. The last house just beside the right of way is 'Lochinvar' originally 'Beechworth' and once occupied by Brigadier Brodrick and his wife Evelyn. The Brigadier had retired from the Indian Army and joined the Golf Club in 1937. Among other owners were Jimmy Kynoch who played only with the Artisans and Hope Campbell and his wife Doctor Joan, who began their married life there.

A wide depression covered by rough clinging grass lies before the tee to punish the topped drive. Beyond that the fairway seems quite wide, and so it is. However it has a subtle hog's back shape to it . A ball struck with a bit of turn on it will be thrown into the right or left-hand rough and suddenly the safe 5 which is so often the plan, is in jeopardy. Particularly as there is a further gully with a long transverse bunker to be crossed or played into before the green is reached. At 35 yards the green is the longest on the course and sits under the eyes of the clubhouse spectators sympathetic (it is a friendly club) - but irreverent - seated comfortably in the lounge or, on good days, outside on the terrace. The drive is, of course, the key to the hole. It is necessary to get far enough down the fairway off the tee to be able to

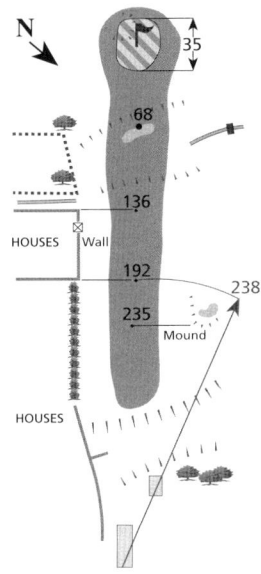

18TH HOLE

HAME
433 yards Par 4

carry the second shot over the dry gully 70 yards from the green. The crucial distance, some reckon, is the beginning of the garden wall of 'Lochinvar'. Short of that point the second shot is in real danger of finishing in the gathering cross bunker on the upper slope of the gully. Realistically, when the west wind blows, only a favoured few can reach the green in regulation. Mere mortals play the hole as a 5.

The top of the gully beside the Clubhouse is where, when snow is on the ground, the young and the not-so-young Longniddry folk have gathered for many years to sledge. They charge down the slope past (hopefully) the burn down on to the 14th fairway. Sometimes on these occasions, soup has appeared miraculously from the clubhouse to help keep the cold at bay.

The following article was written by Gordon Durward for the Carling Caledonian Golf Tournament programme in August 1961. It may be a little out of date now because of changes to the course, but Gordon's advice is never to be disregarded:

Survey from the 19th
"How to Play my Course by Gordon Durward"
(Professional, Longniddry Golf Club)

It is my pleasure to welcome you to Longniddry Golf Club and to take you round the famous links designed by Harry Colt at which I have the honour to be professional.

You can see the sea from every hole and many of the views are quite breathtaking.

The first hole is a comparatively simple par four (395 yards) which should get the field away in good order. The real danger here is a hook from the tee for there are tall trees and gardens on the left. However the fairway is wide and if one can avoid the bunkers on either side of the fairway then there should be little trouble.

If the wind is against at the 436 yards second, the bogey is four and with the wind in your face it takes two good shots for the average player to reach the green, but the players here this week should make it all right. The green is raised and on the left is a deep bunker placed to catch the slightly pulled shot to the green.

Now to the third (461 yards) and the first par 5 on the course. It is slightly dog-legged from right to left but the long hitters will be able to reach the green in two. A good straight second is required for there is a wooded area on the left and a bunker way down the right hand side to catch the pushed out shot.

A tricky short hole measuring 191 yards, the fourth, is played from an elevated tee. The wind plays a great part in the shot here for it usually blows across.

The fifth calls for an accurate tee shot for there is a bog wooded area on the left. The hole itself is dog-legged to a built up green and measures 319 yards. A miss-hit tee shot will mean real trouble for there are cross-bunkers not far from the tee.

The sixth is a good short hole redesigned in the late thirties by A. F. Simpson. Once again the shot is played from an elevated tee.

Danger abounds at the seventh (433 yards) for there are trees down both sides of the fairway. Accuracy must be the key note at this hole. Now on to the eighth where once again a hook will spell disaster for on the left is a field which is out of bounds. Trouble too can be caused by the three cross bunkers.

The ninth 378 yards is bordered by out of bounds on the left. Hookers will be in real trouble here so a good straight shot is required from the tee. A bunker some fifty yards short of the green will catch the miss-hit second.

The tenth is a splendid hole where accuracy is very important. There is trouble in the shape of woods on each side of the fairway and the second must be a very good one for the green is saucer shaped and is guarded by deep bunkers at each side. A burn - yes, like many famous Scottish courses, we have them here too - winds its way behind the green so the second must not go too far.

An accurate drive is again needed at the 343 yards 11th. The fairway goes by the back of the fourth green and the bunker behind this green often catches the pushed shot. There are trees and bushes down the left hand side.

Now the 12th (354 yards) which is dog-legged from left to right with out of bounds on the left. The drive must be carefully placed for there is a mound right down the centre of the fairway. The slightly built up green is guarded by the two well placed bunkers. Beyond the green is another burn.

Crossing the burn we come to the 13th tee from which we play to the green 182 yards away. There is a deep bunker short of the green so a well hit ball is required to find it.

The tee shot is across a burn at the 14th (412 yards) and with another some 80 yards short of the green, careful placing is necessary. The green itself slopes quite steeply and there are two deep bunkers lurking on each side of it.

Playing the 15th hole, if you know the famous Road Hole at St. Andrews, you will recognise that the bunker guarding the green on the left hand corner dominates the tee shot. In fact the position of the bunker was copied from the 17th hole at St. Andrews.

The 16th hole is another short hole (152 yards). The green is narrow, long and well bunkered and an accurate tee shot has to be played if one is to get on and get a three.

Now we turn back towards the clubhouse for the 17th. It is a left hand dog-leg and there are houses down the left hand side, so don't hook or it will cost you dearly. The prevailing wind is usually against, making this a very difficult hole indeed.

The round finishes with a 428 yards hole and once again the left hand side provides the danger. The ground drops just before the green and a well hit second has to be played to find it. This can be a difficult hole in certain conditions.

Gordon's article ended with the slogan *"men like CARLING LAGER BEER"*

Greenkeeping Staff

Having described the course it is timely to consider the men who have nurtured it so lovingly over these 75 years. Assuming that Alexander Wright was the first, there have been nine Head Greenkeepers since 1921:

Alexander Wright. A 1920's report refers to Mr Wright as a man of wide experience and undoubted genius in many ways.

Nancy Jupp describes him as having a thick white beard. 'All the kids were scared of him' she says. Perhaps this was a cultivated fierceness to keep them off his greens and out of his bunkers. Nancy goes on: ' Then one day he invited Douglas Teesdale and me into his house to see his birds' egg collection. They were beautifully preserved and he was very knowledgeable about them'. Nancy and Douglas found that he was really very kind.

W. Brown. The records do not show the date of Mr Wright's departure. It is to be presumed that it was in the early thirties, for in May 1937, the name of the Head Greenkeeper is revealed to be W. Brown in a minute which records his increase in wages from £2.10/- to £2. 15/- per week. He left Longniddry to take the Head Greenkeeper's job at North Berwick.

Alex Samuel. The appointment of Alex Samuel to follow W Brown must have been an internal promotion. Alex is listed as one of the full-time employees engaged in the construction of the new 6th green in 1931. As Head Greenkeeper, he became the first Club tenant of "Fairways" the estate house in Elcho Road. Alex proved a little difficult to trace until it was realised that he had been known to his own family as 'Eck'. It then turned out that he was present-day member John McDougall's great uncle, and that sadly he had died suddenly of a heart attack about 1938, aged 36.

W. Wood. The Board minutes record that a new Head Greenkeeper Mr W. Wood from Wilmslow Golf Club was appointed at Longniddry in 1938. Thereafter there is no further mention of greenkeeping staff until 1964.

Greenkeeping Staff in the Thirties. In the early days there was no play on Fridays apparently. Friday was 'Cutting Day'. For big jobs additional help was needed. It is known that Maurice Dunleavy was engaged to help with the construction of the new 6th green. This work began in 1931. He has written down his recollections for us: *"I did not have a lot to do with the Longniddry Course. The first year we went to Craigielaw. I worked as a casual on Kilspindie for a few weeks; they had the County Cup played there that year. Then they required casual workers to make the 6th green at Longniddry. All the regulars were asked to get someone. So, Archie Dishington asked me; S. Peffers asked M. McAuley; Bob Burnside asked T. Hogg. Alex Samuel also asked (I can't remember the name) a chap from Prestonpans or Tranent, who did barman in the County Hotel, Haddington on Saturday nights. The tractor driver used to sing and preach with the evangelists in Haddington on Saturday nights. His name, I think, was Morris. He went as a missionary eventually. The tractors were Model T Ford conversions by Pattison Stanmore. The units pulled 5 behind the tractors and 3 units behind a horse with boots on. The Estate carter was employed for two days a week as part of his Estate duties. When I went there (that would be in May 1931) the carter was Tom Runciman. He had been at Longniddry farm previously with S. Welch at Spittal as Groom Gardener, Little Lodge by the Bridge. Previous to that the chap's name was Amos. His widow lived at Aitcheson's Lodge with the old housekeeper from Gosford House.*

Of course there have been a lot of changes since then: There was a green over the main road at Cantyhall. All the sand that was taken off the beach at the foot of the Dean, Lorries from Leith and Edinburgh; old Willie Knox and his missus at Fernieness (tollhouse) gathering the tanners. Remember that whale the Fifers towed across the Forth? Baillie's men had to bury it. We also used to do a stint with the boiler (in the clubhouse), cleaning it regularly about every 6 months for the insurance inspector. And, of course, Dick (Dunleavy) used to carry clubs for Connor. He and Tydeswell used to wait for Dick coming from school. He must have been at Aberlady School then. I hope these memories will help a bit."

Tommy Hogg was available at that time because of the miners' strike and was retained at the end of the project, finally becoming Head Greenkeeper.

Tom Porteous present Vice-President of the Club confirms some of this: *"The horse used to be stabled at Craigielaw. It would be brought out each morning and walked along the road to the Cadger Burn and then up the hill to the shed which stood until recently just below the second green. There it would get its boots on, the grass cutter linked to the traces and off it would go plodding its way through the course steadily cutting the grass as it went. In the evening it returned to the shed to leave the cutters and discard its boots before being led back to Craiglielaw."*

Peter Wood adds: *"There were at least six working horses at Craigielaw - all Clydesdales. Three pairs were needed for all the ploughing and there was always an odd horse on the farm."*

Tommy Hogg had a high regard for the abilities of Jim King who was Head Greenkeeper at New Luffness. This admiration was not misplaced; it was shared by many others and the New Luffness greens at the time were the envy of the Lothians.

Tommy Hogg. Although Mr Wood was appointed Head Greenkeeper in 1938 nothing more is heard of him. There is a suggestion that he may have found his job to have been filled when he returned from the war. At any rate, the first Head Greenkeeper to be identified after the war is the ginger-haired Tommy Hogg. Tommy spent a long time with the Club. He was elected an Honorary Life Member in 1954. By 1962 his successor John Campbell had arrived, but Tommy continued to work for the Club in what seems to have been a sort of freelance capacity.

Greenkeeping in the Fifties. Jimmy Hume who is nowadays Club Professional at Gullane, was sent as a young man to Tommy Hogg to get a bit of muscle on him. He recollects his days with the greens staff and remembers working with Bob Burnside who drove the tractor. Bob was employed by the estate/golf course for a period of more than 50 years. He had worked for the contractor who had constructed the course originally. Then when the course was opened for play, he kept the fairways cut, the mower pulled by horse at first and later by tractor. Bob received an Agricultural Award in acknowledgement of his 50 years service. He served in the RAF during the war. He was no mean golfer himself: in April 1947 playing in an Artisan's medal he returned a gross 68 which included only 22 putts.

Jimmy also worked with Harry Chirnside the blacksmith's son who sadly, died quite young. Andrew Chirnside was there too and Bob Foggo an excellent fiddler. The working day began at 7.30 a.m. on the bunkers. The sheep had lain in them overnight so the greenkeepers had to be equipped with rakes, canes and an instrument apparently called a 'suffle' to do the job. After the bunkers were cleared of sheep and raked, the greens and tees had to be caned. Then the fairways had to be tackled. These were allocated on a regular basis:

Tommy took the	14th, 15th, 16th and 17th himself
Harry Chirnside had the	13th, 18th, 2nd and 12th.
Jimmy Hume looked after the	11th, 3rd, 5th and the 1st, while
Bob Burnside took the	6th, 10th 7th 8th and 9th.

Jimmy recalls other names: Kane from Prestonpans, a young apprentice, and another apprentice called Darling. There was also Alistair Paterson from Gullane.

1959 (?) – 1961. John Campbell. Tommy Hogg, while still employed with the Club on the greens staff decided to step down from the Head Greenkeeper post about 1959. The job was taken by John Campbell from the west coast- the information is not specific. John did not stay long at Longniddry. No more than 2 years ,it is thought. In 1964 he left to join the Saint Andrews greens staff. Later he moved on to finish his career at the Foxhills Golf Club outside London.

1961-1994. Duncan Herd. Duncan was Head Greenkeeper at Arbroath Golf Course which he joined in 1954 from Carnoustie where he had been Assistant Foreman and where his brother became Head Greenkeeper. In 1961 Duncan and his wife Agnes moved to Longniddry. Their spell at Arbroath had lasted 7 years. Duncan started quietly at Longniddry giving himself time to get to know the course. He identified three chief problems: firstly a low rainfall, secondly fast drainage combined with drying winds and lastly a high volume of golfing traffic. The water pipes existing on the course had been installed in the early twenties and were heavily scaled so that the original diameter had been reduced by half. This meant that priorities for watering had to be selected very carefully. Large aprons could not be accommodated because they demanded water which was needed for the greens themselves. In due course a new irrigation system was installed ameliorating this problem, but the drainage, evaporation and high volume of golfing traffic have continued until this day. The first big task which Duncan set himself was to establish additional tees, and he built one extra tee each year until he had tackled every hole.

Duncan Herd

Duncan and Agnes enjoyed their golf. They played bowls as well. Most unfortunately Agnes, a very popular lady in the village died shortly before Duncan retired in 1994.

1994-95 Craig Hildersley. Craig had been for a time first Assistant Greenkeeper at Turnhouse Golf Club in Edinburgh. He was offered promotion there, but chose instead to come to Longniddry. His first Assistant was John Kay who had joined the Longniddry staff some years before. Like John Campbell's, Craig's stay was not a long one. He left to take charge of the Hibernian Football Club's ground at Easter Road shortly after John Kay had moved as Head Greenkeeper to the 9 hole course at Musselburgh reputed to be the oldest course in the world still in play. At the end of 1994 therefore, Longniddry was suddenly deprived not only of its Head Greenkeeper, but also of his Senior Assistant. The first step was to fill the Head Greenkeeper post and then to give the new man a say in the selection of his Senior Assistant. Advertisements were placed locally and nationally.

1996- Present Ken Anderson. Ken was appointed at the beginning of 1996. A St. Andrews man, he started his greenkeeping career at Turnhouse as an apprentice in 1979. In 1981 he moved to Murrayfield Golf Club where he qualified as Assistant Greenkeeper in 1983. The following year he was appointed Assistant Greenkeeper at Bruntsfield and subsequently became Deputy Head Greenkeeper there. Between 1987 and 1994 he was Head Greenkeeper at, successively, Torphin, Newmachar and finally Sheringham in Norfolk. In his short time at Longniddry Ken's greenkeeping abilities have won the respect and admiration of many members. Comments of visitors to the course during 1996 have praised its condition and in particular expressed appreciation of the quality of the greens.

Greenkeeping Staff 1996. After Ken Anderson's appointment as Head Greenkeeper, Phil Holmes already a member of the greens staff was promoted to the position of Assistant Head Greenkeeper. Since then he has on his own initiative begun Further Education studies with a view to obtaining formal greenkeeping qualifications. The other members of the current greens staff are David Robson, Steven Russell, Ian Watt and Kenny Mason.

Ken Anderson on the Toro Greenmower.

Today's Greenkeeping Team.
Back row: Phil Holmes, David Robson, Ken Anderson, Steven Russell.

Front row: Kenny Mason, Ian Watt.

CHAPTER II
SOME FAUNA AND FLORA

Curlew

1) *The Birds by Frank Hamilton*

The influence of the rich Firth of Forth on the golf course is felt by any player with even only a passing interest in birds. It is not just the sight of them, but their sounds, that are a splendid background to a round. Curlew, Redshank and Oystercatcher can be heard all the year round, while overhead parties of Lapwing move to and from the fields inland. In winter these are often accompanied by flocks of Golden Plover which move fast in light flocks.

In winter and early spring Pink-footed Geese move to and from Aberlady Bay, often numbering thousands, and usually in the evening in great necklaces across the sky. These birds which breed in Iceland and the North have a wonderful exciting call and it's worth pausing to watch and listen as they go overhead. This is the time too when Fieldfares, thrushes from Scandinavia, in small flocks are attracted to the area by the Sea Buckthorn berries. The fairways and tees of the course are not very attractive to birds. (Crows always excepted).

Oyster Catcher

Oystercatchers feed when players are few but perhaps the most obvious birds are the Swallows and House Martins, particularly in the autumn as they swoop round catching insects that have been disturbed by the golfers. A number of birds feed on the short grass near the adjoining habitat of scrub, tall trees and rough areas. It is here that many of our garden birds are to be found. Blackbird; Song Thrush, Robin, Blue, Great and Coal Tits, Dunnocks and even Goldcrest and Tree Creepers occur.

Great Spotted Woodpeckers are seen and heard in the tall trees in Dean Wood. In these mixed habitats the Finches breed: Bullfinch, Greenfinch and Goldfinch. Summer warblers are limited, but there are a few Willow Warblers and an occasional Chiffchaff, while Sedge Warblers breed in the marshy areas on the other side of the coastal road. Sadly that comparatively rare Scottish Warbler, the Lesser Whitethroat, which used to sing from scrub at the edge of the visitors' car park can no longer be heard. It was present for about three years in the '80's, but with the car park 'tidied up', the birds had nowhere to breed. If wildlife is to have a place in the golf course, the urge to be endlessly tidy needs to be curbed.

Sparrow Hawk

Magpies are striking birds, and it is nice to see them about. Remember, it is said they serve the Devil and if you want luck, (and which golfer doesn't ?) you should always salute them! Both Kestrels and Sparrowhawks are

Scots Pine

regular all the year round, while Meadow Pipits and Skylarks move in parties in spring and autumn. From April to August Terns, especially Sandwich, are often heard over the Forth area, but they are seldom seen over the course. From November till February, players should keep a look out for Waxwings. Every few years large numbers of these birds move from Scandinavia and turn up along the East coast. Up to 250 have been seen at the edge of the course and they are one of the more attractive birds to see.

2) *Trees and Plants*

A former member with a botanical background who still looks on Longniddry Golf Club with affection, has been kind enough to carry out a survey of the course and report on some of the flora to be seen. Admittedly, a few of the items which have been identified may only be found in deep undergrowth. The consolation is therefore offered to the wilder golfers of the Club that they have the opportunity of appreciating these elusive flowers much more often than their straighter-hitting companions.

The northern perimeter of the course is lined with Sea Buckthorn and Scots Pines against the road. These afford a shield which protects golfers and the course itself from some of the harsher winter winds. The chief area of woodland lies between the first green and sixth tee, occupying the high ground beside the houses and the slope down to the fifth fairway. A great mixture of trees is to be found in this tiny forest area. Few Elms survive, but there are Birch and Beech, Sycamore, Oak, Horse Chestnut, Rowan, Aspen and of course more Pines.

Sea Buckthorn

All members must have observed the better known flowers on the course such as the orange yellow blooms of the gorse or the lime yellow of the broom at the side of the 11th fairway. Most particularly, the ladies on the fifth tee will have noticed the dog roses close to their line of shot. Like the May blossom, these always seem to take a long time to bloom. There are many other wild flowers with which members may be unfamiliar or which they may have overlooked: beside the Cadger Burn there is reported to be a patch of Harebells - the Scottish Bluebells - whilst small blue Geraniums are to found beside the right-of-way.

Primroses are well represented throughout the course, chiefly the Cowslips, their deep yellow flowers nodding together in little umbel clusters. The pink Marsh Orchids are mostly found alongside the twelfth fairway, and the deep rough in various corners of the course harbours patches of tall pink Rosebay

Marsh Orchid

Willow Herb. At least two members of the Pea family are to be found: Purple Vetch, a small climber which resembles the Sweet Pea, with leaves ending in grasping tendrils, and Yellow Trefoil which displays between two and seven flowers in an outward facing ring at the end of an erect stalk. Again in the deep rough various Thistles reign and also Ragged Robin, a tall rough-stemmed perennial related to Campion. Its flowers are bright pink and unisexual apparently.

Finally these small white cluster flowers which inhabit the light rough and plague the golf ball seekers, are Yarrow, members of the Daisy family. They display white, sometimes pink florets 4-6 mm across in flat-topped clusters often of golf ball size. Where the growth of the plant is suppressed, the tiny soft fern-like leaves are to be seen growing through the mown grass, betraying the presence of viable roots below the surface.

Pink Footed Geese in flight

CHAPTER III

LONGNIDDRY VILLAGE AND LAND OWNERSHIP

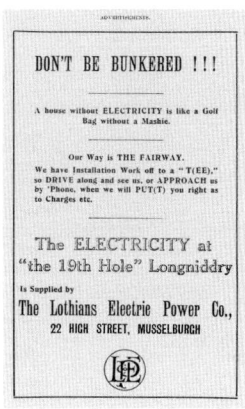

There have been many persons down the centuries who could lay claim to ownership of the strip of land above the beach on which Longniddry golf course and village lie. Some of the earliest would be the hunter/gatherers and fishermen of the middle stone age who left middens of discarded sea shells on the beaches. Without the capacity to clear the dense forest, they would have pursued a nomadic huntin' and shootin' type of life.

By 3/4000 BC it had been realised that herding captive stock and planting seed could save a lot of trouble and keep the menfolk nearer home. Clearance in this new stone age period was accomplished by slash and burn methods. It seems obvious that such operations would work progressively inwards from the beach. The golf course area would be cleared therefore comparatively early in the process. It would be at this time that the standing stone circle was erected which existed until the mid- 19th Century at the bottom of the Dean in the vicinity of the 10th green.

By 2000 BC new fashions and new technology had begun to take over. The use of copper and bronze was spreading and beakers which had been decorated by cord marking before firing, were in use. It is thought that these beakers were associated with beer drinking, so it looks as though alcohol had arrived by this time - probably a necessity to compensate for the loss of the huntin'/fishin' existence so attractive in retrospect. One can visualise the maudlin group of males around the camp fire. Glum and lachrymose, they gaze into the flames contemplating the old days and cursing the politically correct farmist group which had changed things so much. With golf not yet invented there was nothing to do with all this extra spare time but help with the washing up of these damned beakers. Whilst at their feet proto-collie dogs their disconsolate chins on the ground would morosely contemplate a future of herding instead of hunting. Which takes us to bones .... It was during this period that the practice of burying the dead in a crouched position in stone Cysts was used. Cysts of this type were found during construction of the 16th green.

One thousand years further on and the iron age had arrived (except for golf club shafts of course!). With it came the Celts or Keltoi emerging in the historical record. The iron weapons and tools with which they were equipped permitted the clearance of forest areas in earnest.

The Iron Age period continued down to Roman times when the first recorded name of the owners of the land becomes available to us. It is the Gododdin or, as the Romans called the tribe, the Votadini. One of their strongholds, presumably the one from which control over Longniddry was

Recently the remains of an Iron Age village were discovered (sadly now obliterated by open cast mining) north of the A1 just opposite Tranent. It is interesting (but highly irrelevant Ed) to note the comments of a group of experimental archaeologists emerging to the modern world again after a year's existence in such conditions. Asked which of all modern conveniences they had missed most, they replied with one voice 'welly boots'!

exercised, was Traprain Law. King Lot, a Gododdin leader during the early 5th century was said to be a brother-in-law of King Arthur and father of Mordred. The Gododdin were renowned throughout Britain as formidable warriors. They were referred to as Gwr y Gogledd - the 'Men of the North'. Their language was early Welsh, or P- Celtic (i.e. (M) Ap' instead of the 'Mac' of Irish and Scottish Gaelic.) Local historian David Robertson reckons that the name Longniddry came from this language and means something like 'Church of the new settlement'. This would suggest that 1500 years ago a Christian missionary, possibly from St Ninian's Candida Casa at Whithorn had reached the district and established a church.

A contingent of the Goddodin travelled to what is now Wales to help in the battles against pirates and various marauders. They are claimed to have established ruling dynasties there.

Finally the Gododdin played away from home once too often. A powerful contingent was sent south to oppose advancing Germanic invaders. They were badly defeated at what is thought to be Catterick and are not heard of again.

They were replaced by the Angles who came either as invaders or as an expansion of a group of mercenaries originally brought to the country by the Romans. Whatever their origins, once established the Angles took over completely so that very few pre-English place names remain in south-east Scotland. If David Robertson is right Longniddry is one of them. Another is Selkirk named from the Celtic Selgovae tribe.

After the Angles' incursion, much to-ing and fro-ing of the border occurred but in 1018 Malcolm II of Scotland routed an English army at Carham on Tweed. Thereafter Lothian was part of Scotland and Longniddry was to be a Scottish golf course.

Many of the Scottish early records were lost in the course of the wars with England, so that there is little documentation surviving before the re-establishment of Scottish sovereignty by Robert the Bruce in 1314. The records of that time show a very significant redistribution of land ownership in progress. Robert Bruce established at last, years after being crowned, had debts to pay and scores to settle. Those landlords who had been allied to his Scottish enemies the Comyns (Cummings) were displaced in favour of Bruce's adherents. In Longniddry the sitting landlord is recorded as Nicholas de Dispensa. Not only did this family support the losing side in Scotland but the English branch were very close, not to say, affectionate supporters of Edward II. This outraged some of his more conventional and 'butch' aristocracy. The outcome was displacement of the Scottish branch and a sticky end for at least some of the English Dispensas. The immediate beneficiary of Bruce's endowment of 'Langnodryf' was the 'beloved and faithful' Thomas Sympil on condition that one bowman was supplied for the King's army. Neither age nor accuracy were specified. One speculates whether the village sent their best man for reasons of local prestige or whether, boys being boys, they ganged up to persuade Sympil (who may have lived up to his name) to accept a short sighted geriatric of low

Among Robert Bruce's enemies were the Wemyss family.

popularity. The latter may be more likely because Sympil doesn't seem to have lasted long. After him a number of names are connected with the ownership of Longniddry. These include: the Forresters of Corstorphine, the family of Seton and the Halyburtons. One speculates whether the last could have been the ancestors of that splendid Scottish golfer Tom Haliburton, the Wentworth professional who broke the Longniddry course record with a 64 in the 1961 Carling Caledonian Tournament.

The best known family though, was that of the Douglases, who established themselves, David Robertson tells us, in Longniddry at the beginning of the 16th Century. Whether they were the 'Black' Douglases or the 'Red' is not immediately clear, but since the great house of Black Douglas fell about 1460 it seems likely to have been the 'Red', who were said to have risen upon the ruins of the 'Black'. Their castle would probably have been a simple tower house. It was situated at the top of what is now John Knox Road.

In the 1540's the landowner was Hugh Douglas. He engaged a young East Lothian man to act as tutor to his sons Francis and George. The tutor's name was John Knox. For whatever reason: failure of the male line or penury from over-extension, the Douglas possessions in Longniddry were taken over by the Setons in the mid 1600's. By this time the Setons ever loyal to the House of Stuart and staunch Roman Catholics had achieved for their top man, the title 'Earl of Winton'. In the end though their religion and loyalty cost them their lands. Earl George joined the Jacobite rebellion of 1715 disastrously managed by the Earl of Mar or "Bobbin' John" as he was known. Earl George was captured at Preston and lodged in the Tower of London pending execution. In an escapade worthy of 007 he is said to have sawn through the bars of his cell with his watch spring and escaped to the continent. He died in Rome in 1749.

The Seton Lands were sold off and subsequently went by auction to John Glassel, a native of Dumfries who had made his fortune in Virginia. His daughter married the heir to the Duke of Argyll in 1818 and in or around 1852 the Duke sold Longniddry to the Earl of Wemyss who already owned much of the surrounding land. The Wemyss' are first recorded as landowners at Penshiel in the Lammermuirs in the 13th Century. Their name derives from the Gaelic word for caves. There was a society scandal in 1720 when James the 5th Earl of Wemyss eloped with a young lady called Janet. She was the only child of the notorious wealthy rake Colonel Francis Charteris of Amisfield near Haddington and presumably the apple of his eye. The Colonel who appears disreputably in the first plate of Hogarth's "Harlot's Progress", eventually forgave his daughter and left his great fortune and lands to her second son Francis, provided that he took the name of Charteris instead of Wemyss. Naturally it had been expected that Janet's eldest son David would inherit the ancient Wemyss lands and title from his

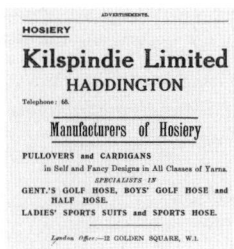
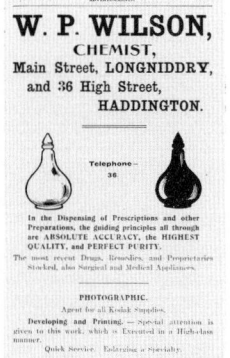
38

father, as 6th Earl. However once again the Jacobite cause intervened. David joined the '45 rebellion and was proscribed. He married a young German lady, late in life; but both she and her baby, a boy, died in childbirth. In these circumstances Francis in 1787 succeeded to the Wemyss patrimony as the 7th Earl as well as to the Charteris inheritance. Janet's third son James, took over the Wemyss Estates in Fife. His descendants are still the Wemyss of Wemyss.

Francis Charteris inherited a golfing tradition and was a keen golfer himself. His seat was at the Colonel's old home at Amisfield near Haddington. Francis used to ride over to Gosford to play golf there. Eventually he bought some of the land and Robert Adam was engaged to design a suitable mansion house.

The 8th, 9th and 10th Earls of Wemyss were all called Francis after the Colonel. The family still seem proud of his notoriety. It was the last of these three, the 10th Earl who finally rebuilt and restored Gosford House as Adam had planned it. The architect appointed was William Young, a native of Paisley, who had a London practice. He had designed the Glasgow City Chambers completed in 1888, and considered risible by Ruskin an artistic reactionary of the time. Ruskin is said to have been overcome by laughter at his first sight of the new building when he emerged into George Square from Queen Street Station. It is not impossible however that this reaction was a premeditated one. Whatever is thought of the outside of the building, internally the City Chambers is magnificent. Certainly Lord Wemyss must have been impressed because he chose William Young for Gosford following his Glasgow City Chambers work. The 10th Earl died in 1914 aged 96 and his successor being his third son was called Hugo Richard. Like Janet's second son he was keenly interested in golf.

Shortly after the 11th Earl inherited the title, the Haddington Advertiser of July 31st 1914 carried an article headed:-

GREAT FEUING PLAN ADOPTED BY LORD WEMYSS
New golf course to be laid out at Longniddry.
Work to be commenced without delay.

(It is said that it was at this time before the start of the First World War that applications for membership of Longniddry Golf Club began to be received.)

The article goes on to relate how it had often been suggested that the Links at Longniddry would make a fine golf course, and that the land to the south, commanding a fine view of the Forth, would be one of the most desirable sites for housing on the east coast of Scotland. The new Earl had decided to realise the suggestions, and negotiations were begun with the agricultural tenants with a view to starting work. The article closes with these words,

Another local man, somewhat lower in the social scale than the Wemyss family was also badly affected by the "45". Indeed he was completely deprived of his livelihood it is reported. James Sibbald rented the extensive rabbit warren on the links where the golf course is now. He lived by trapping and killing the rabbits. In 1745/46 a company of Jacobites quartered at Prestonpans shot "the whole coveys in the warren" for practice and entertainment leaving so few rabbits that there were not enough to breed and provide produce for another year. Not a few golfers would like to see Mr Sibbald or the sharpshooters reincarnated today.

"With the advent of the golf course, a whole new town will spring up near the old red-roofed hamlet, and the whole aspect of things will be changed".

A hundred and fifty acres were put at the disposal of Harry Colt, one of the foremost golf architects of the day. These included the Cowslip Field, used at one time by the Longniddry football team for its matches, Boglehill Wood, and stretches of the links and bents, which were favourite camping places for gypsies and tinkers. A great amount of work had to be done, for the clearing of the site involved uprooting thousands of trees.

On the completion of the golf course a club house was built with stone from Amisfield House and Longniddry Golf Club was formed with G A Connor (the Earl's Factor) as Honorary Secretary and Treasurer. The official opening ceremony was performed in 1923 on 16th June or July (sources conflict).

In parallel with the development of the Golf Course was the establishment in Longniddry of the first-ever Veterans Garden City. Up to the end of the Second World War Longniddry's Garden City for War Veterans was the largest in the UK. Two memorial stones were laid on 23rd September 1916 for twin dwellings under construction in Kitchener Crescent. The ceremony was bravely performed by two bereaved ladies. One was Mrs Parker the sister of Earl Kitchener who had drowned when HMS Hampshire went down. The other was the Countess of Wemyss. The war had taken her youngest son Ivo in 1915. In April 1916 her eldest son Lord Elcho was killed at Katia in Egypt. He had been with a small detatchment of the Gloucestershire Hussars Yeomanry engaged in building a railway east from Suez to Haifa when they were overwhelmed by a Turkish force. Lady Wemyss must have gathered herself with great fortitude to perform this public duty with Mrs Parker. No doubt there would be many similarly bereaved souls in the gathering. Perhaps they all, principals and spectators derived comfort from the ceremony in the knowledge that they were acting for the welfare of comrades of their fallen loved ones.

The sea, the pleasantly wooded surrounding countryside, the Golf Course and easy access to Edinburgh, all combined to make Longniddry a very desirable "residential" area. The land to the south of the golf Course was feued out and slowly but surely "Gosford Road" and "King's Road" began to fill up with large and (for those times) expensive houses, many of them built by Richard Baillie. Those who bought the new houses were mostly professional persons whose way of life was very different from the old country ways. The "auld residenters" like the Chirnsides, Humes and Haddens were now a minority, David Robertson reports, and no longer typical of the population of Longniddry.

For easy access to the Golf course and these feuing areas, one of the Main Street cottages was demolished and "Links Road" was constructed, following for most of its length the ancient "fit road" from the Old Village to the sea.

At the same time as private building started, the County Council also began to build, the first council houses in Elcho Terrace appearing shortly after the First World War.

In 1937 on the death of the 11th Earl and the succession to the title of his grandson (Francis) David, the golf Club and course were quite surely established and prosperous.

CHAPTER IV
THE CONSTRUCTION AND OPENING OF THE COURSE

In 1928 D & J Croal of Market Street, Haddington, published a small booklet entitled 'Longniddry District and its Golf Course'. It gives the following account of the conception and preparation of the course.

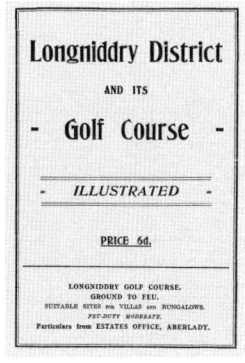

"Previous to the Great War, the little village of Longniddry had remained much the same for many generations - about a dozen houses, a few good market gardens, a school, a smithy, a small village shop, and a Post Office. Now it has developed to such an extent that its old inhabitants of even twenty years ago might have some difficulty in recognising it.

The commencement of this development may be said to have occurred when the Scottish Veterans' Garden City Association cast its eyes upon Longniddry as a very desirable spot on which to begin operations by building suitable houses for disabled soldiers and sailors. Happily the proprietor of the lands here, the Earl of Wemyss and March quite readily agreed to grant a suitable site, and the project was successfully carved out in 1918. Previous to this, however, in 1914, Lord Wemyss conceived the idea of laying out a golf course on part of his own lands lying towards the shore, and to the north-west of Longniddry. On this subject more information will be given further on; but sufficient here to say that these two projects, the building of these Garden City houses, and the laying out of this Golf Course - was the foundation of the more important and popular residential village of Longniddry as we know it today.....

Long before Garden Cities were dreamed of, visitors to the District and some of the more discerning natives as well, used to remark upon the splendid site for building purposes the land around Boglehill presented, never thinking that the day was coming when their idea would be fulfilled as it is today. Boglehill was a mere cluster of three small houses nestling by the side of the public road, now close to and south-east of the Fifteenth Green on the Golf Course. Of course, this road was at the time the main thoroughfare coming eastward from Edinburgh, and foot travellers on that lonely journey were always glad to come in sight of Boglehill, especially as they were able to obtain in those days some welcome refreshment here in the shape of penny ale. It was also on the shore here that, in the year 1869, a monstrous whale was stranded, and lay for some days before it could be removed. This was perhaps, the largest whale ever seen on the East Coast of Scotland. It measured 85 feet in length, and its girth was even greater in proportion. Thousands of people from all parts came to see the monster, and hundreds of them who had never heard of Longniddry became

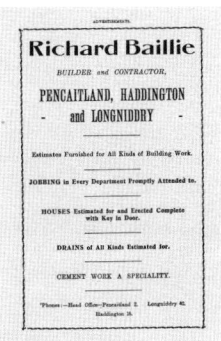

41

acquainted with it for the first time.

It is the unexpected that has happened with the erstwhile obscure little village of Longniddry, for who less than 20 years ago would have thought it was to become famous as a golfing centre. Yet so it is. There is little doubt that the chief attraction it possesses in these latter days, alike for the visitor and the residenter is the first-class quality and various charms of its golf course. The older and long-time noted and golfing links of the county have now this new one added to their number which will further advance the world-wide fame of East Lothian as the favoured land of golf. Even already, it has become a worthy rival to the best of them, and assuredly it has a great future before it.

The laying out of the Course and the work connected therewith were entrusted to Mr. Harry Colt, one of the foremost golf architects of the day. He had ample scope and a splendid site for the purpose – over 150 acres of suitable land being placed at his disposal. The sandy bottom to the turf was all that could be desired; but a strip of planting containing thousands of trees had to be cleared away before a start was made. This was not the only heavy bit of work to be overcome as there was a little stream to be bridged at several points, and a considerable amount of levelling to be done. The ground rises to a fair height towards the South side of the Course, and here one of the putting greens has been cut right out of the face of the hill. It is estimated that this green viz. the 5th, alone cost £700.

The main characteristics of Longniddry Golf Course are those of a seaside nature; but it has also some features, as when for instance you have to play across a little wooded dell, and when you must pursue a dog-leg fairway in order to avoid getting in among the surrounding trees, which remind me forcibly of an inland course. These all help to give a greater variety to the course and to the aspect of its surroundings. If the golfer is not too much absorbed in his game and has an eye for the beautiful, he will be struck at many points by the picturesque bits of landscape, the long strip of bents and brier-topped sand-dunes, and the fine wide sea views that open out to his vision. This fair and far-spread vista of scenes so varied and pleasing to behold is in itself an asset to be counted upon when we reckon up the balance of our contentions in favour of Longniddry Golf Course.

Apart from the situation, and the suitably broken and undulating land which Nature had provided beforehand, Mr. Colt has created here something that will add greatly to his reputation as laying out of golf courses. Many of our most renowned golfers, amateur and professional, have tested the capabilities and possibilities of this course, and are fairly unanimous in pronouncing it second to only a few. The general impression conveyed to one by a trial round is that play should be of a most interesting nature, providing opportunities for all kinds of strokes- except bad ones, of course. For these latter ample punishment is meted out to the player in most cases. The short holes, four in number, have all their own peculiar characteristics, and are all more or less attractive. At the sixth, for instance, which is only 111 yards, the player has to drive across a gully which has both a road and a burn at the bottom of it; and the green is guarded by hazards on both sides. A straight ball carrying the proper distance is a proud achievement, but a topped ball or one much off the line may easily cost an ordinary player double figures. The eleventh, thirteenth, and fifteenth holes are laid out along the sea-shore. Two of these are short holes, and appeal particularly to the sure and steady player. The fifteenth, which is the last short hole of the round, is prettily situated near Bogle Hill before referred to, but is most of all exposed to the wind. Here, again, accuracy counts for much; and on the putting green the player finds himself, should the tide be full, surrounded on three sides by the sea. The fourteenth hole is the longest of all, 576 yards; and, as you stand upon the teeing ground there is a great expanse before you, and you might imagine that you had a whole parish to drive into. The eighth hole is a good example of the compulsory-carry variety with a diagonal hazard, so that players of different degrees of skill may tackle it in their own way. The last three holes all require good hitting, and in making for the home green, which has a deep dip in front of it, the player who has had a long drive will have a rather ticklish problem in playing his second, especially if the wind is blowing from the west. The total length of the course is just over 6,000 yards, and that of the different holes approximately as follows :-

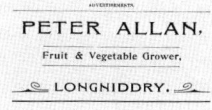
Player's Name .... Date ....

HOLE	YARDS	BOGEY	SCORE	HOLE	YARDS	BOGEY	SCORE
1	395	5		10	367	4	
2	436	5		11	350	5	
3	461	5		12	343	4	
4	191	3		13	166	3	
5	319	4		14	582	6	
6	161	3		15	180	3	
7	433	5		16	422	5	
8	365	5		17	378	5	
9	378	4		18	442	5	
OUT	3131 3139	39		IN	3230	40	

TOTAL LENGTH 6321 6369 YARDS

MARKER'S SIGNATURE

OUT ..
GROSS TOTAL ..
HANDICAP ..
NET TOTAL ..

THIS CARD IS SIX INCHES IN LENGTH

LONGNIDDRY GOLF CLUB

Following upon the completion of the laying out of the golf course a club was formed, taking the name of The Longniddry Golf Club, with Mr. G. A. Connor as honorary secretary and treasurer; and it is now on a fair way to prosperity. A Club-house was erected in proximity to the first tee, and being on a lofty site, has a commanding view of the links. It is a commodious, well-appointed establishment, fully licensed, with facilities for catering for *the wants of the members and friends. A Putting Course, of excellent quality, has also been laid out beside the Club-house, and further adds to the attractions of the place. The present greenkeeper, Mr. Alexander Wright, a man of wide experience and undoubted genius in many ways, may be trusted to keep the course in the best condition. A good professional is also attached to the Club.*

Longniddry Golf Course may confidently be expected to make a great name for itself; and the probability is that, sooner or later, it will become one of the championship courses. The first tee is within a quarter of an hour's walk from the railway station, and half an hour's motor run from Edinburgh, so that it is very conveniently situated for the dwellers in the capital, to whom the facilities of golf may mean health and happiness, and who may find themselves crowded out of the courses nearer hand."

So terminates the section about the golf course in the booklet, which was priced at sixpence. Its objective seemed to be to market not only the golf course, but ground in Longniddry to feu 'suitable sites for villas and bungalows' as well as many local suppliers. It seems likely therefore, that the preparation of the booklet was done with the support of The Earl of Wemyss and his Factor.

The date for the construction of the course and the establishment of the Club is given as 1921. Within two years the course was ready for competitive play. The first full event appears to have been the Spring Meeting on 18th May 1923. The Haddingtonshire Courier reported it as follows: *"With the Spring Meeting, the competitions of the Longniddry Club were inaugurated on Saturday over their fine course in dry but cold weather. The trophies for the competition were a handsome silver challenge cup (Scratch), gifted by Mr. G.H.A. Connor who is officiating as temporary honorary secretary, and an accompanying medal presented by the Club, whilst under handicap a medal was also offered. There were 40 competitors."* Apart from Mr. Connor no Club members' names are given.

A month or two later a bigger event took place. Once more the Haddingtonshire Courier had a first-hand account: *"Spectators estimated at 4000 in number, witnessed Jas. Braid and E. Ray compete against J.H. Taylor and Abe Mitchell in a 36-hole 4 x ball match over the Longniddry Course on Saturday afternoon. The fame of the new East Lothian Course has spread far and near, and on Saturday its beautiful situation along the shores of the Firth of Forth was admired by all. This was the first time since it was opened that an exhibition match by famous professionals has been played over the course. The weather was ideal, there being practically no wind, and the sunshine was not too warm from the point of view of either player or follower. Originally it had been intended that Mr. George Duncan should partner Braid, but at the last moment Duncan had to abandon the idea of taking part as he was unwell.*

The scores for the two rounds were:

	a.m.	p.m.
Braid & Ray	70	67
Taylor & Mitchell	71	73

It was agreed that a great deal was owed to Mr. Connor for the time and devotion he had given while the course was being made!"

At least one member surviving in 1996 saw the match. Dorothy Rennie, a Past Lady Captain, is the daughter of Dr. Robarts, who in the 1920's was physician to the Earl of Wemyss. Mrs. Rennie remembers being taken to the exhibition match by her father and watching the professionals play, and the presentations and speeches afterwards.

CHAPTER V

THE CLUBHOUSE, STAFF AND PERSONALITIES

The Longniddry clubhouse sits high on its terrace above the golf course. Its position commands magnificent views across the Firth of Forth, north to the Lomond peaks of Fife and west to the mountains in the distance beyond the bridges of Queensferry. The cantilevers of the old bridge stretch like lace across the towers of the new one whilst the level of the sea horizon high up the pillars demonstrates the massive curvature of the earth.

The Clubhouse is placed at the very focus of the course with 5 greens and 5 tees within 200 yards. The sandstone blocks which form its walls were carefully retrieved after demolition of buildings on the Amisfield estate outside Haddington.

The building is seen at its best on a summer evening from below on the Shore road. The setting sun across the Forth lights the sandstone to a warm glow while the Wemyss white swan shines above the roof. Looking up to the bright windows, pleasant recollections come to mind of harmony, good fellowship, and friendly antagonists.

The main structure of the Clubhouse comprises three parallel sections aligned east/west, each topped by a blue slate-covered double-pitched roof. The shortest most southerly part has two storeys. It is the Clubmaster's dwelling. From its western end the low level flat-roofed buildings of the boiler room and storerooms project, forming a small enclosed yard with the west wall of the men's locker room. The central section is also of two storeys and includes at ground level, the dining room, kitchen, and part of the men's back bar. Upstairs is the ladies' locker room and lounge terminating in the pleasing blue-slated cupola which is so distinctive. The most northerly part is a lofty single-storey building. It houses the entrance hall, the Secretary's office and the high-ceilinged main lounge from which a large bay window on the north wall looks over the golf course and the Firth.

The Clubhouse appears to have been built in several stages. It has been suggested that the Clubmaster's house was the first to be constructed, intended for the Estate Factor before the plans for the golf course were finalised. Certainly the stonework of the Clubmaster's house is of a different quality from the rest.

To this original building the other two pitched-roof sections appear to have been added at the time of the construction of the course. The photograph taken certainly before 1929 with the anonymous lady putting on the 18th green, shows the west wall of the lounge to be the extremity of the clubhouse. The flat-roofed extension which today houses the men's locker rooms and changing area did not at that time exist. Nor did the cupola section of the ladies' lounge upstairs. Indeed originally, the men's locker room was what is now the dining room; the recess in its south wall is where the men's toilets used to be. The ladies' lockers are said to have been on the ground floor on either side of the corridor leading from the hall. The toilets and changing area for the ladies must always have been upstairs. The houses in the photograph to the left of the Clubhouse are on the south side of Gosford Road. Beechworth (now Lochinvar) had yet to be built.

Lizzie and Ruby Bell in maids uniforms.

The kitchen in those early days would have been quite small because a large part of the present kitchen was originally the dining room. The west windows of that early eating place now face the enclosed yard, but in the 20's the diners would be able to contemplate the first tee and the fine prospects beyond the first hole. From the bay window in the south wall of this small dining room, snacks and sandwiches were served to the caddies such as old Willie McEwan or the young George Taylor.

Ruby Bell joined the staff as a maid in 1927. Later, of course, she became Mrs Robina Paxton, the mother-in-law of the Club's Assistant Secretary Cristine Paxton. Ruby remembers that not long after she started with the Club, the extension to the ladies' lounge and construction of the flat roofed section to the west were put in hand. This is confirmed by the minutes of the Ladies Club which show that Mr Connor advised of the plans for the changes in January 1929.

On completion of this extension therefore, the 1930's visitor entering the clubhouse by the front door on the east side of the building, would find the Secretary's office on the right hand as now. Sometimes this was used as a committee room and it is said that the Board was known to be in session when the tobacco smoke could be seen creeping out from under the door. The dining room newly converted from the men's locker room was on the left hand side of the entrance hall as it is today. The door on the right of the facing staircase led to the main lounge as it still does, but the door on the left opened into a locker-lined corridor which gave access in turn to the men's changing room in the vicinity of the present back bar. Behind the left hand wall of this corridor was a small scullery bar. This occupied the area behind the counter of to-day's lounge bar. It is said to have been usually packed with chatting and jostling male humanity drinking or demanding

In the clubhouse the cleaning proper had to be done late at night when eventually the members had left for home. The maids started work at 7 a.m. In the kitchen, the black coal fired range had to be cleaned out and lit whilst outside the brasses were polished and the steps washed. Inside there was only time for light dusting before the members began to arrive demanding attention from the maids who had to be in their waitress uniforms by this time.

service from the barman behind the tiny eastward-facing hatch. It was the only place those males without jackets could go to be served.

Upstairs what is nowadays the ladies locker room was a bedroom containing a double and a single bed for three maids who lived in. Some of these ladies have been identified. Ruby Bell has already been mentioned but there was her sister Lizzie as well. She married John Gourlay, who became clubmaster first at Kilspindie and then at Luffness. There were also Maud Harvey and Nora and Mary Gaffney. The current Vice-President's wife and former Lady Captain, Bella Porteous was there too on her school holidays. The maids worked hard in those days. Not only for the golf club: they could be required to work for the Estate too.

Apart from the maids' bedroom, the lady members' accommodation upstairs appears to have consisted of a single large room, with the lockers set around the walls. In the early days at least no separate lounge was partitioned off. It is reported that the room was on occasion used for Club committee meetings and that somewhere in the south wall there was a dumb waiter. There was also upstairs, a small bedroom (now the ladies powder room) at the western end of the central section. This was used by Mr Connor and subsequent Club Secretaries when business had kept them exceptionally late. Years later Norman Osborne had a bed for himself placed upstairs under the small round window in the eastern gable.

Downstairs again, members not using the scullery bar were served their refreshments in the main lounge by the maids who responded to a service bell. The push buttons for these bells can still be seen on the walls of the lounge, although the service hatch from the kitchen which once existed has been covered over.

The main lounge was uncarpeted for many years. Members tended to gather round one of the two fireplaces or at a large central table. The chairs were wooden and unpadded. In 1967 Marjory Douglas of 'Inchmahome' generously gifted a carpet for the lounge, but the old wooden floor is still to be seen on social occasions when the carpet has been rolled back for dancing. This reveals a number of deep grooves and indentations in the planks of the floor. The story goes that during the war some members of the Tank Corps were billeted in the clubhouse. The scars on the floor are blamed on them and are attributed either to the feet of the metal sleeping cots or to vigorous bayonet practice.

In the early days, Longniddry was the only club in the district which was open for play on Sundays. Consequently, many from Gullane, Muirfield and North Berwick came to Longniddry to play on the Sabbath. A particular group were known as the Pirates - they would finish off their golf with a supper in the clubhouse and then return to Gullane or Edinburgh for a rubber of bridge. Amongst the names were Hilda and Alex Smith - Alex was

The 'famous thing' on Sundays, according to Jimmy Hume, was 'the bookies'. Several big money matches took place. John Gorman was involved and his wife played too. They lived at Rose Cottage, Longniddry. The Geddies and the Smiths were part of the crowd. Another regular party (quite separate from the bookmakers crowd of course) was a group of priests who turned up for golf every Monday.

a Bookmaker - the Greigs (parents of Tony Greig the England Test Captain) and Freddie Haines who owned the printing firm Morrison and Gibb. There were also Winnie McGuire who had a garden shop called 'Crichtons' in Leith Walk and Nanny and Tim Scott of Portobello. Tim owned a chemist shop also at the bottom of Leith Walk. One of their close friends was Bill McKinlay. There was Harry Stewart the dentist and his wife Ella. Another name was Frank Cooper, a banker. He was friendly with Charlie and Anne Geddie and Willie Cowie. Douglas Tudhope who owned the drapers in Dalkeith called 'Manchester House' was one of the crowd as were Dolly and Bill Cowe who were proprietors of 'Cuskell and Chambers' shopfitters.

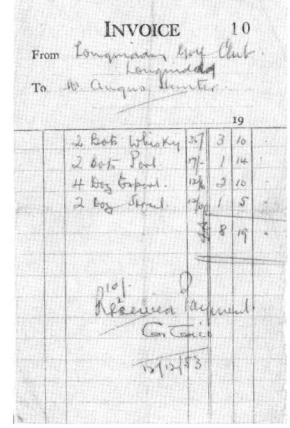

Not only did the extension of the clubhouse permit the enlargement of the ladies' lounge upstairs, it made possible downstairs, the addition of a men's lounge beyond the men's locker room. This small west lounge was originally open on Sundays only. Refreshments were obtained by means of a telephone call to the kitchen which produced a drinks trolley. Later, the trolley was replaced by a small bar built by Club Master Tommy Robb about 1963, and situated in the near corner beside the fireplace. It was only one of the many joinery tasks that Tommy undertook in the Clubhouse. The drinks trolley and the subsequent bar were manned by Angus Hunter one of the Club's longest serving employees.

Angus Hunter. Angus is an Aberlady man. He joined the Club as barman in 1950 and is still an employee 46 years later. He purchased the drinks for his wedding from the Club in 1953 and his receipt for the £8.19/- transaction still survives.

An unassuming person, Angus has an interesting war record. As a driver in the RASC he was at El Alamein with the 42nd (London) Division. He continued with the North Africa campaign to Tunis and then drove his lorry with two trucks on tow back to Suez meeting up with his brother in Cairo for a celebratory meal. He was at the invasion of Sicily where he was obliged to stand in 5 feet of water off the beach (he is only 5'4") and was slightly damaged in action when he jumped over a wall into a bed of cactus. Somewhere in the course of all of this he operated with the Ghurkas and found himself driving donkeys, possibly whilst attached to the 7th Armoured Division.

Angus Hunter

David Cuthbertson. The Club's other long-serving barman is David Cuthbertson - 'Cubby' as he is affectionately known. Son of an early caddy master, Cubby is the same age as the Club itself. Before the war David regularly worked in the brickworks and the pit at Prestongrange. During his time off he caddied at Luffness, Gullane, and Muirfield. One of his recollections is caddying for Sir William Thomson Provost of Edinburgh, when Willie Huish was Caddymaster at Gullane, as was Jimmy Fraser at Muirfield.

David Cuthbertson

David's prowess as a barman was celebrated in the 'Sunday Times' during the reporting of the World Seniors Tournament by that prince of golf correspondents, Henry Longhurst. No sooner had he appeared at the door, wrote Henry, than without a request being uttered, David placed a gin and tonic on the bar to his hand.

Called up during the war, David served in the RAF. He was posted to either end of the country in succession, firstly to Peterhead and then later to Bigginhill. He later got to Hamburg and Brunswick and then back to Scotland to join the Electricity Board.

Looking back on his golf experience, he feels that he enjoyed most the first Seniors Competition in 1970. Among the names he remembers was the winner that year, Max Faulkner. There was also Kel Nagle who won in 1975 and the one and only Bobby Locke who, David says, never lifted coins from the bar counter.

David manages to know everything that is going on in the Club. How he does it is not quite clear. Perhaps he studies humanity as it appears at his bar. He certainly studies equine performance, and favoured members on their best behaviour may be rewarded with some quiet advice. Not that he claims to be infallible of course.

Adept at serving thirsty golfers interpreting and anticipating their requirements, the highly popular David brooks no nonsense keeping any unruly spirits under control.

Heating and the heated

Although the account of the early days of the Club from Maurice Dunleavy refers to his cleaning the boiler, this appliance supplied hot water only. Heating was provided by means of open fires, two in the lounge and one each in the dining room and in the men's lounge. The nine chimneys of the building demonstrate that there were other fireplaces elsewhere in the clubhouse. Eventually of course a full central heating system was installed but this was not until the 1970's. Before that access to the fireplace in the uncarpeted lounge was a matter of prestige and seniority. For twenty years up to the mid fifties Secretary Roy Cutter could often be found with his cronies in front of one of the lounge fires.

Conversations with long-serving members and staff have brought forth many names.

Peter Barr's son Alastair was one of the best golfers whom the Club produced. He turned professional starting his career as Assistant Professional at Musselburgh. Alastair is currently coach to the English Ladies Golf Union.

Peter Barr was often there. He was a Royal Bank man, an excellent golfer and Captain of the Club 1959/60. He used to steep his hands in a basin of water before playing to make them more sensitive - at least so he told his over-awed opponents. The others of Peter's regular four were Peter Cadzow, Joe Mitchell and Gus McVey.

Gus McVey, a category 1 player, was always immaculately dressed, normally in plus fours, or more lately, plus twos. He was a great fan of Henry Cotton. All his shirts were 100% cotton whether for comfort or out of respect for his hero is not clear. It took deep research of the records to reveal that Gus was actually an abbreviation of Augustus. Reflecting on Gus's bearing and authority in the Club his christian name does not seem inappropriate.

Frequently Gus, a Heriots FP, would find himself cast in the role of reluctant straight man to the irrepressible J D 'Johnny' Munro. Johnny was very small and very intelligent. He claimed to be a Communist. He was a provocative argufier and reputedly a terrible maximum handicap golfer. Like Gus he was an insurance man. 'The only prize I ever won' he said 'was for being the tallest dwarf in the 3rd standard'. He is described as often wearing concertina trousers and a suede jacket.

Typical of the goings on would be an interchange at the bar. Johnny would observe Gus entering the lounge and feign to be in the middle of a golfing story "so when I got to my drive" he would pretend to continue "I took out my six iron and hit a real beauty right beside the pin, and stuffed the ball in the hole for a 3". Gus could always be relied upon to fall for it. "Good birdie" he would say "Birdie be damned" replies Johnny "it was at the 16th". Or again: "I see you're wearing a hole in one tie" says Gus who had at least one ace to his credit. "Yep!" says Johnny. "Where?" says Gus. "The third with a following wind" On another occasion Alex Harvey and wife Anne with young son John in his pushchair were on the right of way en route to the beach. They stopped at the edge of the 14th to let the golfers pass. One of them was Johnny Munro. His drive had not been impressive. He stood in front of them and addressed the ball with his 3 wood. He swung and skulled the ball horribly 30 yards along the ground. He turned and bent down to young John, "Remember son, my name is Gus McVey", he said and away down the fairway he went. Both Gus and Johnny were very able and hard working Directors of the Club. Gus of course was captain 1955-57. He was instrumental in the establishment of the Winter League which has been running now for almost 30 years.

J.D. Munro

Then of course there were the Inglis brothers - Alistair and Kenneth, stalwarts of the Club. Gentlemen farmers, they were both bachelors. They lived at Parkeston, Cockenzie. Kenneth was a top amateur rider but he was always exposed to his elder brother's critical scrutiny and comment. They owned a small Landrover which was stopped by the police on the way home one night for driving too slowly.

It is said (though not undisputed) that in the lounge Alistair and Kenneth regularly positioned themselves at either side of the serving counter like noble armorial supporters to the escutcheon of the bar. They have been described more mundanely in that situation as looking like a pair of book-ends. This proximity to the refreshments should not be misconstrued, the pair were deployed there chiefly for debate and the mischievous Johnny Munro rarely failed them.

Another member of the Gus McVey company and still going strong is Bob Anderson. With over half a century of subscriptions to his credit, Bob is one of the Club's longest playing members.

He is a Surveyor by profession. He did his war service in the Merchant Navy and this left him with an arm somewhat damaged. His friends claim that the consequential alteration caused to him has improved his golf swing considerably, much as Douglas Bader arranged his tin legs so that he always had an uphill lie. Of course Bob resolutely protests against these unsympathetic and unjust remarks contending that his numerous golfing victories and championship successes (at Braid Hills particularly) are a triumph of character and technique over both this disadvantage and particularly unscrupulous acquaintances.

Bob joined the Club in 1946. He had just finished supervising the construction of a pier at Barra for Wimpey. It still stands solid and robust today. He and his friend Tom Kemp set off on the bus one Sunday morning in the spring of 1946 for a day's golf. The conductor had not collected the fares by the time they reached Musselburgh and it was a beautiful day, so they decided to give Monktonhall a miss and go on down the coast. They found Longniddry and it looked good. Gus McVey was there. They played two rounds and decided to join the Club. It cost four guineas each and no entrance fee. Membership was cheaper than playing as a visitor.

As well as being a really good golfer and formidable competitor, Bob Anderson has been a most able Director of the Club applying himself tirelessly and meticulously to the welfare of the course.

George Mitchell

A dominating personality in the lounge for many years was local gentleman farmer George Mitchell. His fields stretched right down to the Dean. A powerful thick set figure, George had in the lounge, his very own armchair which no one else was allowed to use. In cold weather it would be placed close to one of the fireplaces. George may well have been a founder member of the Club. He was its proud Honorary Vice-President for many years. He claimed to have driven the 1st green at least twice although friendly sceptics remarked that if so the conditions had been 'bone hard dry with a stiff following breeze'. In his later years George used to motor down (eventually he was chauffeured) to the Club in the evening from his house at Chesterhall. He rolled his own cigarettes or smoked full strength Sobranie. In 1964 he presented the Mitchell Cup to the Club for competition by mixed pairs.

Associated with George Mitchell were Ian Buchanan (Club Captain 1949/50) and the Adairs. John Adair (Captain 1962/63) owned a drapers shop in Leith Street. Jim Adair was a chiropodist. He had been a Heriots hooker and he always used an old tie to hold up his golfing trousers as though he was still in the scrum. Jim played in the same foursome every Sunday with Willie Hackett (who owned a pub situated above the Adair drapers shop), Andreoli and Norrie Smith.

There were many other names. There was Dave 'Old Parr' Taylor from Musselburgh. His regular four every Saturday consisted of J L Johnstone, John 'Pale Face' Paterson and Dave Kirkcaldy.

George (Dumps) Ferguson had been around. He was a foreman with Neuchatel Asphalt when they were laying the Burma road. He claimed to have cut the ribbon when they opened the bridge over the River Kwai. George played regularly with John Adair, Sandy Shearlaw and Anderton. Tommy Waugh was another familiar face and Harry Butcher whose connections were with show business and cinemas. He lived in Gullane and was said to own all the local picture houses.

Before leaving the Clubhouse the formal awards to the Club should be noted. On the south wall of the mixed lounge to the right of the bar, seven wooden plaques are mounted. The uppermost one dated 1987 commemorates Longniddry's selection by the Royal and Ancient as a qualifying course for the Open Championship at Muirfield. A second plaque carries the red lion rampant of the Scottish Golf Union. The remaining five each bear a green shield with overlaid letters representing the Golf Foundation. This is a national charity established to encourage the spread of golf and promising young golfers. Sponsors have included 'Weetabix' and 'Ford Motors'. Each green plaque on the Clubhouse wall signifies a financial contribution from Longniddry Golf Club to the Foundation. The dates on the five plaques are 1979, 80, 91, 92 and 93.

Outside the clubhouse at the first tee there was for many years a starter's box usually occupied by Mr Bob Himsworth, starter and caddymaster. Nancy Jupp testifies that he was a character. 'He could be as officious as he needed to be' she says 'but underneath he had a heart of gold'. Bob was a very good golfer himself; one of the few who, in his latter years, could beat his age. He used to encourage all the young caddies to play the course when it was quiet. He lived in Gullane and would walk up Links Road very straight and erect - he was 6' 2", to get the bus home in the evening. Sometimes the young Jimmy Hume would take over the starting duties when Bob was on holiday.

The starter's box still exists, although not at the golf club. It can be seen from Amisfield Place sitting in the garden behind 32 John Knox Road. Apparently Tommy Hogg took it away as a gift from the Earl of Wemyss when he retired from the job of Head Greenkeeper.

Mr Himsworth who operated as starter both before and after the War, was paid £2 10/- per week in 1936. He was made an Honorary Life member of the Club in 1952.

The terrace of the clubhouse is a grand viewpoint and the seats on it are often occupied on summer evenings. Three of these seats have been gifted to the club. One commemorates Jenny Arnott who was Ladies Honorary Secretary from 1954 until 1966. The second was presented by Derek and Gordon de Vries in memory of their mother Lily who was Lady Captain in 1977/78. A third seat was gifted by the Army in Scotland Officers Golfing Society in recognition of their long association with the Club.

The frontage of the western side of the clubhouse deserves a little attention. It is of course the wall of the men's locker and changing rooms. The small entrance section which today houses the drying room and spike toilet was originally the caddy shed where the caddies gathered hopefully waiting for work under the eye of Bob Himsworth. Further along, above the coping of the flat roof is what, according to stone mason member Bob Anderson, appears to be a cast decorative piece from Amisfield House. A study of the wall below the windows reveals that there was a door here in this west wall. This was the door of the professional's shop in the early 30's. In those days of hand-made clubs it would probably be more of a workroom than a shop. It was replaced by a wooden building presumably on the site of the present shop. The date of this change is not known but it is possible that the use of part of the clubhouse as a foodstore during the war had something to do with it. At any rate the existing professional's shop or part of it at least was constructed about 1948 shortly after burglars had broken into the wooden structure which it replaced.

The Clubhouse and Members 1996. The facilities of the Clubhouse are extensively used nowadays. The back bar has always been busy of course and is much improved by Bert Milligan's renovation.

Although the dress regulations in the main lounge have been relaxed, many members still seem to prefer the informal crowded hubbub of the back bar. It is the headquarters of the Saturday and Sunday sweeps and of the Friday Club. The golfing standards of its inhabitants is generally high therefore, and their competitiveness even higher. While rarely uncharitable, the back bar is no place for the self-important. Its occupants have a genius profound for penetrating comment and irreverent wisecrack. In it are to be found many of the personalities of the Club:

Alex Harvey, Gordon Milligan, Rab Thorburn, George Taylor, Bob Anderson, Steven Thomson, George Harkess, Bert Smith, John Barber, Peter Lowe, Gordon Bonnington, Mike Robinson and Bob Powe to name only a few. Perhaps one of the many stories of the place can be told:

Among professional tournaments at Longniddry in the fifties and sixties were the Martini Invitation and the Carling Caledonian which generated much interest and encouraged convivial conversation with accompanying refreshment. A certain bearded member (ex-Port Seton and now of Gullane) who shall remain anonymous, enjoyed those occasions more than most. One morning on leaving home to watch the play his wife cautioned him to be early and in good condition as they were going out that evening for supper to fastidious friends. Easily led (if only in certain directions) some refreshments were admittedly consumed during entirely necessary post-match analysis. Returning home late (in a sponsor's Rolls Royce it is said) he found his wife gone, so he wended his way to his hosts' house. Drawing himself together, he entered the lounge carefully and sat down with every

On the east side of the clubhouse below the putting green is a practice net where the Clubmaster's garden used to be. Beyond that what is now the lower car park was, in the late 50's and early 60's, a space occupied by a multiplicity of higgelty-piggelty chicken coops. Keeping chickens was an interest of Clubmaster Tommy Robb and the practice was continued by his successor George Morawisc.

appearance of self-control. On crossing his legs though, he discovered that he still wore his golf shoes, studs and all.

It is in the back bar that the television set lives. The original was gifted to the back bar members by Secretary John Gunn. Nowadays it generally operates on the Sky Sports Channel - when it is switched on that is - because it is controlled by 'Cubby' behind his counter, and David can be a strict disciplinarian when necessary.

Through all the chaff and banter senses are alert for the latest sporting news, when activity briefly stills. But the usual happy din collapses to concentrated silence when Raymond Russell is featured. The place was packed that Sunday in 1996 when an anxious eager audience watched Raymond battle home through the last few holes of the Cannes Open. When his final putt fell, Bert's redecorated walls and ceiling reverberated to a great shout of acclaim.

The highlight of the back bar year is the December celebratory dinner enhanced in recent times by the candid video of first tee shots taken by Robin Laidlaw with Dick Burge commentary. Both educational and humbling it is not an entertainment for sensitive souls.

The greatest Clubhouse change in recent years is in the lounge. Now that the dress regulations have been relaxed, many more members use the lounge after a game and dress standards, although more casual, have never seriously deteriorated as some had feared they might. A greater number of ladies are to be seen in the lounge nowadays, particularly if they are having refreshments. The ladies still have their own small lounge upstairs, but with the dumb waiter long out of use, it is seriously inconvenient, not to say hazardous, to carry hot beverages up these long stairs.

While the ladies appear randomly in the lounge there is a more regular pattern to the men's attendances. Different groupings are found on different days. Again it is not possible to give details of them all; the following should be taken as representative.

Apart from the likes of Jim Duncan and Alan Neil who are sometimes out as early soloists, the week is truly and regularly begun on a Monday morning with the Armstrong, Cunningham, Currie and McArthur quartet. Judging by the time of their arrival in the lounge, they must tune up on the first tee about 7.30 a.m.

This group is closely followed by the Frank Webb four: rather senior members usually content to play a steady 13 holes and get to their coffee.

Next comes what might be called the full orchestra or the Recently Indigent Pool. This group began as a twosome of Bill Thomson and Jim Mackenzie in 1990 or thereabouts. It has swollen over the years by virtue of retirements both late and early, to about 14 players. For a time until the numbers got too large, the process of throwing up the golf balls to decide on the playing partnerships had become something of a ritual. There are too many in the group to list them all, but Bill Thomson himself with George Bonnar, Ronnie Herkes, Archie Johnston, Alistair Mackay, Robin Sharp and

The Dawn Patrol:
Duncan Nicolson, Mike Lockhart, Bill Thomson, Jim Bousher, Ronnie Herkes, Jim Davidson, Douglas Marwick.

Douglas Hally form the nucleus of a varied (wild?) bunch whose previous existence ranged from fishing skipper, through bank manager to abdominal surgeon. If the professional performance of the last was as precise as his putting (and it seems that it was), his patients were well served indeed.

No sooner have the catering staff - the faithful Martha or the busy Thelma or sometimes even Jean herself - got this large contingent fed and moistened, when David Morrison and Norman Lang appear like as not accompanied by the Minister Graham Black. They are followed by various partnerships: Sandy Nicoll sometimes with Bill Aitken or Alastair Thomson with friends, and then by Hugo Galloway (having removed his Rett Butler hat), George Taylor perhaps, or John Jardine, and the two McKay brothers Robert and Donald. Scattered among these groups individual random regulars appear: Matt Bilsland having a light lunch, the omnipresent Dick Morris or the more occasional Stuart Fiddler.

Tuesdays are generally given over to the ladies and for want of willing witnesses, their lounge doings are not recorded.

On Wednesdays the variegated retirement pool arrives again. This time it is augmented by the honest lad from Ayr, Alex MacKay, whose small dapper frame contrasts with that of his tall Edinburgh companion, Bill Reid. Another Wednesday arrival is the Alex Good, Jim Mackenzie, Stanley Riddell and Jack Sommerville foursome, when the progress of Hearts Football Club is often contemplated.

Later in the day the Wednesday Club appears. A cheerful lively group among whom Tom Miller, George Arbuthnot and Kenny Kinnear are prominent. Invitations to Wednesday Club Christmas celebrations are coveted. The presence of the Club enlivens and cheers the lounge through Wednesday afternoons. An account of the history of the Wednesday Club written by Jack Little is given in Chapter VII.

Thursdays tend to be quieter days with fewer regular games for the men. Many of the ladies appear again though and a number of mixed couples, John and Ellen Ellis for example or Bob and Celia Bowers.

On Fridays some elder statesmen of the Club appear. Tom Porteous Gilbert Dempster, Dan Abbot, George Morgan or Charles MacGregor, tee off mid-morning, whilst Tom Milne often turns up for lunch.

Saturday and Sundays are of course the big days. First out on Saturdays is usually the fast moving foursome of Jim Scott, Jim Davidson, Ian MacRaild and Reg Curzon. Their game, and the one immediately following of George Bonnar, Ronnie Herkes, Alastair Mackechnie and Bill McClure must have been fixtures for going on quarter of a century. These two foursomes are usually followed closely by Graham Patterson and Ken MacLean, sometimes with Bill Grieve.

After this, a variety of names follow: Alex MacKay again and the Alex Good group, followed by Malcolm Graham with Bill Renton perhaps. About this time Jim Lowe plays as do Ian Watson and Garry Connacher and the Saturday sweep (which is dealt with in detail later) comes into full flow, interspersed perhaps with a few non-sweep matches such as David Bruce and Bill Thomson. Then, about 11 o' clock, the Lochend men appear led by Rab Thorburn with such as Gilbert Wallace, Bert Smith and others in tow.

Sunday mornings are occupied chiefly by a combination of Saturday Sweep and Friday Club members whose post round recuperation is generally in the back bar. Later in the day a considerable number of mixed foursomes are played and the lounge can be really busy with couples like Bill and Mavis Fenton, Robin and Jan Sharp or Gordon and Jenny Morrison relaxing after the day's golf.

The lounge is at its best though upon the occasions of the men's annual dinner each February. The top table runs the full length of the lounge. The Captain, his chain of office prominent, is in the centre place with his guests on either hand: the Earl of Wemyss and the Captains of Kilspindie, Caermount, Tantallon Castle, Dunbar and North Berwick.

From the top table six subsidiary limbs project, running across the lounge towards the bar, manned by 'Cubby' once again. At these transverse tables sit the members and their guests. As usual Rab Thorburn and the 'Lochend' crowd are in splendid form nearest the fireplace – Bert Smith, Derek Naughton and the others. The silver gleams, the conversation hums and buzzes and ceases for the Grace. Then it rises again as the courses are adroitly served to the packed company. Good humour and good fellowship abound and John Kennedy, Master Chef and Clubmaster, joins the company for the speeches and post prandial conversations, on past midnight.

All agree, the Club is in good heart and contented members wander home rejoicing.

Clubmasters

There have been six Clubmasters in the 75 years of the Club's existence.

1921-1929. J Shackleton. Although described as bald and short in stature, Mr Shackleton apparently did not lack authority. He had been the Earl of Wemyss' butler. He is remembered as always wearing black sleeve covers and is said to have kept the Club silver in gleaming bright condition.

He lovingly tended the garden beside the clubhouse growing much of the vegetables and fruit required for the kitchen.

Mrs Shackleton was thin and very lady-like. One Shackleton son Alan lived in John Knox Road and was often to be seen helping in the clubhouse. He also worked on occasions as a gardener for Madame Tensfelt who lived in Gosford Road and whose beautician's parlour in Princes Street was the first to be established in Edinburgh.

There were three Shackleton daughters: Ethel, Eva and Mabel. Ethel married Sandy Shearlaw who worked in the railway office at Waverley (The North British Railway Company). Mabel married Lord Wemyss' chauffeur Jack Saddler and it was said that the pair went south to live at the Earl's Estate in Gloucestershire.

It was a great tragedy when the Shackletons lost their son Maurice. He came off his motor cycle in Links Road. The petrol tank burst and he was badly burned. In spite of prompt treatment in the Teesdale's home at Links Road, next to the professional's house, the young man died.

When the Shackletons retired they went to live at Woodville in Aberlady.

1929-1952. The Shearlaws. Sandy and Ethel Shearlaw took over in the clubhouse. Eva meantime had married a banker and had gone to live in Aberdeen. Unfortunately he died comparatively early and Eva returned to help the Shearlaws in the clubhouse. Ethel did all the baking and the cooking. Nothing was bought in. She made wonderful light 'floury' scones and pastries on an open fire with a griddle. She made great succulent roasts and steak pies. Often it was so hot in the small kitchen that she would go barefoot. Her speciality was tripe. All the tripe lovers used to come when she was making tripe. She kept the fat and sold it back to the butcher as dripping.

Most of the vegetables and fruit came from Sandy's garden below the putting green supplemented by some bartered produce from George Mitchell of Chesterhall. Sunday lunches were particularly popular. Sandy and Ethel were very hard working and are remembered with great affection.

Eva served in the dining room. She would distribute menus to the luncheon parties with the warning that they 'couldnae a' have the same thing'. It would need to be 'spread a bit'.

In the Clubmaster's Garden there were a variety of fruit trees: pears, apples and plums, a regular source of fruit for the youth of Longniddry. A gentleman who shall be nameless but now operates in a professional capacity at Gullane will admit, if pressed, to appropriating 'the occasional windfall' without authorisation.

Ethel's Ginger Cake recipe has come down to us via Ruby Paxton:

$1/2$ lb margarine
$1/2$ lb soft brown sugar
1lb plain brown flour
3 eggs
1 teaspoon ginger
$1/4$ pint milk (warm)
$1/2$ teaspoon bicarbonate of soda
1 teaspoon vinegar
$1/2$ lb syrup (warm)
$1/2$ lb treacle

Cream margarine and sugar. Add the rest of the ingredients. Line tin and cook at 325 degrees for about one and a half hours. Enjoy!!

The Shearlaws were made Honorary Members of the Club in 1953. They were followed by Major and Mrs Gill.

1952-1956. Major and Mrs Gill. Angus Hunter describes Major Gill as a short man, always very well turned out. He had a black moustache and his bearing was a military one. He had served in Burma. In those days of 'bona fide' travel, Sunday was the big social day at the golf Club. The rules tended to be flexible. In the evening, the legend goes, the closure of the bar was decided upon by the Major. When it was feared that he would be about to 'call time' it would be a tactic to engross him in conversation to prolong the conviviality as long as possible. Burma got most thoroughly discussed therefore on many occasions.

While Major Gill supervised the bar, Mrs Gill did all the cooking and directed the maids as Ethel Shearlaw had done before her. Mrs Gill was an exceptionally pleasant person. She had a bad leg which caused her to limp noticeably.

Angus Hunter particularly remembers an unfortunate accident involving the Major. There was no running water for the bar or the drinks trolley in the small Sunday-only west lounge. Angus kept a bucket of water, therefore, on the floor beside him at the end of a duckboard. Major Gill came in to relieve him one evening and the poor fellow missed his footing, tripped on the duckboard and plunged head first into the bucket of water. Fortunately the only damage sustained was to his dignity.

The Gills stay was comparatively brief. They were followed by the Robbs.

1956-1962. Mr and Mrs Tommy Robb. Tommy Robb an old 8th Army man, had owned the first butcher's shop in Longniddry. It was situated in the vicinity of the British Legion memorial. When he gave up the shop both he and his wife Elizabeth were employed for a time by Commander Donald Ross who lived at Cockenzie House, long since vacated by the Cadells.

It was subsequent to this that Tommy Robb was engaged by Major Gill to assist in the golf clubhouse. When the Gills departed, Tommy and Elizabeth took over. It was a family affair. Their son Telfer helped from the beginning even though he was often away during the first two years on National Service with the RAF. Telfer's wife Margaret did the cooking for the Club.

It was Tommy who established the multiplicity of chicken coops on the site of the clubmaster's garden - now the bottom car park. There may have been pigs as well, his daughter Nancy Hay suggests. If the Club's own fresh vegetables were no longer available to members, fresh eggs and bacon certainly should have been. Nancy remembers particularly that the Club's kitchen sinks in those days were of wood, blackened with age.

Eventually Telfer and Margaret left to take up the Clubmaster/Mistress job at North Berwick Golf Club and Tommy and Elizabeth retired.

*Commander Ross owned the up-market L'Aperitif Restaurant in Frederick Street, Edinburgh, popularly known as 'The Ap', **the** place to be seen. Commander Ross kept a boat, the Jason, in Cockenzie Harbour at that time.*

George and Jean Morawisc. George had also been employed by Commander Ross at the L' Aperitif. He and his wife Jean had assisted the Robbs in the Clubhouse towards the end of their tenure. When they retired, George took over. A friendly man, his stay was quite brief and he resigned at the beginning of 1965. George's departure was quite sudden: he and Jean were thought to have disappeared without trace, until Alex Harvey and Alistair Barr went to Burford to play in the Oxfordshire Foursomes and, there behind the bar as large as life, were George and Jean.

1965-present. John and Jean Kennedy. George Morawisc had departed suddenly. Tom Porteous was Captain at the time and was keenly aware of the need to appoint a new Clubmaster quickly. Mrs Rodgers who owned the Golf Hotel at Gullane knew of John Kennedy's growing reputation at Darling's Hotel in Edinburgh, and recommended him to the Board.

John Kennedy

John Glendinning Kennedy was born at Newfarm Cottage a stone's throw from the Solway Firth. His schoolmate, Jean Riddick was born at Haugh of Urr.

John joined Longniddry from Darling's Hotel after gaining experience at top hotels in Scotland, the north of England and Switzerland. He recalls that Jean and he arrived just after Winston Churchill's funeral and that the price of lunch at the Club at that time was 3/6 (17$\frac{1}{2}$p)

John had had wide experience of food production and treatment. His past includes arable farming, waiting at table, cocktail bartender, and in Switzerland, Chef de Range. Even administration and clerical control activities were within his ambit.

His two years national service found him square bashing alongside football manager to be Jock Wallace he recalls, and took him to Singapore with the KOSBs 1st Battalion.

Of course John had management experience too. He was catering manager at Darlings for 4 years and when he left the Marine at North Berwick it was to start in a managerial capacity at Peebles Hydro. This was when he had to use his savings to buy his 'working clothes' - morning and evening suits.

John's army discharge reference describes his military conduct as *'very good'*. It goes on: *'Private Kennedy has been employed as a senior Officer's Batman since joining the Battalion in May 1954. He is most suited to this type of work having a pleasant personality, smart and well-dressed at all times, reliable and completely trustworthy.'*

Somewhere in the middle of all this - actually while he was working at the Cally Palace in Gatehouse of Fleet - he met up with Jean Riddick again and married her. Jean had gone to the de Bear College in Dumfries taking a business course including typing, bookkeeping and shorthand, as well as the management skills which she would need to deal with John. She had also been Cub Mistress at the Haugh and taught at the Sunday School where she played the organ like her mother before her.

Whilst at Longniddry, John has added to his experience and qualifications, gaining membership by examination of the Hotel and Catering Institutional

Management Association and the Royal Institution of Public Health and Hygiene.

When John and Jean arrived at Longniddry, they already had one son, Ian, and Jean presented John with a daughter Kate when the World Seniors Championship came to Longniddry. Bruce arrived just over a year later.

John and Jean have been extremely happy at Longniddry. 'If given the chance' says John 'we would do it all again'. Their recollections cover much of the Club's past. The Carling and Pringle Tournaments are very vivid. Both Ladies Home Internationals were great fun and the family have made personal friends of many who play at the Club, members of course but also visitors such as the Jensons from Denmark who sent 60th birthday congratulations to John. 'Bring our regards' they wrote.

Jean Kennedy

Of course the job of clubmaster demands many qualities. John seems to embody most if not all of them. Even Matadorial skills have been required. It happened when a cow (suspected but not confirmed to be a Morrison animal) broke free and wandered on to the eastern part of the golf course. Alarm signals were received at the Secretary's Office from perturbed members enquiring whether a cow could be described as a burrowing animal. By this time the beast itself was approaching the putting green and something had to be done. The noble Gilbert is said to have thrown himself into the breach. However the cow was not impressed. Chartered Accountancy was not a profession which she recognised. John Kennedy took charge: waving a tablecloth and reciting bits of Rabbie Burns, he danced elegantly around the beast in his best bullfighting fashion. No doubt the cow sensed his agricultural background. At any rate the bewildered animal was secured safely and John hung up his tablecloth.

This was a privileged cow. John's Burns recitations are widely appreciated. His address to the Haggis at the beginning of the Club's Scots night every year is delivered in rousing and dramatic style. It is the foundation of the evening. Not content with that he has later in the programme delivered a full recitation. Tom O'Shanter or, dressed in ample night-shirt and woolly night cap a saucered candle in his hand, Holy Wullie's Prayer.

The Kennedys' stewardship has been very much a family affair: John would be the first to admit that Jean does the lion's share of the management and administrative duties leaving him free to run the kitchen and personally supervise the cooking and catering operations. It is said that on one occasion having much impressed legal gentlemen from the South, John was offered the post of Chief Chef at Sunningdale. After careful consideration John and Jean decided to stay on at Longniddry.

The three offspring are all familiar to the members. Ian as the eldest particularly in the early days, was often seen helping. Even now dedicated

John can compose a verse or two himself when the notion takes him: he has in fact already written at length upon the story of the golf club. Hopefully he will not object if the first verse is given here:

'In the year of our Lord 1921

The course was opened and golf begun

A new use of the land had started and sprung

For the people with position and wealth

No more need of sheep and dung

Just common sense and a bit of stealth'.

Kate Kennedy

Martha Cuthbertson

Thelma Johnston

Isobel Munro

as he is to automobile servicing and renewal he gives support on occasion: he took charge of the outside barbecue at the Jubilee day celebrations for example. Kate's ability to serve at the bar and the tables, take orders, give change, wash glasses, find trays all seemingly simultaneously and quite unflappably is truly remarkable. She seems equal to any task in the clubhouse, whilst in her own right she is a qualified artist and at her local studio, produces intriguing and decorative glasswork. She is no mean golfer either. Bruce the youngest is also popular with the members and it is thought that his wedding to Pauline in the dining room recently was the first to take place in the clubhouse. Bruce has set himself up as independent bench carpenter but he also has a real facility for barkeeping and waitering. He has a friendly welcoming manner which the members greatly appreciate.

John and Jean emphasise that the friendliness of the members and the loyalty of their staff has made their task over the 31 years of their service – thought to be the longest for a Club stewardship in Scotland – most rewarding and pleasurable.

The Clubhouse Staff. Several names in the clubhouse staff have already been mentioned. There are others who must not be omitted. Such as Martha Cuthbertson, David's wife who has served so pleasantly and reliably for nearly 50 years, and whose length of service with the Club may exceed that of her husband.

Thelma Johnston also. She joined the Club for a week in 1972 at the time of the Seniors Tournament and is still in post. For many years she ran the bar on Friday nights keeping the irrepressible Friday Club members under some sort of control. She is rightly proud of her barkeeping skills, professionally rolling the Angostura bitters round the glass. Another is Bella Johnston who was a regular for a long time. She is now replaced by her daughter Mary O'Rourke. Mary's beat is the week day one.

Marina Ross and Linda Hume are encountered at weekends and special occasions, while unseen in the kitchen is Helen Ogg, Jimmy Hume's sister. Of course there have been many more down the years. Peggy Edmond is one. She was serving drinks one day when the floor gave way and poor Peggy disappeared. No permanent damage was done, thankfully, but repairs to both the Clubhouse floor and Peggy were required. Another popular waitress was Isobel Munro. She generally served in the dining room welcoming members with her beaming smile and serving fast and efficiently. Isobel retired in 1995 after 30 years with the Club.

It has been the Club's policy to endeavour to employ local people as far as possible and persons with family connections are particularly welcome. Girls who have recently joined the staff are Gillian Hope, Ruth Hubbard and Alison Hendrie.

Club Secretaries

There have been nine Secretaries of Longniddry Golf Club

1921-1936. G H A Connor. George Harry Adams Connor was the first Secretary/Treasurer of the Club. He, in collaboration with his employer, the 11th Earl of Wemyss was responsible for much of the golf course and clubhouse characteristics as they exist today. Harry Colt was the course architect which the pair of them fixed upon, but it seems clear that the hire and direction of the labour and equipment required, were George Connor's responsibility. In the circumstances he must have regarded the Club with a fierce and protective personal pride.

G.H.A. Connor

George Connor was a twin son of the Dean of Windsor. He had come to East Lothian in 1884 as Assistant Factor to the Wemyss Estate. Two years later he was appointed Factor in his own right. Subsequently he was designated Commissioner. In 1932 when he retired from the Factorship of the Estate he had 46 years of public service to his credit. He continued to discharge his golf club duties from his new home at Huntington near Haddington. During that time he had, according to the 'Courier' filled almost every office connected with the County Council to which he was elected in 1928. At his death he was Vice Convenor.

Although he had briefly considered living at the Clubhouse site, Mr. Connor's home before retirement was at Craigielaw beside the Estate Office. He would arrive at the Clubhouse in his car with his doggy Airedale companion, 'Major', sitting beside him in the passenger seat. The perceived similarity of the two faces peering through the windscreen as the car drove up caused secret amusement to the Clubhouse staff. Another story told is that the family name had originally been O'Connor and that the prefix had been dropped at some stage possibly in deference to the fashionable anglisization prevalent in the high noon of Empire. The story continues that a subsequent generation has replaced the discarded vowel so that the old name is now restored.

George Armstrong Connor died suddenly in the autumn of 1936. He had been about to begin a game of golf when he collapsed on the first tee. Throughout his stay at Longniddry he had been a very effective Factor. He was the man who, with the whole-hearted backing of the Earl of Wemyss, saw the Course and Club designed, created and brought to maturity and success.

1936-1956. Roy Cutter. Roy Cutter had been (among other things) a judge in Africa and his appearance and demeanour were in full accord with this background. He disliked medal competitions and considered that there were far too many of them.

Roy was born at the historic Blackheath, the cradle of English golf. Nevertheless cricket was his first love. As well as playing cricket at Cambridge he got his soccer blue there and twice went to the Argentine as a member of the famous Corinthians Football Club. On the second occasion though, due to the outbreak of the first world war, the ship had to turn at Rio and come home. Back in Britain, Roy joined the Royal Fusiliers as a private. He served in France was wounded on the Somme and rose to the rank of Captain. After the war he had a period as a barrister before his appointment as a judge in the Sudan where he served for fourteen years. On his retirement he decided to link up with golf and after studying secretarial work at Royal Wimbledon, he had a short spell with the Sandiway Club in Cheshire before taking the Longniddry post.

First and foremost, Roy remained a cricket fan and he loved to reminisce on the test matches which he had seen as a boy. It was his normal practice once back in Britain to attend all the tests in this country and other cricket events as well. He was often accompanied on these occasions by Nancy Jupp's father and founder-member George. Roy was one of the principals who so dominated the Clubhouse in the late forties and early fifties. They would congregate in the evening about 7 p.m. around the lounge fire. The group included Maurice Yorke from Greencraig, Ian Buchanan and George Mitchell.

The Cutters lived at 5 Links Road and later it is thought at 'Kingswood' in Kings Road behind the 4th tee. One of Roy's walks was down the 4th to the 12th tee where he would join the players. He is known to have offered a £1 on occasion to anyone who drove the green. On the course V B Hilton, Captain 1947/48, and Hunter Murray the Factor, were among Roy's companions, but his regular four seems to have been the Inglis brothers and George Mitchell. Roy's caddy was often young Jimmy Hume. Although the names of the other caddies are not remembered, the going rate of 2/6 per round for the young caddy certainly is.

The minutes of the Board meetings of the Club which Roy maintained for the 20 years of his service are admirably clear and concise. Unfortunately no minutes can be traced after his retirement in 1956 until 1964. In consequence the details of his departure are obscure. There is a brief reference to ill-health, but perhaps he decided to go when the new structure of the Club as a Limited Company was implemented. It is possible that he considered that the changed set-up was a task for a new man. The 'Courier' of April 1965 regrets his departure saying that a genial and popular personality had been removed from the game.

1956-1963. A. P. H. 'Lawrie' Lawrence. 'Lawrie' was a retired banker who had worked in Chile. He lived immediately across from the first tee in the house now called 'Namara' by its present owner Harry MacNamara. In

Lawrie's time it was called 'Dormie', though such a name might be thought more appropriate for a house nearer the end of the course.

Lawrie has been described as always in control of events, or at least appearing to be, displaying a poised and unruffled demeanour at all times. In contrast to Roy Cutter, he seems to have had no cronies. A very laid-back character, he appeared detached from the changes taking place in the Club and Clubhouse. These developments in the running of the Club must have been quite profound with significantly greater responsibilities falling upon the Secretary's shoulders now that the administration of the Club was independent of the Estate. In the absence of evidence to the contrary, everything seems to have run sweetly enough and one speculates that perhaps Lawrie's detachment was something of a pose, and like the feet of a swan gliding placidly on the stream, he was working furiously out of sight.

Because of the gap in the minutes, the exact duration of Lawrie's stay is not known. His successor was R.W. Burt ('Wally')

1961-1964. R. W. Burt. Wally was born in Tranent but he spent virtually all his professional career in East Africa, where he finished as Chairman of Smith Mackenzie and Co. Ltd., the Inchape Group subsidiary. He retired from this post in 1960 and brought his family to Longniddry in 1962. They took up residence in 'Divot' previously owned by the Hiltons. Wally's tenure as Secretary probably began therefore between 1961 and 62.

R.W. Burt

This may not have been his first spell of membership of the Club. It is thought that he may also have been a member of Longniddry in the twenties. Certainly after the war he was a member of Gullane and the R & A and as a Watsonian he played in the Halford Hewitt in 1964 and possibly on other occasions.

Wally Burt's golfing record in Africa is a most distinguished one. He was by 1952 the only man to have won the Uganda, Tanganyika (Tanzania) and Kenya Championships. (1936, 1950 and 1952 respectively). He also won the Kenya Coast Championship (which is different from the Kenya Championship itself) 4 times, his last win being in 1957. There is another golfing achievement to his credit which at a slight stretch supports a claim for Longniddry to have defeated a top-level US/ Australian professional partnership. This extract from the 'History of Golf in East Africa' tells the tale when Walter Hagen, the first US professional to win the British Open accompanied by Australian trick-shot artist Joe Kirkwood visited Kenya in 1937 on one of their exhibition visits:

'Visit of Hagen and Kirkwood to Kenya

These two famous professionals came on a golfing visit towards the end of 1937 and played on a few courses .... Hagen of course is world-

famous for his 4 wins in the British Open and his two American Open victories. He beat Bobby Jones in a 72- hole match-play Championship of the United States of America in 1926. His feats are too numerous to recount. Kirkwood is not quite so famous on the field of play although he has done many good things, but his trick shots are quite amazing and with his first -class line of patter he is worth going a long way to see and hear.

*The two professionals had teamed up some years before and had gone all over the world giving exhibitions. Kirkwood stated when he arrived in Mombassa that they had played in about 2,600 courses and therefore browns were not unknown to them. Their first game was at Kilindini where they **played against R.W.Burt and R.Forest who beat them 3 and 2'***

What fortifies Longniddry's claim for this international success is that Bob Forest retired to Longniddry and joined the Golf Club, as Wally had done. Not long after joining Longniddry, Wally Burt's health broke down. He never played a full round after the winter of 1962/63. He resigned from the post of Secretary of the Club during John Adair's Captaincy in 1964.

1964-1970. Norman C. Osborne. Norman is a local man. His father had been Church of Scotland Minister at Cockenzie. Norman was already a Director of the Club when Wally Burt resigned. Indeed the meeting which gave notice of Mr Burt's resignation went on to nominate Norman for the Vice-Captaincy, a proposal which was confirmed by the membership at the AGM a few weeks afterwards. However a little later it was decided to accept the offer which Norman had made, to perform the duties of the Secretary pending the appointment of a new man (or woman).

Norman C. Osborne

Mrs Osborne was secretary to the Ladies Club for several years, and she and Norman still consider Longniddry to be their home golf club.

Joe Sykes, a local Headmaster replaced Norman Osborne as Vice-Captain therefore. The Secretary's job was never advertised, so Norman soldiered on in a part-time capacity for some seven and a half years at the princely honorarium of £150 per annum. Norman Osborne's other employment was as an accountant to the fishing industry in the East of Scotland covering an area from Gourdon in the North to Eyemouth in the south. His office was in Port Seton.

In Norman's first year of office the Clubmaster's post fell vacant and Norman was involved in the selection of John and Jean Kennedy as Steward and Stewardess, a decision of which he is justly proud. Later, extensive alterations were carried out in the interior of the clubhouse making the Bar and Lounge area a real showpiece at the time. The back bar was also established. These changes were planned and overseen by a small committee consisting of the Captain, Dr Ian Forbes, Tom Porteous and Norman Osborne, with occasional welcome comment from Gordon Durward.

Other events in which Norman was involved as Secretary were two occasions when the Club hosted the Martini Tournament and two when the British Seniors was played at the Club.

Norman left Longniddry in 1970 when he was invited to apply the post of Secretary of the Royal Burgess Golfing Society. He was secretary there, again in a part-time capacity for 8 years. Now he and his wife have retired to Malaga where they run a very successful Bridge Club on the Costa del Sol.

1970-1977 and part 1981. John Gunn. John Gunn is a tall and erect good-looking chap. He now lives in North Berwick but when he was Secretary of Longniddry Golf Club his home was the 'Anchorage' in Links Road.

John Gunn

John Gunn's career had been in Insurance. When he decided to retire he was Deputy Head of the Commercial Assurance Company in Edinburgh. This meant that his grasp of the book-keeping and financial aspects of the secretary's job were excellent. However John also brought to the post experience of handling public sporting events at the highest level. He had for some time been chief steward to the Scottish Rugby Union. In this capacity he had been responsible for the marketing and management of the major international rugby matches held at Murrayfield. When John took up the Secretary's post at Longniddry, he worked very hard to gain recognition for the Club. It was his and Gordon Durward's efforts which brought the Pringle World Seniors Tournament to Longniddry. This only after John had lobbied Dai Rees himself.

Outwardly a strong and authoritative figure, John was known to his friends as a kindly person and he and his wife Dorothy had many friends at the Club, notably Mr and Mrs 'Jocky' Forbes, the Durwards, and Dan and Chris Abbot. When John left after 7 years of service, he gifted a large television set to the back bar with whose patrons he had had some full and frank discussions in the past. In his own assessment, his greatest achievement was to have engaged Cristine Paxton as Assistant Secretary, but it is doubtful if John's significant contribution to the overall standing of the Club, was fully known to members.

John Gunn, ever a loyal servant returned for a few months to tide the Club over when Captain Davis departed.

1977-1981. Captain S.W. Davis. Captain Davis is a small man, neat and dapper, with a military manner and a moustache to match. He favours sports jackets. The Board minutes which he produced are tidy, comprehensive and succinct. They were once more typed (John Gunn's had been handwritten), presumably reflecting Cristine Paxton's presence in the office where Captain Davis was usually very cheerful and good-humoured. Shortly after the 1981 AGM, he resigned. The Board appointed Gilbert Dempster as the new Club Secretary from the list of 18 candidates who had applied. Gilbert was unable to take up the post immediately and as stated John Gunn loyally agreed to fill the gap.

Gilbert Dempster

1981-1993 Gilbert Dempster. When Captain Davis departed, Gilbert Dempster was already on the Club Board as Finance Convenor. At that time he was Managing Director of the Edinburgh Crystal Glass Company. Upon retirement a few months later, he took up the post of Longniddry Golf Club Secretary almost immediately.

Gilbert is a Glasgow man from south of the river. He filled the post of Club Secretary with expert dedication and friendly authority. Involved in the Territorial Army at the outbreak of the War, Gilbert saw military service for its whole duration in theatres from Palestine to Austria. Gilbert is a member of the Army in Scotland Officers Golfing Society which visits Longniddry regularly.

Gilbert's long-suffering wife Elsie helped on occasions, for his hours of attendance at the office were away beyond those contracted. He made a particular point of being available to members on Saturday mornings. When medal cards were to be processed, Sundays were involved too. He gathered a small pool of loyal members who could be relied upon to help when needed, like Billie McNeill and Robert Kerr, who had been Directors of the Club.

In the clubhouse Gilbert achieved a high standard of staff morale, encouraging by his example a collaborative team concept with himself, the Kennedys and Cristine Paxton as principals. He presented to the Club the Dempster Rosebowl played for annually by Adult/Junior teams of two on a stableford basis.

Perhaps Gilbert will be best remembered for the very successful Scots Nights which he organised and compéred each January. On one occasion the main speaker called off late on the day before the event. There was no replacement to be had so Gilbert sat up half the night (says Elsie) writing a script. Next evening not only did he compére the show as usual, he delivered an entertaining substitute address which was interesting and original. He also found time to run the East Lothian Junior League, managing to attract both Dunbar and Winterfield into the fold.

Gilbert Dempster also provided services to Golf outside the Lothians. In his final year as Secretary before announcing his intention to retire, he was elected Captain of the Association of Golf Club Secretaries Scottish Region.

His great achievement as Secretary of Longniddry Golf Club was that he began the modernisation of the whole book-keeping and financial processes introducing computerisation and putting the Club's operations on a modern commercial footing. The chief highlight from Gilbert's own point of view was the Open Qualifying competition at Longniddry in 1987. It went off extremely well. Gilbert was responsible in liaison with the R & A for all the arrangements.

His would be a hard act to follow. Tom Porteous, Vice-President of the Club who perhaps was closest to Gilbert during his 12 years has written: 'No praise can be too high for this great servant of the Club'.

1993- Present. Neil Robertson. Where Gilbert is a Chartered Accountant, his successor Neil Robertson's training was as a scientist. He was born in the Borders where his parents farmed, and he developed this background by taking an Honours BSc in Agriculture followed by an MBA in Business Studies. His early post-graduate work was as a consultant in farm and estate management. Later he turned to golf administration, joining Thornton Golf Club in Fife as Managing Secretary.

Neil Robertson

Since coming to Longniddry from Thornton, Neil has applied himself to streamlining and further modernising the administration of the Club. He has overseen the selection installation and commissioning of up-to-date computer/word processing equipment in the office. With this done, a number of useful applications have become immediately available such as the internally produced news sheet 'The Course Record', and the player input system for medal scores. The various improvements and redecorations which have taken place in the clubhouse since his arrival have seen Neil's close involvement throughout. These include the refurbishment of the ladies' locker-room, and the men's toilet as well as various repaintings and renovations. With his agricultural background he also takes a keen interest in the welfare of the course itself and was a particular advocate of the revetting of the bunkers which was begun recently.

On moving to Longniddry, Neil and his wife Belinda set up home at Saint Germains like a few golf stalwarts before them and since then Neil has become a father twice over as Alice and then Hamish arrived. One of Neil's chief tasks in 1996 was, in liaison with the LGU, to achieve in September a highly successful Ladies Home International Match. Neil is proving himself to be a dedicated Club Secretary whose highest priority is the welfare of the Club and who is a worthy successor to Gilbert Dempster.

1970-Present. Cristine Paxton. It is difficult to get ex-Secretary John Gunn to talk about himself and his past services to the Club. However one question brings an enthusiastic response: "What was the best thing you did for the Club?" "Engage Cristine Paxton as Assistant Secretary" he replies. "When she poked her head round the door and asked if there were any jobs going, it was the best thing that had happened to the Club for years".

Christine Paxton

Cristine Begarnie was born in Tranent. Her first job after school was with the Commercial Bank of Scotland in Shandwick Place. The travelling was a problem though and after two years she got a transfer to Haddington. She got all-round training in all aspects of banking, but the task which she enjoyed most was that of teller which required her to be face-to-face with the public. Cristine got married to Reg Paxton in 1963 and left the bank to have son and heir Bruce in 1967. She went back to work at the Royal Bank of Scotland Head Office, but when they introduced night working in 1970 she thought one day that she would give the golf club a try and poked her head round John Gunn's door.........

Club Professionals

The roll of the Club's Professionals is as follows:

George Thomson

Hugh Watt, who of course became professional at Gullane, worked as a young clubmaster to Jack at one time.

1923-1930. George Thomson. George came from a large family of good golfers. Several of his brothers were very successful in the U.S.A. He was related to the famous Ben Sayers of North Berwick. Ruddy-faced with a ginger moustache, he was one of young Nancy Jupp's favourite people. George Thomson is to be seen in the photograph in front of the Clubhouse associated with the professionals' inaugural match in June/July 1923. He stands second from the left in the second row beside the professional E. Ray who substituted for the indisposed George Duncan.

1931-1932. Jack White. Described as short and dapper, Jack White from North Berwick originally was professional at Sunningdale until 1926 when he moved to Gullane. He had won the Open Championship in 1904 at Royal St George's, finishing ahead of Vardon, Taylor and Braid. With his score of 296, he was the first man to break 300 for four rounds in the Open. He scored better in each succeeding round of the competition finishing with a 69. With an average of 74 strokes per round, he also bettered the performance of young Tom Morris whose 149 for two rounds with the gutty had stood for 34 years.

1932-1957. Bill Morris. Bill was a Fifer – a Leven man. He came to Longniddry from Lundin Links in 1932. He had been seriously wounded in the First World War and he never married. He lived with his sister in Elcho Road, Longniddry. Nancy Jupp seems to have been rather in awe of Bill in those early days. Perhaps his manner was a bit brusque. Certainly, later in his career, customers asking for proprietary clubs with the Bobby Lockes or Henry Cottons engraved on them were given short shrift. None of those stocked. Only personally crafted William Morris clubs. Some of these have survived and are in the possession of the Club (along with examples of George Thomson's and Jack White's handiwork).

Bill was a dedicated servant of the Club and like Bob Himsworth he could be kind. Jimmy Hume (nowadays professional at Gullane) remembers in his young days, Bill eyeing his meagre collection of clubs '*I see you've still got hickory shafts*' he said '*Here, try out these steel shafts of Mrs Gorman. See how you like them*'. (Presumably Mrs Gorman would not have objected. She and her husband used to arrive at the Club in their Rolls Royce). And when Jimmy having left school at 15, told Bill that he wanted to be a professional golfer, Bill said, '*Na Na you're too wee. See Tommy Hogg* (the Head Greenkeeper) *Get a job from him. He'll get some muscle on you.*'

Bill was much respected by his colleagues. In December 1946, the Edinburgh and District Professional Golfers Association was formed to encourage and promote the interests of professional golfers in the East of Scotland. The first Captain of the Association was Bill Morris and the first competition which they held was at Longniddry on the 23rd April 1947. The event constituted the inauguration of the post-war reconstructed course and the players competed for two cups donated by the Earl of Wemyss. In 1948 Bill was made an Honorary Life member of the Association which he had captained at its inception.

Life is full of ups and downs though. At the beginning of August, 1946, Bill's shop was burgled. Golf clubs which he had made for exhibition were stolen, together with his allocation (things were still rationed) of 18 dozen golf balls.

Bill died on the course as George Connor had done, twenty years before, at the first tee. He had been about to referee the final round of the 1957 Club Championship when he collapsed. Doctor C R D Leeds, one of the finalists, did his best to revive him but was unsuccessful.

1957-77 Gordon Durward. Gordon came from Banchory to the professional's job at Longniddry. Betty Adam remembers playing at Banchory when he was there and being impressed with him then. He was described towards the end of his career as living entirely for Longniddry Golf Club. He was always extremely punctual and made meticulous preparation for competitions beforehand. A good teacher too. "If you want to knock some strokes off your handicap" he would advise, "give yourself half an hour on the practice ground before you tee off". Gordon's wife, Gladys also worked very hard for the Club. She was often in the starter's box assisting him or sometimes holding the fort. 'Watchi Watchi' she used to caution people.

Gordon Durward

Gordon's parents had been involved in shoe retailing so that in addition to his all round excellence as a Club professional, he really knew about footwear and his advice on golf shoes was worth taking. Gordon was such a good Club professional that his abilities as a player were sometimes overlooked. In fact he was a formidable competitor. Within 12 months of his arrival at Longniddry he won the East of Scotland Professional Stroke Play competition for a record third time. It was played at Cruden Bay on that occasion and Gordon's second round 67 was a record for the course.

The 1971 Golfer's Handbook includes Gordon Durward in its list of "Who's Who in Golf". The entry for him is as follows: "*Durward, James*

Gordon. Born Banchory 13/9/06. Clubs: Banchory and Deeside. Turned professional 1927. Joint runner-up Scottish Professional Championship 1947. Tied East of Scotland Professional Championship 1947, runner-up 1951. Runner-up Scottish Matchplay Championship 1934. Tied for Northern Open Championship 1936. Tied second place Scottish Championship 1939. Tied Victory Tournament Glasgow 1945. East of Scotland Professional Champion 1949, 54 and 57. Won North East Alliance Championship 1956."

Gordon Durward became President of the Scottish Professional Golfers Association and in 1975 was awarded a thoroughly deserved OBE. He was elected Vice-President of Longniddry Golf Club in 1981.

John Gray

1977- present John Gray. John Gray was for some years Gordon Durward's valued assistant before departing south to Oxford to continue his career. Upon Gordon's retirement, John returned with his wife Dorothy to Longniddry. One of his innovations at the Club, with the encouragement of Club Secretary Gilbert Dempster, was the introduction of the 'Professionals Day'. Arranged and organised by John and well supported by local sponsors, the 4-ball team competition held in early August is one of the most enjoyable events of the season.

A most likeable and knowledgeable professional, John is particularly valued for his teaching abilities. Steven Thomson, Club Champion on four occasions, pays a warm tribute to the early tuition which he got from John Gray. By 1996 John who is also a skilled badminton player, had not participated for 17 years in external competitive events. However, that year he agreed to partner Club Captain Gordon Bonnington in the Volvo Captains Challenge. The pair of them won the East of Scotland qualifying round at Gullane and participated meritoriously in the finals at Wentworth.

John Gray, during his years at the Club has seen several very promising young men begin their professional careers at Longniddry as successive assistants to him.

Supporting Professionals and Assistants

Glyn Jenkins was already in post when John returned to the Club. Glyn is now a Club professional in Thailand.

David Yates who is now in Chester, was Glyn's successor.

Mike McLaren winner of the Longniddry Boys Open, competed in the tournament circuit before moving to Thailand as Glyn had done.

Paul Wardell was the next in line. After a couple of years under John he moved south to a promising golf range/retailing project. He has now returned and is operating from the Club in a freelance capacity.

Derek Scott was Paul's replacement. He moved to Dubai in his turn and in 1996 both John and the Club were well served by **Justin Fiddler,** son of popular Club members Stuart and Janet. As with his predecessors, Justin proved to be a promising golfer and a hard-working conscientious assistant to John.

Raymond Russell. There can be no argument that the most outstanding golfer produced by Longniddry in recent years has been Raymond Russell. In 1995 he came equal second with A. Crerar in the Scottish PGA Masters only one stroke behind P. Lawrie's 274. He secured 19th place at the PGA European Tour Qualifying School with a total of 433 made up of 70, 73, 71, 76, 71, and 72. The following year he was winner of the Cannes Open and just pipped at the post for Rookie of the Year. His prior achievements are given in Chapter VII.

Raymond Russell

Raymond was never Assistant to John Gray although for a time he was a hard working and valued member of the greens staff. Raymond got his formative coaching from Bob Torrance, showing very considerable personal dedication and resolution in travelling to Largs frequently. Nevertheless he pays tribute to John Gray's support and encouragement which strengthened his early determination to do well at the game. Raymond was made a Life Honorary Member of the Club in 1994. He is also nowadays, a golf columnist with the Herald Newspaper.

Several other young men came from the Longniddry Junior ranks to a career in professional golf.

Graham Shed was one of these. He was for 8 years Assistant to Jimmy Hume at Gullane and is now the fully qualified Club Professional at Kilspindie. Others who followed a similar path are **Peter Downie** now in Dubai and **Eliot Gray** in South Africa.

Just starting out are the two promising young men **Simon J Mees** and **Steven Burton.**

CHAPTER VI
LONGNIDDRY LOG – EVENTS, INCIDENTS AND PERSONALITIES DOWN THE YEARS

Early members

In the records of the Royal and Ancient Club of St. Andrews a proliferation of Leslie Melville Balfours and Leslie Balfour Melvilles occurs as winners of the Royal Medal and the Gold Medal for the Autumn Meeting and the Silver Cross and Silver Medal for the Spring one. A Leslie M Balfour is also mentioned. These entries are for the ten years around 1890. How many persons they represent it is difficult to say but it seems likely that our Leslie Balfour Melville was one of them.

Alex McPhail's Silver Badge

One source gives the month of the professional's match as July, another as June.

1921 is given as the year in which, after a pre-first world war statement of intent, Longniddry Golf Club was formally established. It has not been possible to identify the founder members with certainty. There are several names however, who were clearly associated with the Club from the very early days.

George Colville was certainly one of these. He was the author of a book 'The Five Open Championships' which described the old 9 hole Musselburgh Course and the five players who won the Open Championship there. A suggestion that George Colville applied for membership of Longniddry before the First World War has not been substantiated, but there seems little doubt that he was one of the very early members.

Similarly it is known from Ella Vlandy that some time around 1920 Maurice P. Vlandy (it is originally a Greek name) contacted Leslie Balfour-Melville saying that he was going to put his own name down for membership of the new Golf Club at Longniddry. He undertook to put Mr Balfour-Melville's name down too. Leslie Balfour-Melville had been an international star at both tennis and cricket and was a long-jump champion.

Another possible early name has been reported by Mr James Mackay of Milton Keynes. Mr Mackay's father and his father's friend Alex McPhail who lived at Windmill Street near the Meadows in Edinburgh, were both keen golfers. They would quite frequently put their canvas golf bags over their shoulders and set off down the coast by bicycle or tram. James Mackay believes that Alex McPhail was a member of a golf club along the East Lothian coast. Tragically Alex McPhail was drowned towards the end of the First World War and Mr Mackay's father treasured a medal or membership badge which Alex had given him. James Mackay has gifted it to Longniddry Golf Club. It is silver and comprises three intertwined letters 'LGC', similar to the Club's flag. The other obvious candidate for the source of this medal is Luffness, but that seems a little too far from Edinburgh to meet the circumstances. One is left therefore with the possibility that some sort of membership or even a few early holes were available at Longniddry before the end of the First World War.

Some important photographs from the very early days of the Club survive. One of them, taken in front of the Clubhouse on the occasion of the inaugural match by the four Professionals in June or July 1923, shows the Earl and Countess of Wemyss with their guests and Club personalities.

Unfortunately not all are named. Mr Balfour-Melville is one who is and in the photograph he sits beside the Countess of Wemyss. One speculates as to whether he was Mr Vlandy's Balfour-Melville and whether in view of his place of honour in the line-up, he had formally opened the Club.

Others identified in the photograph who may well have been founding members are John Gillespie, James Shields, G. Jeffs and George Cruikshanks. Both James Shields and John Gillespie were later to be associated with the formation of the subsidiary Home Club in 1925.

Stuart Forsyth.   Prominent in the early photograph wearing a bow-tie, standing tall behind the Countess of Wemyss is Stuart Forsyth.

He was the proprietor of the retailers R W Forsyth which had large prestigious shops in Glasgow and Edinburgh. Always very well turned out, he played with a new ball every round, passing the surviving old ones to the two Jupp sisters or Douglas Teesdale. Stuart Forsyth twice reached the finals of the National Mixed Foursomes Tournament held annually at Worplesdon. On the first occasion when his partner was Doris Park they were beaten by Joyce Wethered and her partner the Hon. Michael Scott. Stuart's partner on the second occasion was Jean Hamilton but they fared no better than before. Stuart Forsyth was elected in 1935 as the first full Captain of Longniddry Golf Club.

The Jupps.   George Jupp was an Englishman and a good friend of Stuart Forsyth . He seems to have been a gifted sportsman because he played cricket for Somerset at the age of 16 and continued to represent the County

Front Row: GA Connor, the Earl of Wemyss, Mrs Connor, the Countess of Wemyss, Mr Balfour-Melville, Miss H Carey, Miss J Wilkinson

2nd Row: John Gillespie, George Thomson, E Ray, Abe Mitchell, Stuart Forsyth, JH Taylor, James Braid, James Shields, G Jeffs, George Cruickshank

when he was on holiday. When he left school at 18, he joined the Civil Service and was sent to Edinburgh where he played his cricket at the Carlton Club. Up to the time of his death in 1938 he was the only Englishman to have captained the Scottish Cricket Team. During World War I, George Jupp served as a Captain in the Royal Scots. After a brief spell in London at the end of the War when his second daughter Nancy was born, he was transferred back to Scotland in June, 1921. The family moved to No. 1 Elcho Road, Longniddry, in 1923. George became head of the Office of Works for Scotland and was responsible for the upkeep of all Government buildings and ancient monuments. Although cricket was his first love, his golf was not to be sneezed at; he got his handicap down to 4.

George's wife, Ethel, was elected first Lady Captain of the Club. She had been a very good singer in her younger days. The two daughters, Rhoda and Nancy, were excellent golfers. Although Rhoda was considered the better player, it was Nancy who collected the honours; at the age of 13 she won the British Girls Championship and four years later captained the Scottish Girls team against England in the first match of the series. Later, she was the ladies amateur champion of Norway and she went on to make a career in the USA on golf tournament management. She now lives in active retirement in Tulsa, Oklahoma.

The Sawers. The Sawers family had long connection with Port Seton. For many years until her death in 1946 Mrs Sawers lived in old Longniddry House. Both her son Tom, her daughter Emma and her grand-daughter Nancy had close associations with the Golf Club. Tom Sawers was an Edinburgh Baillie, he lived at 'Woodburn' (the north-facing house at the bottom of Lyars Road). He was elected Club Captain in 1939 and remained in that capacity throughout the War. The stained glass window which he and his wife donated to Longniddry Church, in memory of RAF personnel who served in the area, is prominent behind the holy table. Tom's sister Emma was a Justice of the Peace and Honorary President of the Women Artisans. For thirty years, she was also Honorary Secretary of the Ladies Club. Tom's daughter, Nancy, was elected Honorary Secretary of the Lady Artisans.

W. B. Torrance. It is not clear whether Bill Torrance, the 1922 Walker Cup Player, was a founder member of Longniddry Golf Club or not. He was certainly a member by the autumn of 1923. He was associated with several Lothian Clubs and his chief love seems to have been Duddingston, whose recently published history 'Pillars of the Temple', gives a full account of his golfing career. Nevertheless, Bill Torrance was certainly connected with Longniddry from the early days, and played for Longniddry on occasions in inter-club matches. He was a close friend of George and Ethel Jupp, having

Tom and Nancy Sawers were enthusiastic members of a local flying club. One of their aerial diversions was to pretend to dive-bomb the golf course. Nancy was taken seriously ill during the War and the sun lounge extension on the west gable of 'Woodburn' was built to assist her convalescence. Her name is now Mrs McGlagan and she lives in Scone.

been best man at their wedding in 1916. Bill had two daughters: Jean who played hockey for Scotland and Margaret who is said to have run Netherhurd for the Girl Guides.

Among Bill's many successes was the winning with his partner G. Seymour Noon, of the Evening Times Trophy at Longniddry in 1931, defeating Denholm and Flynn of the Bass Rock Club 2 and 1.

The Roses. J C (Tim) Rose brought his family to Longniddry in the early 20's. They had previously lived at St. Andrews where Tim had begun his banking career. When the Royal Bank of Scotland persuaded Tim that he was needed in East Lothian he established his family in 'Shalimar' on the corner of the 17th fairway. It was said to be the first new house built under the Earl's feuing scheme. Tim was elected Captain in 1938, but unusually, he had been beaten at the post by his wife who had achieved Captaincy of the Ladies Club two years before. Dorothy Rennie recalls that Tim Rose used to enter the course through his garden gate in the evenings and practice iron shots to the 17th green much to the exasperation of some of his neighbours.

Sadly, Tim Rose died suddenly in 1939 during the second year of his Captaincy. Daughter, Kath Rose, is currently Lady Vice-President of the Club.

A F Simpson. In September 1935 the 'Haddingtonshire Courier' reports the AGM of Longniddry Golf Club at which *"Arthur Simpson was appointed Captain for the following year"*.

Arthur Simpson was a Quantity Surveyor and his drawing of the Longniddry Golf Course dated 1930 is an invaluable surviving record of the early days of the Club. He was also a distinguished golfer having been runner-up in the British Amateur Championship at Muirfield and previously Captain of Lothianburn and Royal Burgess. When his period of duty as Captain of Longniddry ended he continued to serve on the Board until changes which he had initiated were completed.

Charlotte Stevenson (Mrs J. B. Watson, Mrs E. C. Beddows). Charlotte Stevenson was born in 1887. Her family had a draper's shop in Princes Street. Her brother Tim was killed in the First World War. By the time Longniddry Golf Club was opened Charlotte was an established first rank player. She had been a Scottish Internationalist since 1913, and as Scottish Ladies Champion, had taken over the Captaincy of the Scottish Team in 1921. A full account of her long golfing career is given later in the section on the Ladies Club.

Other Early Members

Other early members include Vernon Hilton who lived in Gosford Road, Philip Snowdon and his step-son Norman Campbell, who died in South Africa recently, Walter Cranston and the very popular Kello Henderson, a banker, who lived next door to the Jupps at 3 Links Road. Kello retired to Troon eventually. James Teesdale was another possible founder member. His name is perpetuated in the Club's Teesdale Trophy presented in his memory by his son Douglas. Jimmy was said to be great fun and always had a cigarette drooping from the corner of his mouth.

Peter S. F. Tensfeldt was a naturalised British subject. He had come from Kiel, Germany, about the turn of the century. He had hairdressing businesses in Shandwick Place and Princes Street and with his wife, advertised Madame Tennsfeldt's Beauticians Establishment. Peter joined the Golf Club in 1922.

A little bit later, but still early in the story, were Commander Purdon and the Nashes. Their children Andrew and Ruth and Isobel golfed with the Jupp sisters. Andrew Purdon died recently in Cheshire while playing golf. He had just birdied the 14th hole Nancy Jupp reports when he bent down to retrieve his ball and died on the spot!

Events and Incidents

1921. No information has been discovered about events at the Club in the first year of its existence, but it is reasonable to presume that preparation of the course layout and construction work on the clubhouse would be chief activities. Meantime in the wider golfing world there was the usual round of tournament play and some significant departures and arrivals:

For example the Open Championship was won in 1921 by Jock Hutchison\, a St. Andrews born Scot, resident in the USA. The deeply grooved clubs which he used were to begin a prolonged controversy. According to the Daily Telegraph he came within a fraction of two consecutive holes in one during the tournament held over the Old Course at St. Andrews. Having holed in one at the 8th his tee shot at the 9th finished within an inch of the cup.

In that year too, John Ball, eight times winner of the British Amateur, chose to compete in it for the last time, whilst Joyce Wethered's developing golf career took her to the final of the British Woman's Amateur where she lost to Cecil (actually Cecilia) Leitch. With her brother Roger, Joyce also lost to Eleanor Holme and Tony Torrance (W. B.'s brother) in the mixed foursomes inaugurated at Worplesdon that year. By 1929 Joyce was to become acknowledged as the world's leading woman golfer. Robert Green's History tells us that Willie Wilson, a contemporary Scots professional, said of her "Good swing? My god man! She could hit a ball 240 yards on the fly whilst standing barefoot on a sheet of ice".

Lady Internationalist Doris Park who lived in one of the cottages across the railway from Canty Hall was also a long standing member, but perhaps not one of the very first since her name does not appear in the records until 1929.

Another arrival on the scene was Bobby Jones' rusty blade putter gifted to him after he had putted badly against Francis Ouimet. Jones christened it "Calamity Jane". It was also in 1921 that the USGA and the Royal and Ancient ruled that the ball should not be more than 1.62 ounces in weight and 1.62 inches in diameter.

1922. The record remains silent about Longniddry during 1922. At St. Andrews, the Prince of Wales became Captain of the Royal and Ancient.

The big international development was the first Walker Cup match held at the National Links, Long Island when Great Britain and Ireland were beaten 8 - 4 – an ominous indication of things to come. At that time the USGA still opposed the use of steel-shafted clubs in championship play. W. B. Torrance played in this match. One of his opponents was 'Bobby' Jones.

1923. The following year saw 'Bobby' Jones' first major championship victory when he won the US Open after a play-off.

Meanwhile at Longniddry Golf Club events began to be noticed: The Spring Meeting of 18th May 1923, when the course was first opened for competitive play, has already been described. The trophy presented by Mr Connor on that occasion for the best scratch round is therefore the oldest in the Club. It was won that first year by Mr J. C. Rose (Tim). Then, one or two months later (reports differ), the inaugural 36-hole match between the four famous professionals took place. Three of them were Open Champions and the fourth, Ted Ray, had been an Open runner-up. Even more resounding was that two of them, James Braid and J. H. Taylor, were of 'The Great Triumverate." Only Vardon was missing. The fourth contestant Abe Mitchell has been described as the cleanest striker of a ball of his generation. With regard to J. H. Taylor, the Editor's father recalls him giving a demonstration in the Glasgow outfitters Rowans of Buchanan Street. "Sit back on your heels for chip shots", Taylor advised.

Later in 1923 Longniddry Golf Club held its Autumn Meeting. A trophy for the best scratch round was presented by Stuart Forsyth. The first winner of the Longniddry Stuart Forsyth Trophy was W B Torrance.

The Ladies Club. The history of the Longniddry Ladies Golf Club is dealt with separately, but it is appropriate to note here that it was on 10th September 1923 that the Longniddry Ladies Golf Club was inaugurated.

1924. In the Ladies County Championship held at Longniddry in 1924 Midlothian beat Ayrshire. This appears to be the first external event held at the Club.

The Artisans. The same year saw the establishment of the Longniddry Artisan's club. This was a wholly male organisation. The women's Artisans Club would not be set up until 1936. A full account of the Artisans' affairs is given elsewhere so it is sufficient at this point simply to record that the very first Honorary Secretary and Treasurer was J. R. A. Johnston junior of the Garden City, Longniddry.

1925/26/27. 1925 was the year that Willie Macfarlane, born in Aberdeen won the US Open after two playoff rounds against Bobby Jones. It was also the year when the R & A, in reaction to the Jock Hutchison affair, banned deeply grooved club faces.

1922 was also the year when Walter Hagen became the first American-born professional to win the British Open. Meanwhile, back in the States the 5' 4" Gene Sarazen suddenly emerged on the scene to win both the US Open and the US PGA.

The second Walker Cup Match was held at St Andrews with the home side doing a little better this time only losing by five and a half to six and a half.

Further afield in 1924 Walter Hagen won the Open for the second time and the British Walker Cup Team suffered their third successive defeat.

At Longniddry there was renewed activity: Two Challenge Cups were presented - presumably by the Club itself - one for each of the Spring and Autumn Handicap Meetings. Another of the Club's oldest trophies awarded to the winner of the handicap knock-out singles competition was gifted the following year by Emma Sawers J. P. It was won on that first occasion in 1926 by Captain T M Guilford. Since then, many more trophies have been added to those first few. There are now about 60 presented at the Club's annual prize giving.

The Home Club. At this remove, it is difficult to be certain, but it does appear that there may have been, in those early days, some local dissatisfaction with the structure of the Club. Its affairs were run on a day-to-day basis by Mr Connor who reported directly to the Earl of Wemyss. In a photograph of the opening ceremony, the Earl and Mr Connor can be seen standing paternally authoritarian and enthusiastic at the side of the speaker (J H Taylor). The appointment of Golf Club officers and personnel was entirely in the hands of the estate. In these circumstances, it is possible that there was a local perception that the course was intended for visiting bigwigs and dignitaries rather than the Longniddry hoi polloi. Whether this is true or not the Haddingtonshire Courier reported on 1st May 1925 as follows:

'*A Club under the title of the Home Golf Club has been formed by members of Longniddry Golf Club, and is composed of players resident in the district. Office bearers have been appointed as follows:*

Captain: James Shields, Honorary Secretary: John Gillespie, Committee Members: T Elder, P Malcolm, G Gillespie, R G Leishman, Dr Boyle.'

Unfortunately, after this detailed and intriguing start, there are only a few other references to the Home Club. In May 1927 the Ladies Club decided to arrange a match with them-outcome not recorded. A little later "Haddingtonshire Courier" reported the result of the Home Club monthly spoon on August 29th 1930 when there was a tie for the scratch prize between A Wemyss and C E Black. Only a few months after this the demise of the Home Club seemed imminent. The Ladies minutes of 20th February 1931 state: "*A meeting (which Mr Connor had had - Ed) with the Home Club representatives reveals that the Home Club will now be merged in the Main Club ...... a committee to run the competitions formerly run by The Home Club should be formed consisting of two representatives of Longniddry Club, four from the present Home Club and one from the Ladies Section.*" It is not until twenty years later that the Home Club appears again in the records when Miss I M V Park raised the question of reviving it. The minutes indicate approval of this intention. The initiative does not seem to have been successful because two years afterwards Mr F Wood, an architect by profession, obtained the support of the Board to attempt another revival. His efforts were overtaken by the reorganisation of the Longniddry Golf Club itself in 1954/55 when the idea of a Home Club became completely redundant.

1928. Moving back however to 1928, we find Longniddry involved in the County Cup.

The County Cup. The Inter-Club Competition for the East Lothian County Cup originally presented by the Earl of Wemyss was initiated in 1867. In 1928 at the request of the Earl of Wemyss Longniddry was added to the list of Clubs competing. The match was played at Longniddry that year for the first time and the cup, reputedly the oldest team trophy in golf, was won by the Longniddry quartet: A F Simpson, H Pollock, G C Killey, W B C Miller.

The East Lothian Cup – thought to be the oldest team trophy in Golf.

1929. Several entries of Golf Club interest appear in the 'Haddingtonshire Courier' records for 1929:

The Ladies. The first report records that on the 31st May, the ladies played for their new championship trophy presented by Stuart Forsyth. It was won by Doris Park, who was also Lady Captain in that year. It was to be 66 years before this double achievement was repeated.

The Sawers Cup. A couple of weeks later, Mr Connor reported to the newspapers that in the final of the Home Club Golf Competition for the Sawers Cup Mr G S Noon had beaten Captain Guilford by one hole.

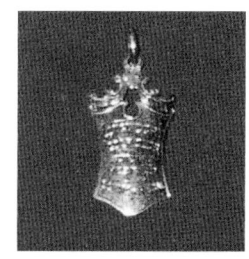

The Gold Medal awarded to WBC Miller for the best scratch score in the 1928 Longniddry Autumn Meeting.

Accident. The newspaper then reported the blackest day in the history of the Golf Club. On 21st July the accident to Christina Dickson Lawrie occurred. Harry Reid, Director of Thorntons the sports retailers, was playing the course and witnessed the events. Christina was sitting in a bunker at the 11th hole near the beach when she was struck by a golf ball. She seems to have considered herself not seriously injured for she subsequently travelled home on the bus. Most unfortunately, she died later that day. Her father Hugh Lawrie of Great Junction Street, Leith, considered the club and consequently the Estate to be responsible; their having displayed no warning notices of any kind. He took the Estate to court claiming £600 damages but the outcome two years later went against him.

Although major changes to the course did not take place until post-war it is possible that this sad incident triggered reconsideration of the layout and concern about the proximity of play to the beach and public road. Certainly it was about this time that a decision was made to change the 6th hole.

The Gold Medal awarded to WBC Miller for the best scratch score (71) in the 1930 Longniddry Autumn Meeting.

1930. A glimpse of caddy rates is obtained from a court action in December 1930 on behalf of Mrs Annie Donaldson or Conisby against her erstwhile husband Terence Conisby of Canty Hall. He had paid not a penny of the £1 per week alimony she had been granted. In response our Terence made two pleas: he hadn't understood the decision in the first place and in the second,

Ladies v Gents
The first Ladies
versus Gents Match
took place on July
10th 1931. All
played off the men's
tees. The normal rule
of 3/4 of the
difference in
handicaps applied
but the ladies
received 6 shots in
addition. The Board
minute stops there,
but the
"Haddingtonshire
Courier" is less
discreet: it reveals
that the ladies won
by nine and a half
matches to five and a
half.

1932 was the year
when a member
approaching the 7th
green sliced his
mashie shot into the
whins on the right.
He found his ball
lying upon four eggs
in a blackbird's nest.
The eggs were
unbroken and four
days later the four
fledglings had been
hatched. The ruling
is presumed to have
been that the lie was
unplayable.

he hadn't any money. The rate for a caddy at Longniddry was only 2/- per round, Terence's sole source of income. The judge was unimpressed and Terence departed to the local jail, where his opportunity to pay poor Annie anything at all would be further reduced.

On December 26th 1930 the "Haddingtonshire Courier" reported the appointment of past Open Champion Jack White to the position of managing professional to the Longniddry Golf Club. He was to take charge of the caddies (minus Terence for a time!) and the professional's shop. He was to begin his duties on 11th March 1931.

Just recently a steel shafted driver made by Jack White during his tenure at Longniddry, has been kindly donated to the Club by Mr Alex Gray, a retired employee of the Estate.

1931. Match against the Bass Rock Club. The first record of a match between Longniddry and an external Club is found in May 1931, once again in the "Haddingtonshire Courier". Longniddry appears to have lost at home to the Bass Rock Club by 9 matches to 11. Some familiar names are listed in the Longniddry team: H Watt, R Ritchie, A Dishington, N Moran, R Himsworth, J C Rose, S Forsyth, R B Denholm, and J F Foggo are among them. This match was followed a week later by a return fixture, in which W B Torrance played for Longniddry. It resulted in a draw.

External Competitions. Two external competitions were held at Longniddry that year. Firstly there was the Evening Times Trophy won on behalf of the Royal Burgess Golfing Society by Bill Torrance and his partner G Seymour Noon. They defeated Denholm and Flynn of the Bass Rock Golf Club by 2and 1. Then in the East of Scotland Ladies Championship Mrs J R Watson beat Doris Park 3 and 1.

1932. This was the year of the first official Curtis Cup match, and the year when the term "bogey" was officially replaced by "par".

In August Hilton of Leven, playing in the Longniddry Open Amateur Competition, is recorded as having a second round 69, "two strokes above Denholm's" record. Clearly the course record at that time must have been 67, held by R B Denholm although the details have not survived. The cup had been gifted by the Earl of Wemyss and it was won on this fourth year of competition by the record holder R B Denholm with scores of 72 and 71.

In December 1932 the "Haddingtonshire Courier" reported a social event in the clubhouse as follows: *"The Annual Whist Drive and Dance ... was held on Friday evening. Dance music was provided by a radio gramophone superintended by Mr Greig - the garage. The catering carried out by Mr Shearlaw was all that could be desired."*

1933. 17th February the following year, was the occasion of Lord Elcho's coming of age. It was also the year of the arrival from Kinghorn of a Mr Weston as Longniddry Station Master.

Another glimpse of the social side of things is given in the 'Haddingtonshire Courier' of March 10th : '*A whist drive and dance, the second of the season, took place in the clubhouse on Friday evening, by kind permission of Mr Connor. After whist, the company adjourned to the dining room and the prizes were presented to successful ladies. The members of the committee are to be congratulated on the success of the function.*'

A record of another match with the Bass Rock Club is found on 12th May 1933 once again in the 'Courier': '*In a hole and hole match with the Bass Rock Club, JC Rose, Captain registered the first win for Longniddry going round in 71 to defeat G B Laing.*' The title of 'Captain' in this report refers to Team Captain. The first full playing Captain of the Club would not be appointed for another two years.

Again the 'Courier' reports in 1933: '*In the Club's Spring Meeting in 1933, John McCredie the holder and A F Simpson tied at 74 for the Connor Cup (scratch). This was the first occasion when the new short 6th hole was used and it gave general satisfaction*'.

The 'Courier' report of 30th June 1933 is also important: '*Miss Doris Park (Longniddry) partnered by Miss Greenhorn played for Britain yesterday in the Women's International Golf match against France at Weybridge. Miss Park and her partner settled their match at the 15th, their golf being much too steady for their opponents.*'

1934. Presumably in compensation for the late raspberries the introduction of 1934 was marked by one of the worst gales in living memory on the 19th January. Windows were broken, roofs damaged and bathing boxes blown over.

British Girls Championship. It was in 1934 that Nancy Jupp who lived in Elcho Road, Longniddry, brought to the Club the British Girls Championship Trophy. She was 13 at the time and is thought still to be the youngest ever winner.

The Links Affair. Through the summer of 1934 the pages of "the Haddingtonshire Courier" record the beginning of a heated dispute about control of the links beside the shore. It appears that a group of Longniddry residents who had formed a Feuars Association chaired by Bailie Sawers of Woodburn, had closed off a section of the Links as a private car park located close to the bathing huts. The action was opposed by Longniddry residents and tenants led by Thomas Millar who objected that access to the beach for ordinary Longniddry folk and the general public was being unlawfully restricted. The battle raged to and fro with much ink used

Apart from the picking of ripe raspberries in the Cadell's garden on the 28th November, perhaps the last noteworthy event of 1933 at the course was in December, when Frank Beckett managed to keep a six off his card on an inward half of 34 which used all the digits remaining between one and seven namely: 3,4,3,1,7,2,5,4,5.

Nancy Jupp

83

in the correspondence section of the 'Courier'. Mr J K Stewart of Inchmahome became involved - he was now retired but had been Comptroller of Stamps and Taxes for Scotland. The local authority was drawn in too. The matter did not subside until spring of the following year.

AGM. In September 1934 the Golf Club AGM took place in the clubhouse. For the only time recorded - although there may well have been similar occasions in the 1920's now lost to us - the "Captain Lord Wemyss" as the "Courier" puts it, presided at the meeting. This confirms the situation which had been suspected that the Captain of the club from the outset until 1935, when Stuart Forsyth took office, was Lord Wemyss himself. The other office bearers on this 1934 occasion were: Vice Captain Sir David Kinloch of Gilmerton, Honorary Secretary and Treasurer Mr G A Connor, and Messrs J C Rose, G W Jupp, A F Simpson, G M Gillespie, J McCredie and G Mitchell.

1935. Apart from the appointment of Stuart Forsyth as Club Captain with the Earl of Wemyss stepping up to President, golfing activities in 1935 tend to be obscured by gun smoke from the "Battle of the Bents" which was still rumbling! In May 1935 the Longniddry Feuars Association were asked to give an undertaking that no further fences would be erected on that portion of the bents leased to them. They were also requested to remove the wire of the fence of their private car park to allow people on foot free access to the beach and their bathing huts. It was proposed that Lord Wemyss should let the County Council take control of that portion of the bents westwards of the "sand depot at the new road to the shore up to the Estate boundary".

Lord Wemyss in reply made it clear that he had never wished to encroach upon public rights or push his own position. He was concerned about the adverse effects on the bents of general motoring and camping. Had the County Council come forward with a plan he would have welcomed it. The land had been let to Richard Baillie but the results had been negligible. The Feuars had come forward to offer control and within a year the place was different. It was now a pleasure to drive along the road.

After this, the correspondence began to tail off. There are still some revealing comments. For example it is pointed out the Feuars were not necessarily the same as the Golf Club members. Also that there were barbed wire entanglements to be negotiated by tenants in getting access to the beach. Apart from a brief sequel in June, the matter disappears from the "Courier" columns but the overall result seems to have been that the right of public access was upheld at the expense of the Feuars. This had significance for the golf course because it became increasingly difficult to restrain campers and walkers on that part of the course north of the shore road. Eventually this led to the reconstruction of the course and its confinement south of the road.

In September 1935 the "Haddingtonshire Courier" records the AGM of Longniddry Golf Club at which A F Simpson was appointed Captain of the club. For once the newspaper report seems to be in error. It advises that Mr Simpson *"holds the honour of being the Club's first playing Captain"*. This conflicts with the record that Stuart Forsyth had been Captain the previous year and was an active and able competitor. The other golfing news to survive is that in October of 1935 Longniddry hosted the Scottish Professional Golf Championship. It was won by J McDowall of Turnberry with a 4-round total of 280.

1936. 1936 was the year when Alf Padgham beat the full-swinging Scotsman Jimmy Adams by a stroke to win the Open at Hoylake.

Nearer home, Longniddry's Miss Doris Park won the Scottish Women's Amateur Championship and was presented with a diamond and pearl brooch by the Longniddry Ladies Club. In June, in what was presumably the seal of the peaceful settlement of the bents affair, the Feuars Association presented a changing hut to the Bathing Club.

Port Seton Golf Club. Mr Matthew Cunningham who is researching the history of Port Seton Golf Club advises that in June 1936 a Home and Home match was played with Longniddry. The first leg took place at Longniddry where the Home Team won 7 and 5. The result of the return match at Port Seton was a 7 - 7 draw so that overall Longniddry won the encounter 14/12.

The Longniddry Team was recorded as:

J. K. Adamson	J. Morrison	W. Rankin
J. Brunton	W. Neil	W. Wood
J. Brown	A. J. Davis	W. J. Henderson
W. J. McKay	T. Hare	J. E. Teesdale

Within a few years the Port Seton Club closed and many of its members became affiliated to Longniddry. George Taylor was one who as a youngster played the Port Seton Course. While he caddied at Longniddry and some young people played there such as the Walls boys, Nancy Jupp and Peter Teesdale, it was easier just to go to Port Seton. George reports the rate for a caddy in those days as 1/6d. It was decided not to break the news to him that Jimmy Hume had got 2/6d.

Board Meeting. During 1936 some changes were being made to Longniddry's 15th hole which like the 6th had originally been played across a main road. This is revealed by the first surviving minutes of the Club Board dated 20th September 1936. They record the proceedings of the Annual General Meeting. Sir David Kinloch Bart., now elevated to Vice-President, was in the chair and J McCredie was elected Captain for 1937.

In the Curtis Cup the ladies fought out a tie with the Americans over the Gleneagles King's Course.

The retiring Captain, A F Simpson, was to be retained on the Greens Committee until the alterations to the 15th had been completed.

The 1936 extract from the Tatler is included by courtesy of the Illustrated London News. The commentary upon the MEL cartoons suggests that some holes were in play at Longniddry in 1914.

Mr G A Connor. The minutes of the Board meeting which followed on 31st October record the death of Mr Connor and appreciation of his services to the Club. It transpired that Mr Connor had been about to start a game of golf when he collapsed and died on the first tee. He had given forty-six years of public service to the community in East Lothian and with Lord Wemyss had seen Longniddry golf course created and matured during the fifteen years of his stewardship. The new representative of the Earl of Wemyss, Mr Hunter Murray, was co-opted as a permanent Board member. There appears to have been no intention that he should serve as Honorary Secretary/Treasurer as Mr Connor had done. Indeed the new Secretary would be Mr R C Cutter. The postcard notifying Mr Cutter's appointment has been preserved by the Lady Artisans.

Further Alterations. An important development with regard to the course was the decision to ask James Braid to advise on the 2nd hole. By the time of the next Board meeting a month later James Braid had visited the course and was preparing his report. Meantime portions of the cross bunkers at the 8th, 9th, 17th and 18th were to be filled in, though subsequently the last two were reprieved.

Miscellany.

At the final Board meeting in 1936 the grant to the Ladies Club was increased from £10 to £20 and a sorrowful decision was also reached that a plan to convert the men's smoking room into an up-to-date cocktail bar would not proceed because of the high cost involved.

Matches with Dirleton Castle and the Bass Rock Club were renewed and a new one against Rhodes, North Berwick introduced

On the 29th November 1936 the Board met to consider the detail of Braid's proposals. Interestingly in view of the original enquiry, the 2nd hole was not mentioned at all. The proposals were:

1) The 6th to be unchanged meantime.
2) Changes to the 13th (then across the road).
3) The 14th to be made into two holes:
   a) A new tee to be constructed 70 or 80 yards behind the existing one (presumably still across the road)
   b) A new green to be constructed east of the first burn (the Cadger) and short of the right of way on the right hand side of the then 14th fairway.
4) A new tee on the east side of the Cadger Burn to the unchanged 14th green (presumably to become the 15th).

No decision to implement any of these proposals is recorded.

1937. This was the year when Henry Cotton won the Open Championship at Carnoustie finishing ahead of the whole US Ryder Cup team.
At Longniddry the Board began the year by raising the Starter's weekly wages from £2.7/- to £2.10/-.

GOLF CLUBS AND GOLFERS

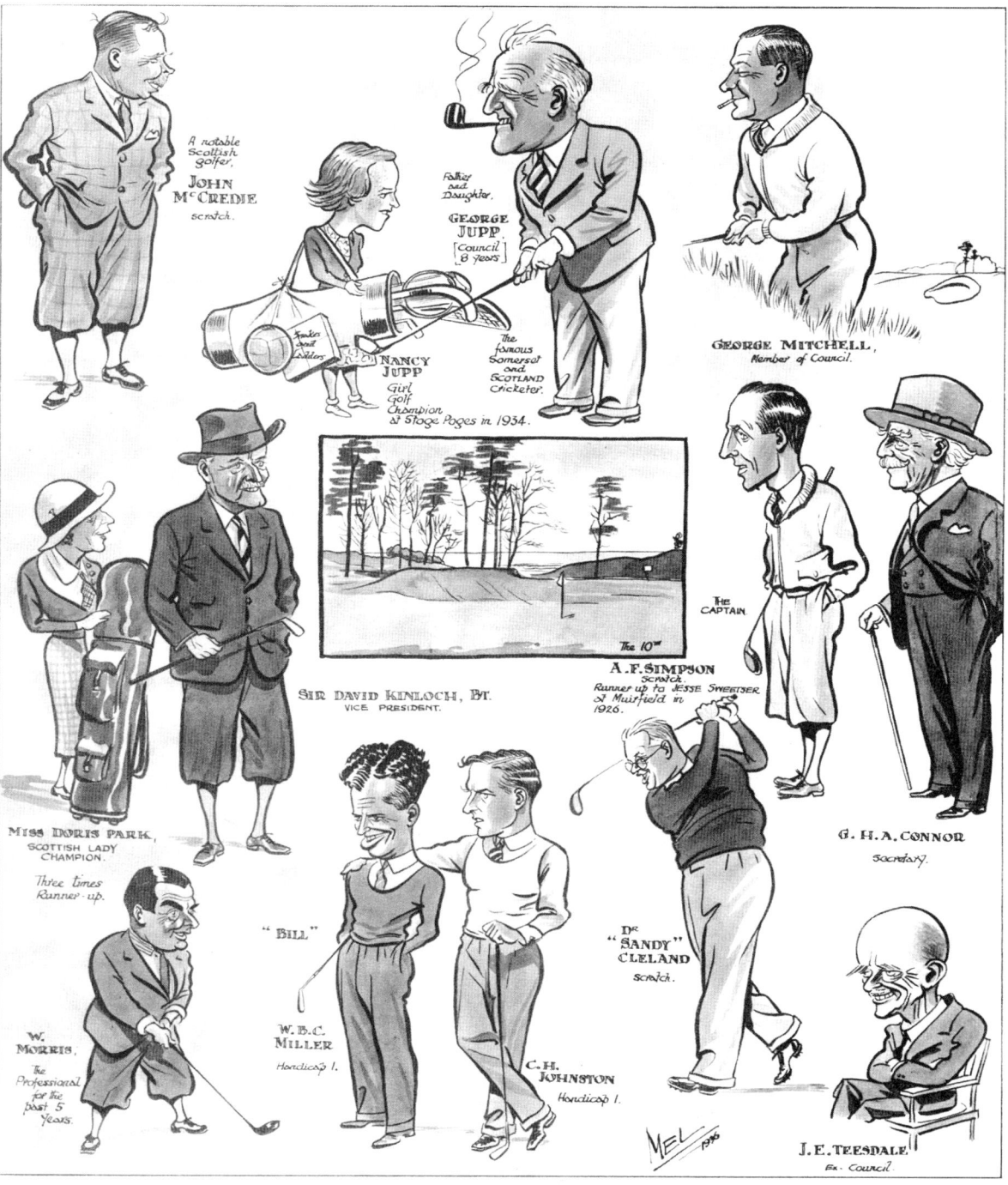

A notable Scottish golfer, **JOHN M℃CREDIE** scratch.

GEORGE JUPP [Council 8 years] The famous Somerset and Scotland Cricketer.

Father and Daughter.

NANCY JUPP Girl Golf Champion at Stoke Poges in 1934.

GEORGE MITCHELL, Member of Council.

MISS DORIS PARK, SCOTTISH LADY CHAMPION. Three times Runner-up.

SIR DAVID KINLOCH, BT. VICE-PRESIDENT.

The 10th

THE CAPTAIN

A.F.SIMPSON Scratch. Runner up to Jesse Sweetser at Muirfield in 1926.

G. H. A. CONNOR Secretary.

W. MORRIS, The Professional for the past 5 years.

"BILL."

W. B. C. MILLER Handicap 1.

C. H. JOHNSTON Handicap 1.

Dr "SANDY" CLELAND scratch.

J. E. TEESDALE Ex-Council

MEL 1936

The MEL cartoons in the Tatler were.accompanied by the following text:

Longniddry Golf Club by MEL

As this page goes to press, news has been received of the regretted death of Mr G H Connor, the Honorary Secretary. Mr Connor, who was formerly factor to Lord Wemyss, did a great deal for the club, and his death is a great loss. Lord Wemyss, who is chief landowner of the district, laid out a private golf-course in 1914 and from this has developed the important course known as Longniddry to-day. It is interesting to note that in the times of Mary, Queen of Scots, Longniddry House, now vanished, belonged to the Douglases and that John Knox was resident there, in his younger days, as Tutor to the Laird's son. The main characteristics of Longniddry Golf Course are those of a seaside nature; but it has also some features, as when, for instance, you have to play across a little wooded dell, and when you must pursue a dog-leg fairway in order to avoid getting in among the surrounding trees, which remind one forcibly of an inland course. Longniddry may, sooner or later, become one of the championship courses.

Estates Office,
LONGNIDDRY,
East Lothian.

October, 1936.

Mr. R.C. Cutter has been appointed Secretary of Longniddry Golf Club, and all communications relative to the Club affairs should be sent ad-:dressed to him at the Club House, Longniddry.

R. HUNTER MURRAY.

EDINBURGH EVENING NEWS, MONDAY SEPTEMBER 17, 1934

GIRL GOLF CHAMPION WELCOMED HOME

Rhoda and Nancy Jupp under the arch.
Holding the Clubs
Left: Tommy Beattie (killed in war), Dougie Teesdale, Kathleen Rose.
Right: Ivor Davies, Tony Davies, Colin Mair and Betty Rose

The Great Dandelion Project. Then they began the dandelion project. It was decided to spend £30 to eradicate dandelions on the first fairway. Five girls were to be employed for a period of 5 to 6 weeks applying Wikeham Weed Eradicator to the dandelions. At the same time a square section was to be marked out in which dandelions would be cut out with knives instead of receiving the weedkiller. The results would be compared. Most infuriatingly the outcome is not recorded. One is left to speculate whether the knife did better than the poison, or did the Lucretia Borgias' have more success than the Charlotte Cordays'?

Greens Policy. It was also at this meeting in February that it was decided to take out of commission the bottom tier of the 5th green. In future it would be treated as part of the surround and not the green (It would be 50 years before the decision was reversed, at the instigation of Vice-President Tom Porteous it is whispered). At the same time a general policy of reducing the size of the greens was agreed upon, probably to reduce costs.

Bathing Huts. In May, Mr J C Rose obtained permission to run an extension pipe from the water main at the 13th green to service the bathing huts at the beach. In time with greater public access and mobility the preservation of the bathing huts became more and more difficult. Certain anonymous sources (now highly respectable it should be emphasised) have referred to adolescent recollections of assisted disintegrations and of the unauthorised construction of boats from the debris.

The 11th Earl of Wemyss. At the AGM of August 1937, the death of the 11th Earl of Wemyss was recorded with great regret. Hugo Richard Wemyss Charteris had died in July 1937 only two months after his wife had passed away. They had had 4 sons, one of whom one died very young, and 3 daughters. Two of the boys were killed in the Great War, the youngest Ivo in 1915 and the eldest Lord Elcho in 1916. The succeeding Lord Elcho, (Francis) David was at that time serving in South Africa under the Resident Commissioner for Basutoland. The Countess of Wemyss had been, like her husband, an enthusiastic supporter of the Golf Club. She had been particularly interested in the Ladies Section, although whether she ever became President of it, as her successor did, is not recorded.

The passing of both Lord and Lady Wemyss within less than a year of George Connor, meant that Longniddry Golf Club had suddenly lost three stalwart supporters. It would have been understandable if there had been considerable anxiety about the future of the Club at that time. Such fears, if they existed at all, were soon shown to be unfounded. The succeeding 12th Earl of Wemyss (the grandson of the 11th Earl) had signified his willingness to accept the Presidency of the Club and was duly elected at the AGM. The continuation of Sir David Kinloch as Vice-President was also approved while Mr J C Rose was elected Club Captain in succession to J. McCredie.

Ladies Footbath.
Intriguingly in April 1937 the Board considered the ladies' request for a smaller foot bath. One struggles to rationalise this request - the ladies' minutes do not help - unless of course hot water was in such short supply.

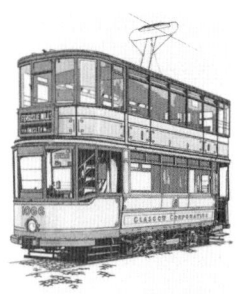

Glasgow Corporation
Tramways Standard Car
1066. Built 1912-1919.

In June 1938, the price of whisky was fixed at, in today's money, 7 to 8p per glass with beer at 3p per pint.

And in August a new course record was set by W C Menzies an Edinburgh University student with a round of 66 compiled as follows: 4,4,3,4,4,3,4,4,3, 3,4,3,3,4,4,4,4,4. Menzies won the Club Championship the following year and due to the wartime break, he held the title until 1947 when Peter Burt displaced him.

Rather strangely, at a Board meeting in November 1937 held in the North British Hotel (The Balmoral), it was decided to discontinue the Open Scratch Competition for the Earl of Wemyss Cup, hitherto held annually in June. It was also resolved to employ a course Ranger on Sundays to ensure that players kept their place.

1938. Club Member E. R. L. Fitzpayne and Glasgow's Tramcars. To a Glaswegian, a particular entry in the minutes of the Board meeting of 28th January 1938 is quite fascinating. At one time or another all people brought up in Glasgow in the 30's and 40's have stared at the orange sides of Corporation Transport vehicles and read printed there in small red letters "E R L Fitzpayne, General Manager"! It was rumoured that Mr Fitzpayne hailed from Sheffield. His name was taken very much in vain when the vehicles bearing it did not arrive on time or when they did appear were found to be full, and defended by a green-clad termagant who declared 'there's nae mair room on this caur'!. When, therefore, one encounters a Mr E R L Fitzpayne in the Longniddry Golf Club minutes proposing the adoption of J K Inglis of Cockenzie as a new member, one feels that a long-sought quarry has been run to earth at last. Is this where the blighter was when one was shivering on an exposed traffic island at Anniesland waiting on a green tram to Scotstoun West? Eventually a tram would arrive with a retinue of 3 others (when the poker game broke up, it was darkly muttered). It was said that the Glasgow trams travelled in convoys in case there was an inspector (Duncan Ayton's father perhaps) submerged in a close somewhere at periscope depth!

Dandelions again. At the same meeting the dandelions which seem to have counter attacked were considered once more. This time the caddies were to be given 1/- an hour to deal with them. The methods to be employed were not specified.

Miscellany. It was also decided to purchase a new Honours Board which begs the question of what happened to the old one.

In the final of the East of Scotland ladies Championship held at Longniddry Miss Jessie Anderson beat the Club's own Doris Park 4 and 2.

The Captaincy. In September 1938 the decision that the captaincy should be for a period of two years was taken and this is a rule which has continued ever since with a few variations due to wartime and special circumstances.

George Jupp. Towards the end of the year the death of George Jupp is reported in the Minutes. The impression given is that his sad decease was quite sudden and unexpected.

1939. In February it was agreed to play a match against Caermount. Dr Gavin Boyd who has searched Caermount's records, advises that this was the first Longniddry/Caermount match and that it ended in a 3 all draw.

Tim Rose. The 1939 AGM was chaired by Bailie Tom Sawers in the absence of the Vice-President. The meeting continued the tragic sequence of the previous three years: Tim Rose, Captain of the Club and founder member had died in office. The minutes record sympathy for Mr Rose's family and appreciation of his valued service. Bailie Sawers was elected Captain to fill the vacancy so regrettably created.

World War II. At the AGM on 30th September 1939, the country had been at war for some days. Mr James Teesdale said that members were anxious to discover what the policy of the Club was, and if it would carry on during the war. The Captain replied that the Club would certainly be carried on, and that he hoped that members would assist by playing whenever the opportunity presented itself.

Nevertheless at the next Board meeting in October it was decided to suspend all competitions for 1940 and not to issue any fixture cards. Club members who were also members of the armed services or whole time members of attached nursing services, would be asked to pay a nominal subscription of 5/- to retain their full privileges as club members.

Maisie Walls remembers seeing the first German plane to be shot down over Britain. It was 16th October 1939. Maisie and her mother Mrs Dodds were putting on the 6th green when they heard the pop-pop-popping of the plane's engines. They looked up and saw above them the German plane, a Heinkel, quite close with little lights flashing from it and its swastika prominent. It was heading west. Its target was the Forth Bridge which it failed to damage. Later that day it was shot down in the Forth. The crew were picked up by the fishing vessel Day Spring whose skipper was John Dickson. Club member Archie Johnston remembers the airmen being marched through Port Seton under guard.

Maisie Walls also remembers her mother driving down from Dalkeith with her in a pony and trap to play at the course. Though what on earth she did with the pony when she got there Maisie can't remember. Maisie's other wartime memory is of the Home Guard "creeping about in the tatties" in the dug-up section of the course. Bella Porteous adds that the Home Guard equipment, when it eventually arrived, was kept secure in the brick building which existed until 1995 amongst the trees between the 10th green and 7th fairway. An anonymous suggestion has also been made that certain essential supplies/ refreshments were stored in this small quartermaster's establishment and that frequent inspections and replenishments of the stocks were necessary. A photograph of this fine body of men under the command of Russel Patrick was unearthed by Jenny Morrison.

The Home Guard did fight one battle. This was a golf match in aid of the Red Cross against the civil defence personnel. In a foursomes format the Home Guard were defeated but the Red Cross received £4. 7/6.

The following minute of the meeting of 27th August 1939 is well worth repeating: "Honorary Member: It was decided that Mr S B Williamson should be made a Life Honorary Member to commemorate his magnificent victory in the British Boys Championship of 1939."

At this time of course, Nancy Jupp was still playing at Longniddry, so that the Club could boast the membership of both a Girls and Boys British Champion as well as having had an Open Champion as club professional.

LONGNIDDRY COMPANY, 2ND BATTALLION EAST LOTHIAN HOME GUARD

Back Row: David Douglas. Ben Mackintosh. Tom Greenlaw. John Paxton. ? Bruce Johnston. ? Peter Scott. ? James O'Donnel. Andrew Honeysett. Walter Montgomery. Bob Porteous. Jack Buxton.

Middle Row: ? Peter Sanderson. Roy Cutter. John Howie. Gordon Morrison. ? Bill Skane. John McRaw. Claude McDougal. ? ? Harry O'Niel. Peter Dickson. ?

Front Row: Henry Barris. Jack Black. Willy Mcleod. Jack Park. George Walls. Russel Patrick. Archie McLelland. Frank Smith. Davie Park. John Brown. Dave Morris. ? Florrence.

1940. The minutes of the next committee meeting after a gap of nearly a year are very brief. There were five persons present: Bailie Sawers in the Chair, Mr R C Cutter as Secretary, Mr M F Yorke as Estate representative and two Board members, H V Hilton and A Morton Young. Hunter Murray at the beginning of the war had entered the Military Land Service; Lord Wemyss's cousin Maurice Yorke replaced him as Factor throughout the war and for some years afterwards. It was decided to recommend to the AGM that the existing officers and committee should remain in office 'for the duration' (a common phrase in those days) of the war. This proposal was duly accepted at the AGM held later that same day. Club competitions were to continue in abeyance and the whole course had now been fenced and sheep were grazing.

1941. The next committee meeting was in March 1941 and appears to have been convened to consider a response to the Department of Agriculture who wished to put part of the course under cultivation for food production. The Committee agreed and offered the 16th and 17th fairways with the stipulation that the greens should be preserved. This condition does not seem to have been observed - possibly it was not really practicable. In any event a formal directive for ploughing up 14 acres was received by The

Secretary of the Agricultural Executive Committee for East Lothian (AEC) towards the end of May 1941. There is a tone of relief in the Club's Board minute of October 1941 which records that there was no prospect of any further ploughing of the course in the immediate future. Two letters were noted at this meeting: one from the Food Controller South East District thanking the Committee for allowing the changing room to be used as a food store, and the other from the O/C the 5th Battalion King's Own Scottish Borderers expressing appreciation to the Club for their hospitality to officers and men.

1942. In those years of the war it had clearly been a struggle to keep the Club going. Matters must have come to a head at the end of 1941 because an Extraordinary General Meeting was held on 17th January 1942 with the object of reconstituting the Club. Accordingly, Longniddry Golf Club was formally wound up as at 31st January 1942 with R C Cutter appointed as liquidator. One can only speculate that perhaps with so many members in uniform the reduction in income had become very serious. At any rate, it was not a knockout punch. On the count of nine the Club was on its feet again slightly groggy perhaps, but vertical. Immediately following dissolution it was agreed that the reconstituted Longniddry Club would be started as of 1st February 1942 with Committee and Office Bearers unchanged. It seems clear that Maurice Yorke on behalf of the Earl of Wemyss had had a significant hand in saving the Club. The minute pays tribute to this generous intervention which had enabled the Club to carry on in these difficult times.

In 1941 also, Edinburgh Corporation decided to cultivate 160 acres of what had been public golf courses. They suggested to private clubs that they might extend the courtesy of their course to golfers who had been deprived in consequence. Longniddry was among the first to respond with the offer of such a facility at the going rate of four shillings per round.

Further Ploughing. Later in the year it is apparent that the October 1941 optimism about the extent of the ploughing had been misplaced. The records contain a copy application for a ploughing-up grant dated August 1942 in respect of 9/10 acres to support an oats crop in 1943 – not to be re-seeded with grass afterwards. If this is additional to the first cultivation then about 24 acres went under the plough. Certainly tradition has it that the course was cultivated for crops up to the right-of-way. In October 1942 the Golf Club dutifully reported that the bunkers had been filled in and the course was ready for ploughing.

1943. RAF Connection. The story of the Club's two Royal Air Force trophies is told in articles in the "Haddingtonshire Courier" in consecutive months in 1943. The first is in the issue dated 17th September. It states:

*"**RAF Gift to Golf Club.** An interesting momento in the form of a silver rose bowl has been presented to Longniddry Golf Club by the personnel of a RAF station in recognition of playing facilities given them by the Club. Wing Commander Gibbons expressed appreciation of the great benefit it had been to all ranks to have the golf course available for this off-duty time. Councillor Sawers (Edinburgh) Captain of the Club in acknowledging the*

In February 1943 arising from the cultivation work on the course a report on the soil constituents of that part of the course was received. It was good on lime, very good on phosphates but low on potash.

gift said that it would form a silver link between the airmen and the members and would be a constant reminder of the great debt everyone owed to the RAF. Councillor Sawers promised that when the Club resumed its normal activities there would be an annual competition for the trophy."

Since there were at least two different air stations which might have made the presentation there is at first some small exasperation that the donor station is not specified in the report. That is until it is recognised that this may have been a deliberate omission for security purposes.

The first trophy having been received and reported in the press the second air station clearly felt obliged to do something too. Perhaps somewhat chagrined that their neighbours had got in first they could take comfort in that the superior qualification of their Wing Commander more than compensated. Once more the Haddingtonshire Courier witnessed the ceremony. It reported on 8th October 1943 as follows:

*"**RAF Gift to Golf Club.** At the conclusion of a match played on Longniddry course on Saturday between an RAF team and a Longniddry Club team, Wing Commander Sheem DFC and Bar, a Battle of Britain pilot, presented a silver cup to the Club in acknowledgement of the facilities for play granted to the personnel of a station under his command. Councillor Sawers (Edinburgh) Captain of the Club said that they were honoured in having with them one of the "Few", and it would have been more appropriate had the Club been presenting a momento to the RAF in recognition of the great debt owed to them by the "Many". The trophy, he added, would be one of the Club's treasured possessions."*

The identities of the airfields concerned are established when the engravings on the two trophies are examined. In fact they were Macmerry and Drem respectively. The Macmerry Bowl is contested annually on a scratch basis while the Drem Cup is played for under handicap.

1944. Meantime, with the increasing success of the Allies it was becoming more and more difficult to convince men of the need to continue to turn up for Home Guard duties. General Sir Andrew Thorne GOC Scottish Command arrived to inspect the units of the Home Guard during their Sunday training programme. On February 4th the "Courier" reports on his visit:

"When a visit was paid to Haddington Company, General Thorne saw gun crews at drill with an 18 pounder. He asked if they had any opportunity of firing practice at an artillery range. On being told that they did not have the opportunity, he said he would take up the matter with the Royal Artillery. 'I have been much impressed by your bearing and drill' he told them. He pointed out that although the risk of general invasion might be past there was still that possibility that the enemy might make diversionary landings.

In such case East Lothian was a likely place to choose 'You', he said 'Are on the right of the line and the Country depends on you.'"

One can sympathise with General Thorne. After all, Italy had capitulated 6 months before and it was common knowledge that the Second Front was imminent so that perceived need for Home Guard duties must have been waning. However, to say that in East Lothian they were on the right of the line, the place of greatest danger, was perhaps stretching it.

Crop Cultivation. In September Maurice Yorke wrote to the AEC saying that he proposed to plant early potatoes for the 1945 crop and adding, *"please could this be the last crop taken? We do need 18 holes."*

1945. The year began with correspondence between Club Secretary Roy Cutter and Golf Course Architect Philip Ross Mackenzie whose letter dated 21st January 1945 is shown below by the courtesy of the Earl of Wemyss

"Dear Sir   Longniddry Golf Course   January 21st 1945

I am honoured by your enquiry regarding the re-construction of the golf course and I would very much like to be associated with the work.

On my walk round the course with you on Thursday it was made clear that it would be necessary to scrap two holes by the sea, Nos 11 and 13, and find two new holes on the main ground South of the road, and also to construct four new holes on the land under plough on the East side of the course.

My fee for planning and supervising this work would be 135 guineas plus 10 guineas expenses, and half of that fee if my plans are used with no supervision. I am willing to submit a plan for your approval, together with an estimate for the cost of the work, for a fee of 15 guineas, this to form part or my total fee if my plan is accepted.

It is understood that the Estate will likely undertake the sowing of the new fairways. The best time for this operation would be from the third week in August to mid/September. Messrs Sutton & Sons of Reading, the well known seed Firm, advise sowing of fairways with a non rye grass mixture of Agrostis and fescues at the rate of 2 cwt per acre, the cost of their seed would be £32.10/- per acre. A heavy rate of sowing is necessary if the areas are to be brought into play within twelve months.

For your information I append a list of courses on which I have been employed on layout or re-construction work.

Yours faithfully, P. Mackenzie Ross "

In the meantime permission had been obtained from the AEC to sow grass seed after the removal of the 1945 early potato crop. This did not quite conclude the cultivation matter. Some years later the Department of Agriculture advised the Club that claims could be made in respect of the restoration of land cultivated during war time. The correspondence reveals that the land was cultivated for five years, namely 1941 and 1942 at 14 acres and 1943, 1944 and 1945 at 24 acres. The profit, worked out as a proportion of the whole farm operated from Craigielaw, was £800. 0s 8d for the five years.

The first recorded Club Board minutes after January 1942 refer to a meeting in March 1945. Victory in Europe is almost secured. Minds are turning to happier prospects. The monthly spoon competition between April and October is reinstated and a mixed foursome competition arranged for June. Ladies Summer and Autumn Meetings are to be arranged and participation in the restarted County Cup is planned. The two cups presented by the RAF aerodromes, Macmerry and Drem would be allotted to the Summer Meeting, one for the Scratch and one for the Handicap prize.

Detailed proposals from Mr Mackenzie Ross were dispatched to the club on 10th March. Unfortunately the plan to which they refer has not survived but the narrative of the letter, for which we are again indebted to the Earl of Wemyss is as follows:

"Dear Sir,   *Longniddry Golf Course,*   *10th March 1945*
I send under separate Cover a tracing from the map which outlines the scheme which I recommend for the reconstruction of the golf course. It being understood that the two holes across the main road by the sea are to be abandoned. Under this scheme the length of the course would be approximately 6170 yards from the back tees and could be stretched further. It will play normally about 6000 yards, which I regard as sufficiently long for the average golfer.

I have examined the bunkering of all the holes and have made suggestions for the filling up of a certain number which do not come into play or which simply worry the long handicap player. Bunkers should be filled in such a manner that they can be cut with a gang-mower or at any rate with a scythe. A detailed estimate for the cost of the work will be found on page 4 of this report.

Regarding the construction of the greens and bunkers. No good result will be obtained unless an expert is employed who can stay on the Job all the time, it costs no more to employ a trained man because he knows exactly what to do from the word 'go' and there is no fiddling about on the ground trying the effect of hill work here and there with consequent loss of time and wages.

I have written recently to four Firms who construct golf courses and I know of only one foreman who might be available. Messrs Sutton and Sons of Reading have a really first class man in Chapman who constructed the Estoril course near Lisbon for me and also the one at Cramond near Edinburgh. If German labour is to be employed then I believe everything would go smoothly with Chapman in charge, I have seen him getting a lot of work out of the Portuguese without knowing anything of the language. I suggest as strongly as possible that you should apply for this man, he is most reliable.

I suggest that work should start in June on the new greens (6) and (11) so that the gang would be working as a team when the time came to take over the ground under potatoes, where four new greens are to be made with accompanying bunkers and fairway bunkers. Work on this area should be completed in six weeks, enabling sowing to take place during the last two weeks in August. Messrs Sutton assure me that the second half of August would be the best time to sow.

I will now pass to a detailed examination of the suggested new holes.

(6) Length 160 yards. This should prove a very sporting hole and popular too if a local rule is made under which a player can pick from the burn and drop near the L.G.U. tee under penalty of one stroke. On very windy days when it might be impossible to control the ball from the top tee the hole could be played from a new tee below the 5th green.

(11) Length 200 yards. The tin shed would have to be removed, but it could be placed at the corner of the Dean road and the main road. A good length hole and no walk to the 12th tee.

(l3) This green should be placed on the natural plateau as marked on the plan. When the plateau has been slightly reshaped I believe that it will make a very interesting green, good fun to play and real seaside golf, something between "Pandy" and "Foreman's at old Musselburgh.

(14) Tee to the right of the 2nd green, a good length hole.

(15) As per plan, a good length.

(l6) A short hole to the corner of some 145 yards. A short hole can always be as good as one likes to make it. A raised tee would be constructed but would conform to the ground slopes and have no abrupt square sides. Bushes would be planted between the tee and the road.

(17) Played dog-legged from near the wall, bushes would be planted in clumps along the wall to discount any tendency to play too close to the gardens.

(18) Tee should be well forward to enable players to make a fairly easy carry to the green with their second shots. A back tee would be constructed for anyone who might care to play from it.

Suggestions regarding bunkering of the present holes:

(1) Fill in all the bunkers and reconstruct as per plan, similar to the first hole at Muirfield.

(2) Leave all bunkers as they are at this hole.

(3) Fill in the 1st and 2nd fairway bunkers on the right and the 2nd fairway bunker on the left, near the trees.

(4) Leave all the bunkers.

(5) New bunker on right as indicated on plan, to safeguard new green (11) and enforce line of play. Cut six trees on left of fairway to encourage shot to that side of course.

(6) From the top tee a peephole should be cut through the trees to the left so that any traffic coming down the road can be seen.

(7) Fill in left half of centre fairway bunker. Fill bunker behind green and half of the bunker on the right side of the green.

(8) Fill in two fairway bunkers on the left in the rough but the height of the present hillwork must remain as it is. Fill left half of bunker left of green but the hill work must remain untouched. The bunker at the back of the green does not come into play, it can be filled or left rough.

(9) Fill right hand fairway bunker on hill. Fill one third on right of 2nd fairway bunker on right.

(10) The hillwork at the back of this green is unsightly but an open ditch runs round two thirds of the back of this green and the hillwork certainly does prevent a ball running into the ditch. The bunkering at this hole is good unless the green is too easy of approach owing to its enormous size, it could be tightened up. The green was relaid at the end of 1939 and since then it has had very little fertiliser, it should be given a chance to see how it comes along under treatment.

Pine trees in the vicinity of a green always have a bad effect poison being blown from them to the grasses.

Actually there is only three inches of topsoil under this green, there should be at least six inches.

(12) Leave all bunkers at this hole, all very good.

(13) Fill or grass first half of first right hand fairway bunker and fill or grass all of 3rd and 4th fairway bunkers on right.

No figure has been put in the estimate for the cost of filling in bunkers as it is assumed that this work will be undertaken by your own staff. Congratulations are due to your greenkeeper on the excellent condition of the course when considering all the difficulties.

In conclusion I will say how much I enjoyed my visits to Longniddry and would thank you for your kind hospitality. I shall be glad to reply to any questions which you may care to put.

Yours faithfully"

Some explanatory comments are necessary:

5th Hole.   The proposal envisaged the 5th tee to be east of the 4th green which is why the bunker was required to protect the 11th green.

6th Hole.   This suggests that they were contemplating restoring the 6th hole to its original east west line across the Dean Road and burn.

The estimated cost of the changes was £1,930.00 exclusive of architect's fee and cultivation work to be done by the Estate.

Course Reconstruction.   The plan for reconstruction of the course submitted by Major Mackenzie Ross was approved, and it was decided to instruct him to make arrangements for the work to proceed. His drawing of the new Longniddry layout displayed in the clubhouse is dated 1946, at least 9 months after acceptance of his proposal. In the process of reconstruction some departures from his original plans must have been decided upon. There are also a few discrepancies in the plan as compared with the course today.

German Recollections.   The Mackenzie Ross letter supports Duncan Herd's story that German Prisoners of War from the Camp in Gosford Estate helped to restore the Golf Course. Duncan says that they worked particularly on the reclamation of the ploughed section from the right of way eastwards. In light of this the following letter printed in the Scotsman on 1st June 1948 is interesting:

"20 Sperberweg (24) Lueneburg, British Zone Germany   20th May 1948

Sir, a copie of your esteemed paper having come accidentally in my hands again remembers me the days of my POW time in Gosford Camp near Longniddry where I could subscribe your paper by the kindness of the then British Paymaster. I am sorry that there is no possibility for any subscription for me at present. But nevertheless let me show my gratitude and thankfulness to the Scotsman.

Your paper has given me an all-comprehensive general view of the British policy and with much pleasure I have read all the interesting spaces like: the London letter, science notes, music notes and not to forget the points of view. Often I could read here many a good word for us Germans. But besides all the Scotsman has done a great share in getting to know the people and life of Scotland.

And then I have to thank all the Scotsmen who helped completing the picture of Scotland by giving me a good view of your poetry, history and the customs of your people. Here I express my warmest thanks to that farmer of Pencaitland who as a Robert Burns worshipper introduced me in Burns poetry. I don't regret having learnt by heart some of his poems. And never I'll forget the time which I could spend in the Edinburgh Castle acting as interpreter of a German working command. Although I was bounded in my

Sir David Kinloch.
In April the passing of Sir David Kinloch who had served the Club so well as Vice-President, was recorded with regret and appreciation.

99

freedom I must confess that Edinburgh is the most interesting city I have ever seen. The beautiful Princes Street and opposite of it the huge castle rock with the wonderful Edinburgh Castle. Here I visited all the historic rooms and last not least the capital War Memorial which gave me an overwhelming impression of hero worship. Often I guided my fellow POW through these historic places. In an article of the former POW Camp paper I tried to show them the beauty of Edinburgh and its royal castle.

Then I remember the Scotsman who told me much about Scottish customs and songs. All these signs of good will and good understanding I will never forget. May there be a time where I with my wife and now as a free man can visit all the beautiful and historic spots once more and so enlarge my knowledge of Scotland and the Scottish people. Don't think that these lines are put down by a young enthusiast, no they are written by a 47 year old former POW whose love to your country and people is true, genuine and lasting.

I am yours sincerely, Walter Donath, Senior Inspektor of the Landeszentral Bank."

Children in Clubhouse–Take 1. There seems to have been a problem about children in the clubhouse. It was proposed from the floor of the 1946 AGM that no children under fifteen be permitted. At the Board meeting following therefore, restrictions on children in the clubhouse were finalised (or so it was thought) and written into the Bye Laws.

1946. In August 1946 in a preparatory Board meeting before the AGM, a new constitution of the Ladies Section was approved. At the AGM itself, 5 weeks later Bailie T Sawers who had captained the Club through the long war years was elected Vice-President - surely well deserved. Major V B Hilton became Captain. Also at this meeting, four members who were to become well known names to future generations in the Club, were elected to the Board. They were: J J Mackersy a banker, A Dudgeon a seedsman, J A (Gus) McVey an insurance executive and Peter Barr another banker. The last three became captains in due course.

It was at this meeting that the requirement to make a copy of the Accounts available to the members was accepted.

Bill Morris Professional. Bill was made an Honorary Member of the Club towards the end of the year. His time was so taken up with starters duties apparently that he had no opportunity to play with members. A proposal was put at the AGM that he should have an assistant professional. Bill had that year been voted Captain of the newly formed Edinburgh and District Professional Golfers Association (of which Charlotte Watson was Honorary Vice-President).

The problem of the professional's availability was resolved by re-employing R Himsworth as starter.

Complaints Book. Finally, that cross for Committees to bear, a complaints book, was to be obtained.

100

1947. Although it is not specifically recorded in the minutes, it appears that on or about 23rd April 1947 there took place a formal ceremony officially opening the new course. This is indicated from the statement of the Board meeting on 15th April: *'The Greens Committee should inspect the course in the evening of April 23rd after the official opening and decide whether the new holes should remain in play'*.

The 'Courier' reveals that the inaugural match on the new course was the very first competition by the Edinburgh and District Professional Golfers Association. The Earl of Wemyss had put up two trophies for the contest. Each professional was accompanied by an amateur player so that both a professional and amateur record for the course were established that day. These proved to be 75 by J Brash and 77 by T A Fairburn.

Rationing. Interestingly, it is also recorded that if it was necessary to continue with a 'meal-less' day in the Clubhouse, it should be altered from a Thursday to some other day of the week. Nowadays even people who can remember the Second World War tend to forget how long restrictions on food, fuel and clothes continued after 1945. In this connection, a most important decision was made by the Board on 3rd May 1947:

Essential Refreshments. It was decided to divide the estimated amount of whisky for the year into weekly allotments. The weekly allotment should be put out on a different day in each week, i.e. Monday the first week, Tuesday the second and so on. Each member should be allowed one small whisky per day while supplies were available. In this year also the introduction of draft beer was proposed and seconded.

The New Course. The 'Courier' of May 2nd, after reporting the Ladies Spring Meeting took time to comment on the new course:

Two outstanding features of the recast layout of Longniddry Golf Course designed by P Mackenzie Ross, are the disappearance of the holes on the shore side of the public road, and the introduction of 6 new greens and 5 entirely new holes in the eastern part of the course which had to go under the plough during the War emergency. Only the old 18th hole remains. The alterations which make the course comparatively self contained are attractive, and excellent opinions were expressed regarding them when the inaugural competition, that of the Edinburgh and District Professional Golfers Association was played last week.

Ladies Open Championship Gullane. It was in June of 1947 that the Ladies Open Golf Championship was held at Gullane. Several familiar Longniddry names are to be found in the list of competitors. These included Nancy Jupp and Annice Latta (Lady Captain 1937) as well as Betty Adam who was probably egged on by Mabel Nicol ("Mabel with the beret - a wonderful iron player"). Gullane entries included Mrs C M Park and Mrs Beddows.

Children in Clubhouse – Take 2. At the same Board Meeting there was further debate about children in the clubhouse and it was decided to hold an Extraordinary General Meeting to finalise the matter. This duly took place on 14th June 1947 and the decision reached declared firstly that children of any age should be permitted in the dining room. The recorded text of the second part of the decision accidentally reflects the conflict which there seems to have been: 'No children under the age of Eixteen shall be allowed in the lounges.' Perhaps this could be read as eighteen or sixteen according to circumstances.

This was the "Babe" Zaharias Championship. Mildred Zaharias was the lady golfing phenomenon from the States. It is probable that it was due to her that the USGA produced a rule that only men could enter their Open Championship. She hit the ball a formidable distance but complained "If ah didn't have these (gesturing), ah'd hit it twenty yards further". Babe defeated Jacqueline Gordon 5 and 4 in the final as well as giving, (Betty Adam says) the socialising competitors in Gullane Clubhouse an impromptu homily on the evils of drink. Mildred Zaharias was the first transatlantic player to win the British Ladies Open Championship.

County Cup.

The 1947 County Cup Competition was held at Longniddry. The Home Team won the trophy. The team was: J. A. McVey, G. Henderson, H. Johnston, T. Corrie.

Burglary.   Early August brought to Longniddry an incident which deplorable as it was illustrates several features of the times:
These were: the quality of Bill Morris' hand-crafted golf clubs, the continuing shortages of every day items such as golf balls in the post-War period, the fact that the Longniddry Professional's shop was at that time a wooden structure separate from the Clubhouse, and finally some Sherlockian overtones to the police investigation. The 'Courier' of August 8th carried the following report:-

Exhibition Clubs Stolen. Golf clubs which had been specially made for exhibition purposes were stolen during last weekend from the shop of Mr Tom (sic - clearly if you were a professional golfer with a surname Morris the first bit just had to be "Tom" - Ed) Morris the professional to Longniddry Golf Club. Mr Morris' hut is situated near the first tee at the south corner of the clubhouse, and entrance was gained by the men concerned removing boards from the back of the structure. It is believed that the theft took place between 11 p.m. Saturday night and 12.30 a.m. on Sunday morning as about that time on Sunday two men were seen carrying clubs across the course towards the coast road. The thieves removed amongst other things two sets of clubs each comprising 3 woods, and 8 irons, 3 golf bags, head covers for the clubs, a golf jerkin and other accessories. In addition the month's allocation of 18 dozen golf balls, which had been received by Mr Morris a few hours before the theft, was also taken. The thieves had also entered the clubhouse and there had wrenched an electric clock from the wall. The clock which had stopped about 11.30 p.m. was found on the course on Sunday morning. The East Lothian police are investigating.

1948. Although the course had been restored to 18 holes, the grazing of sheep introduced during the war had continued. Consequently, the Board in February 1948 decided (not without opposition) upon a local rule that *'If a ball played into a bunker is found lying in a sheep's hoofmark, it may be lifted and placed in the bunker not nearer to and in line with the hole...'*

Subsequently there was a decision to try to get a couple of Sunday trains stopped at Longniddry; one from Edinburgh in the morning and another returning to Edinburgh in the evening - petrol was still rationed it should be remembered. The outcome is not recorded unfortunately.

Later that season almost two years after its introduction, the Complaints Book was withdrawn *'as it served no useful purpose'*.

Open Championship – Muirfield. 1948 was the year of Henry Cotton's third triumph in the Open Championship. He had emerged in the 30's as an outstanding British golfer, and the Second World War must surely have robbed him of other Open victories. The 1948 event was held at Muirfield. Henry's caddy was Longniddry Club member Jackie Dickson to whom, it is rumoured, Henry handed the entire cash prize. Subsequently Jackie, a plumber to trade, was disqualified from the Longniddry Club Championship on the grounds that his caddying activity had rendered him a professional player.

Garden Party. On July 9th the 'Courier' reported as follows : - *The Cosy Corner Circle of the League of Pity held a most successful garden party on Saturday at the Sycamores (adjoining the Professional's shop) by courtesy of Mr and Mrs Webster. Mrs Johnston (Culag) President of the Circle introduced the 7 year old daughter of the Earl and Countess of Wemyss, the Lady Elizabeth Charteris who performed the opening ceremony in a most gracious manner, delighting the large company who had assembled. It was a unique occasion as seldom does one hear of so young a child acting in this capacity. Master Leonard Lowe presented Lady Elizabeth with a basket of beautiful roses.*

Miscellany. The minutes of the Club's AGM for 1948, which took place at the end of September, reveal a practice of filling the two annual Board vacancies by one person recommended by the Committee and one by the members. They also record that at the meeting the Committee was urged to run a full programme of competitions.

Meanwhile Peter Barr had won the Leven Open Amateur Tournament

Restoration.

The Winter Foursomes competition was introduced in September 1947 and at the AGM at the end of that month, Major V B Hilton as Captain, referred to the fact that the Club now had a full 18 hole course once more. External competitions had been staged as well as Club events. Longniddry Golf Club was fully operational again.

Cigarettes.

Cigarettes were still in short supply. It was decided that they should be sold to club members only and that they should be limited to 20 per member per day.

defeating John Orr of St Andrews by one hole.

1949. In March in view of dissatisfaction about the 12th hole (perhaps because George Taylor and several others had driven it or perhaps it was costing Roy Cutter too much), it was decided to lengthen it by 30 yards by moving the tee back towards the 11th green.

Three evening meetings were arranged between the Ladies and the Men but no results are recorded.

The Club hosted the East of Scotland Ladies Championship. In the final Jean Donald beat Charlotte Beddows 8 and 7.

Course and Clubhouse. At that time there was a practice of not playing from the 4th tee until the 5th tee was clear. This was the reason given for a proposal to erect a protective net around the 5th tee, thereby cutting down waiting time at the 4th tee. This net existed for a while but was found to be ineffectual and was removed. Of course the tree beside the 5th would have been much smaller than it is today. The proposal was not carried at the time but a suggestion was made that a practice ground behind the 14th tee in a westerly direction should be considered.

At the end of the year the SSS was amended to 73 with the 14th hole reduced to a 4 whilst the 17th and 18th were both put up to 5. It was also decided to erect a board in the lounge carrying the names of the Club Captains. Perhaps the "Honours Board" purchased in 1938 had listed the Club champions only.

1950. The mid-century year seems to have been pretty uneventful. Board meetings in these times were infrequent and disagreements - the word "conflicts" seems too strong for these well-mannered days- appeared to be few - children in the clubhouse apart. Of course the minutes may have been written with a view to displaying a serene harmony to future generations. Certainly, if they are taken at face value proceedings were comparatively brief and straightforward.

The Foreshore Again. 1950 appears to have finally seen the end of the foreshore arguments. Richard Baillie died only a few months after the County Council decided to take charge of the foreshore and bents. In May it was agreed that the County Council should lease the area from the Earl of Wemyss and control it in the public interest.

Honorary Membership. Two important events in the Club that year were the well-deserved elections of Charlotte Beddows and Emma Sawers to Life Honorary Memberships.

Scots Pines are a feature of Longniddry Golf Course. This harmonious triplet stands between the 4th green and the 3rd fairway.

The prospect back to the Clubhouse from the angle of the dog-leg on the 5th hole.

1951. This was the year that the international authorities decided to abolish the stymie.

At Longniddry an important decision appears to have been the fixing of the price of lunch at 4/- (20p). The lunch consisted of soup, meat, sweet, biscuits and cheese with coffee at 6d extra. Indeed it had been necessary to call an EGM in December 1950 in order to raise the annual subscriptions by one guinea to 5 guineas for the men and 4 guineas for the ladies.

Dunlop Executive I M Buchanan (Ian) was a good golfer and had been a very active Captain since 1949. He stepped down early in the year and Alec Dudgeon replaced him. Alec's first love was cricket of course. He had been Secretary and Treasurer of Haddington Cricket Club since 1919, a post which he relinquished in 1952 more or less coincident with his accepting Captaincy of Longniddry Golf Club. He remained the Golf Club Captain until mid 1954 and although he may have given up office in the Cricket Club, the elegant firm signature at the bottom of the Board minutes suggests a man very much in his prime.

Later in 1951, Sandy Williamson got another Scotland cap and J K Henderson was selected to represent the Lothians.

1952. The Clubhouse. Attention turned to the clubhouse in 1952 with electric boilers replacing the old coal one. Member George Taylor's quotation for installation of additional lockers was accepted and the kitchen was painted. The prices of 3/6 for high tea and 1/9 for plain tea were approved. Wartime privations still existed: the Clubmaster proved to be completely opposed to serving 'a la carte' lunches and also advised that with the then degree of rationing (April) it was impossible to increase helpings of butter. Perhaps this 'a la carte' demand was the last straw for the Clubmaster because Mr Shearlaw resigned as from the end of September. His departure was most amicable, it should be said, and accepted with regret. He and his wife Ethel had served members faithfully for 23 years. A testimonial fund was set up which resulted in a presentation of £150 and a party which Mrs Shackleton (Ethel's mother) also attended. Both Shearlaws were awarded Life Honorary membership of the Club in the following year.

Course Record. The Evening Dispatch of Saturday June 21st 1952 reported "R. M. Lees of Liberton broke the course record for Longniddry by three strokes with a round of 65 including a brilliant inward half of 30 in the Lothians Team Tournament today ... Lees' total was of course far ahead of the next best ...

Lees who is unofficial record holder of his home course with 64 produced a fantastic inward half 3, 3, 4, 3, 3, 3, 3, 4, 4, largely through brilliant chipping and putting. For his inward half Lees holed two pitches, had five single putts, and had two double putts in nine holes. Going out Lees had been much more orthodox, but he had missed the green at the second hole,

Prize Money. Distance in time diminishes the significance of some changes made. For example the 50% increase in the money prize to 3 guineas for the Club Champion seems insignificant now. It was a considerable step in 1950.

Scottish Professional Championship. *Another big event at Longniddry in 1950 was the Scottish Professional Championship. John Panton had won the title in 1948 at Luffness and he had held it since. In the event he retained the trophy at Longniddry with a total of 276. He was to win it seven times in all.*

For the first time, the arrival of golf trolleys on the scene at Longniddry was registered with the request for 'stabling' arrangements at the 1951 AGM.

pitched on and got down in a single putt, and then at the short 4th he got his tee shot under the trees and pitched on and needed four to get down. He had a birdie at the short 6th however holing a six yard putt, but took three putts at the 7th missing a yarder. At the next hole however he holed a five yard putt for a birdie to be out in 35 having taken 16 putts on the outward journey.

The home Club Longniddry had three very steady rounds and might have beaten the Gullane total (221) but their third player L. Drennan pulled his tee shot out of bounds at the 17th, and the hole cost him a six. The other two Longniddry players J. K. Henderson Club Champion and Peter Barr were round in 73.

Gullane:	G. W. Mackie	79	*Longniddry:*	J. K. Henderson	73
	W. C. D. Hare	69		P. Barr	73
	G. Robertson Durham	73		L. Drennan	75"

Twenty years later Mr Lees' wife Louise was to become Longniddry Lady Club Champion and since 1979 their daughter Patricia has been Champion eight times. An earlier mother/daughter Club Champion combination at Longniddry had been Ethel Rose and her daughter Kath.

Tom Sawers. Sadly in May 1952 the death took place of Vice-President Bailie Tom Sawers who had Captained the Club through the war years.

By the end of September 1952, Mr Maurice F Yorke Honorary Member was elected Vice-President to replace Bailie Sawers. Mr Yorke lived at 'Greencraig'. He must have been something of a botanist and/or a collector of rare books. Perhaps both, for in 1947 he had sold 'a remarkable collection of books on flowers. These were the three celebrated works of P J Redoute, whose 'Les Roses' had fetched up to £600 and his 'Choix Des Plus Belles Fleurs' £880, in recent sales', according to the Haddingtonshire Courier.

In the Clubhouse Major and Mrs Gill had been appointed to take over from the Shearlaws, having apparently undertaken to provide cold meals on Thursdays, the hitherto meal-less day. The 'a la carte' situation is not recorded.

1952 ended with a party to celebrate the Longniddry Team which had won the Lothians Club Tournament.

1953. 1953 is remembered by all long-standing Longniddry residents as the year when the fast mail train crashed at Longniddry. The fireman was killed and the derailed locomotive rolled down the roadside embankment near the newsagent's. This was in December however. A few noteworthy events had taken place affecting the Golf Club throughout the preceding months.

Firstly Isaac Rosenbloom had passed away. He had owned the Craighouse

Cabinet works and had presented the magnificent Coronation Cup to the Club. His daughter is remembered as a particularly fine golfer. August 1953 had seen another important success for Nancy Jupp when she won the Women's Amateur Championship of Norway. She had beaten Mrs Annie Berg 12 and 10 in the final match.

Meanwhile back home at the Club it had been decided following the burglary to replace the professional's wooden shop with a more substantial structure. The work was generously carried out at cost price by Club member Mr H Cruden. The possibility of installing showers in the men's locker room began to be considered.

The Club Dance had become a regular feature. It seems to have had enthusiastic support: 120 tickets were sold for it that year. This is more than can be said for the prize-giving which took place at the end of the October AGM. There is a dry note to the minute: *'Mrs Dudgeon then presented the trophies to such of the winners as condescended to put in an appearance.'*

Mr R Himsworth, the long-serving starter was made a Life Honorary Member 'to acclamation'.

1954. Midway through 1954 things seemed to be proceeding normally at the Golf Club; the Shearlaws and Tom Hogg the Head Greenkeeper had just been made Honorary Life Members and the question of getting the Home Club going again had been raised. Young Jimmy Hume had entered for the British Boys Championship at Hoylake and would get as far as the fourth round.

But things were about to change quite profoundly. The Club had written to the Estate asking that sheep should be removed from the course. The Estate was also asked to consider the installation of shower baths. For some time though the Earl of Wemyss and his Factor James Rogers had been concerned that the Golf Club regularly made a loss which the Estate had to fund. Lord Wemyss decided to try to put an end to this situation which arose from the generous terms granted to the Club in 1942. The deficiency borne by the Estate was to reach £4,111. 14s. 4d by the end of February 1955. Accordingly at the AGM in October 1954 Captain Alec Dudgeon, as one of his last duties, before handing over to 'Gus' McVey announced that the Wemyss Landed Estates had asked the Club to take over the course and clubhouse on a lease, and to assume full financial responsibility. At the same time, the Captain advised that the sheep would be removed from the course by 1st April 1955.

1955. A Committee was formed to negotiate with the Estate on the rental proposed. It consisted of Gus McVey (Captain) Alex Dudgeon and Roy Cutter, Secretary. Negotiations continued through 1955. By mid August a starting rental of £407. 10s. excluding private dwellings had been agreed

15th Green

At midsummer in the records of 1953, attention turns to the 15th green once more. This green seems to have given frequent dissatisfaction since the course reconstruction. Eventually Mr Mackenzie Ross was called back to advise alterations to the 15th green. What these were is not recorded. Perhaps the intention that the 15th green should duplicate that of the Road Hole at the Old Course was proving too difficult to achieve.

Children in the Clubhouse – Take 3. The matter of children in the clubhouse had become a vexed question. A proposal to implement the appropriate Bye Law fully (it seems that it had become relaxed somewhat) was countered by an amendment to rescind the Bye Law completely. The final outcome is not entirely clear - understandably perhaps.

upon. The question of staff accommodation in the clubhouse seems to have been a problem, because the maids still 'lived in'. It was decided therefore to approach the Estate to see if the Club could acquire a lease of Links Cottage. This was successful and the records show the Clubmaster and his family in occupation of the cottage by November 1955.

1956. The minute book maintained so meticulously by Roy Cutter for 20 years ends with the acceptance of the new constitution of the Club by the members on 14th January 1956, just two weeks before Mr Cutter's retirement from the office of Club Secretary. The duration of the lease agreed with the Estate was 21 years. The record of the Board Minutes stops at this point for several years unfortunately. Some information from other sources has been obtained, for example:

The records from the Estate Office show that the first meeting of the Directors of the new company was held on 29th January 1956. The Earl of Wemyss also reports that by chance the notion of the East Lothian County Council laying a sewer across the golf course (to serve Tranent and part of Longniddry, it is thought) came early in 1956. The Golf Club agreed that the Council of the Club would accept responsibility for the operation and deal with all claims for damages. The sewer was duly laid across the 18th and 14th fairways. As a result of the compensation afforded by the County Council, the Golf Club made a profit for the first time for many years – a sum of £73. 18s. 9d.

The new Club Secretary Mr Lawrence, wrote to the Earl of Wemyss reporting the outcome and concluding *"Your own generous attitude in allowing the Club to settle directly the matter of the course restoration compensation is fully recognised and most keenly appreciated."* With this fortuitous starting profit the Club was launched as a Limited Company responsible for its own operations and leasing the golf course and Clubhouse from the Wemyss and March Estates.

The first external competition to be held at Longniddry under the new Constitution is revealed by the 'Golfers' Handbook' to be the Edinburgh and East of Scotland Golfers' Alliance Championship. Hugh B Watt, Jack White's old assistant, and at that time Professional at Gullane, won the event with a two round total of 145.

1957/1958. Two years later the same Championship again at Longniddry was won by J S Anderson of Bruntsfield with a 138 total. He must have found the course to his liking because later in the year also at Longniddry he won the East of Scotland Professional Championship. His score was the same: 138.

1959/1960. Martini Professional Tournament. The Haddington Courier reports on 7th August 1959: *"The final round of the two day Martini*

The Lothians Amateur Tournament was held at Longniddry during 1955. The final is recorded in the *"Golfers Handbook"* as having been won by A M M Bucher who beat the club's own S B Williamson 3 and 1.

The Evening Times Foursomes also held at Longniddry in 1995 went off satisfactorily with Haggs Castle beating Ranfurly Castle in the final.

Professional Foursomes Tournament was played in brilliant sunshine over the Longniddry Course on Wednesday. The winners were the Irish pair H. Bradshaw (Portmarnock) and J. Henderson (Warrenpoint) with a two-round total of 134."

And again on May 27th 1960 the same paper reported Dr Joan Campbell's hole in one at the 6th. The other recorded Longniddry event in 1960 was the Scottish Assistants Championship. It was won by R T Walker of Downfield with a 2-round score of 141.

1961. In August 1961 the Carling Caledonian Golf Tournament was held at Longniddry. To Mr Bob Jackson of the Wednesday Club we are indebted for the survival in excellent condition of a copy of the programme and of the draw on the third day, 4th August 1961. First prize for the Tournament was £1,000 and the awards went down to £20 for the 30th place. The introductory note on the programme begins:

"The first Carling Golf Tournament in Great Britain was held in 1960 at Pannal Golf Club, Harrogate. It was officially called the Hammond's Carling Jubilee Golf Tournament after three different beers produced by the sponsors UNITED BREWERS LIMITED."

The programme also advises that the United Caledonian (formerly Caledonian Breweries Limited) was the management company in Scotland for United Breweries and in 1961 it had been in existence for just over a year. The two products which could be found in all houses belonging to the group in Scotland were Carling Lager Beer and Fowler's Wee Heavy. In addition each brewery of the group continued to brew its own beers and market them locally. They were: Aitchison Jeffrey, Edinburgh (previously Peebles), James Aitken & Company, Falkirk, James Calder & Company, Alloa, John Fowler & Company, Prestonpans, George Younger & Son, Alloa, William Murray & Company, Craigmillar, J. G. Thomson & Company, Leith

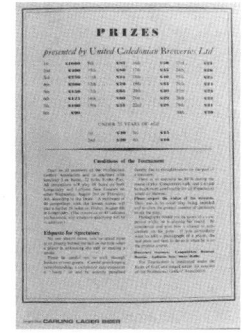

It was in this Carling Tournament that Tom Haliburton and Bernard Hunt broke R. M. Lees' course record 65 by one stroke. Christie O'Connor of Royal Dublin won with a total of 269.

1962. After a brief gap of three years the Edinburgh and East of Scotland Golfers Alliance Championship returned to Longniddry. J S Anderson had not forgotten the course for he won once again. This time his score was higher: 143.

Interregnum As stated, no minutes of the Club can be traced from Roy Cutter's retirement in January 1956 until the board Meeting of Sunday 14th June 1964. Many changes had taken place during this eight-year interval. Bill Morris had died, and Bob Himsworth was in well-earned retirement.

Tommy Hogg, though still working, had relinquished the Head Greenkeeper job. In the office, Roy Cutter's immediate replacement, Lawrie Lawrence, had been long gone and Lawrie's successor Wally Burt had just resigned. George Mocawisc reigned in the Clubhouse now having taken over from the Robbs who had succeeded the Gills. The office of Vice-President to which Mr Yorke had been elected in 1952 was vacant.

Captains. The Captain, when the curtains open again in 1964, is John Adair. There had been three Captains since Gus McVey; Russel Patrick, Peter Barr and Archie McLellan.

Directors. The Board consisted of Tom Porteous (Vice Captain), J Sykes, W McNeill, J D Munro. Peter Barr and Doctor Rose Donaldson.

The Village. The other change was in Longniddry itself. The Earl of Wemyss had feued substantial areas of land for new housing, transforming the size and character of the village. The consequence for the Club was quite profound. Pre-war its local membership had been quite small. Many Edinburgh-dominated subscribers had used it as a second course for weekend play.

1964. When we open Norman Osborne's minutes we find the Board on Sunday evening the 14th June 1964 discussing the vacant Secretaryship. The meeting went on to appoint Mr Osborne as acting Secretary and within a month he had been confirmed in the position. The other chief matter decided upon was the reduction of the age limit for senior competitions from 55 to 50.

In July 1964, Duncan Herd's name turns up in the record for the first time. Apparently Duncan had felt that it would be wrong to water the tees. He also advised against making aprons of any significant size in front of the greens. In the end though, he bent to Tom Porteous' persuasion by saying that 'he was aware of the desirability of having aprons and would do what he could'. Duncan's problem was that the water supply was limited. That water which was available was needed for the greens themselves.

It was at this July meeting that the format of the Club Championship knock-out stages was established with the first round on Tuesday, the second on Wednesday, the semi-final on Friday and the Final on Sunday. In the mixed Foursomes Competitions, it was agreed that the men would drive off the first tee and the ladies would drive off the LGU tees at the even holes.

At the AGM which followed later in the month, George Mitchell was formally elected to the vacant office of Vice-President and Tom Porteous stepped up to Captaincy of the Club. Norman Osborne was elected Vice Captain. Three Life Honorary Members were elected, Mr A H Lawrence, Mr W H McNeill and Mrs J. J. Latta. The new Directors appointed were

Mr A D Sproull and Dr I A Forbes. Fruit machines were demanded from the floor.

At the subsequent Board meeting it was clear that the new Captain was ready to put plans into force which he had long contemplated. Firstly, a caddie shed was to be established beside the professional's shop. This would clear the bottom end of the clubhouse building so that the way would be open for a new bar and locker rooms - perhaps funded by the profits from the projected fruit machines. With Mr Osborne's appointment as Secretary the Vice Captaincy fell vacant again and J Sykes was appointed by the Board.

Later in the year it was decided to replace the men's Foursomes competition with a spoon event. A new competition called the Men's Invitation Foursomes was to be started in which members entering must each bring one visitor. In September the Board finalised the Junior Membership Rules and the Club Bye Laws were revised. It was at this meeting in September 1964 that the 100-mile rule for country membership was established.

It is apparent from the frequency of meetings (9 in 7 months) and the detail of the minutes at this time, that the old relaxed days had gone. There is an air of all-embracing activity now in the records of the Board. 1964 ends with preparation for the Pringle Tournament being put in hand, and considerable improvements in the clubhouse introduced. The New Bye Laws were finalised and preferred lies put into effect over the winter from 19th October.

1965. The year began with the departure of Club Steward George Mocawisc. By mid February John Kennedy had been appointed. He had been working at Darling's Hotel in Edinburgh where the downstairs steak bar had been gaining popularity. At that time his family was wife Jean and son Ian. Kate and Bruce had yet to appear.

Other developments were the decision to arrange toilet facilities at the 11th and the intention to name the holes individually. Unfortunately, the Earl of Wemyss did not find the 11th tee toilet proposals acceptable. Meantime it was decided to investigate excavating under the clubhouse for locker room space.

Before he relinquished the Captaincy, John Adair had begun the establishment of a staff pension scheme. This was finally implemented in May 1965.

For the first time in the Board minutes, a long-standing concession to Loretto boys is mentioned. The Board had realised that the rights which had been given to the boys from Loretto exceeded those of the Club's own junior members and felt obliged to rescind the concession, by means of a letter to

The condition of the clubhouse was beginning to cause concern. Nothing had been done to improve the clubhouse for some time and the outside paintwork was deteriorating, an unfortunate situation in which to host the "Golf Illustrated" Junior Vase Tournament which was imminent. The winner was A M Fleming of Glasgow University with a score of 138.

the Headmaster. At the same time a similar privilege which had been afforded to Edinburgh University was withdrawn.

By summer 1965 the Directors were congratulating themselves on the much improved catering service in the clubhouse. This justified the considerable outlay which had been made in new kitchen equipment.

The Scottish Assistants Championship and the Lothians Champion of Champions contest were held at Longniddry during the summer. The first was won by David Huish with a two-round score of 139, and the second by J G McGregor of Murrayfield.

A salutary tale from David Huish:

On the morning round of the Assistants Championship at Longniddry he stood on the 14th tee at level 4's. He finished with five straight 3's for a 67. He was still going well in the afternoon. On the 13th tee he stood at 6 under 4's for the round and 11 under for the Championship. He struck a magnificent tee shot just 4 feet above the pin. And then hubris. If I hole this for a 2, he thought, and finish with five 3's like this morning, it'll be a 59. Well of course, he 3-putted the 13th and went 6, 6, 4, 6 to be level 4's for the round on the 18th tee. He was immensely relieved to get his 4 at the last to win.

Winter League. On 1st August 1965 it was agreed to support the idea of a Winter League which had been put forward by the Tantallon Club. Subsequent notes in the minutes make it clear that Gus McVey was a prime mover in the establishment and running of the league in those early days.

Gordon Durward. In September the Directors unanimously agreed to an increase in salary for Gordon Durward in recognition of the long hours which he and his wife spent on starter and professional duties.

The Clubhouse and Car Park. The Directors' determination to improve the clubhouse was undiminished 12 months after it had first been expressed. The first reactions of Architect Mr Hall were reported. He had been cautious about the Captain's wish to excavate under the clubhouse. Captain Tom Porteous still felt that this would be the best thing to do if it were practicable. A sign of the times was the problem of nicotine staining of the lounge walls. The idea of a car park below the putting green was registered, together with the proposal to have a car park attendant on a Sunday.

On the Course. Arrangements were made for T Hart the builder to tip material behind the 15th tee with a view to lengthening the hole. Tree planting was to be carried out and the practice, which was to continue for the next thirty years, of having a high pole placed beside the tee of the day at the 4th and 6th holes was established.

County Cup
In 1965 Longniddry won the County Cup for the first time in eighteen years. The Longniddry team had been beaten in 4 consecutive finals in the fifties. The successful 1965 team was: A. Harvey, L. Reilly, A. Barr, P. Burt

112

Bank Holiday Bookings. It was agreed at the December meeting of the Board, after long discussion, that visitors' bookings would be accepted on the May and August Bank holidays. However the ruling was to stand whereby no club be allowed on statutory holidays.

1966. The year started with concern about the fixing of the SSS. The Longniddry practice apparently had been to decide the SSS at midday on the day of the medal. This was contrary to the recommendation of the R & A that the SSS should be decided at the end of the day's play. The Captain reported that Mr J McGregor of the Lothians when consulted had supported the Longniddry practice. The proposal that it should continue however met opposition in the Board meeting and a decision was deferred.

At the same meeting an offer from Henry Cotton to provide on-the-course lessons to members at a cost of £100 plus expenses was turned down.

In the Scottish Ladies Foursomes Tournament at Longniddry Gullane beat Elie and Earlsferry in the final.

In February the Board accepted Mr Hall's proposals for the alterations to the clubhouse and they were submitted to the Estate for comment. The idea of excavating under the clubhouse seems to had been dropped.

In March the outcome of the Winter League was reported; Alex Harvey of Longniddry had been the winner of the individual competition and T G Gass had finished third. The result of the Dunbar versus a select match had been a draw. Longniddry had been represented by A Harvey and P Barr. This was a Muirfield Open Championship year and the courtesy of Longniddry was to be offered, during the competition to Muirfield, Gullane and New Luffness members.

The proposal to alter the clubhouse was put to the 1966 AGM held in July. Joe Sykes had now taken over from Tom Porteous as Captain. The proposal to proceed was carried by 57 votes to 32. It appeared that out of a total cost of £20,000, £9,000 was available within the club's resources while the remainder would need to be raised elsewhere.

At the following Board meeting it is seen that the clubhouse alterations are well in hand. Tom Porteous had stayed on the Board as House Convener (possibly to see the changes through) and it was decided at the August meeting that the new refreshment bars were to be installed at once.

The September minutes record the installation of a drinking fountain though whether at the 10th or 14th tees is not clear. The existence at that time of a seat at the 7th tee is also revealed, together with the fact that some adjustment had been made to the line of the 17th hole. A mysterious note saying that the position regarding a golf ball machine was to be discussed by the House Committee is intriguing. What was a golf ball machine? (Later it is revealed to be some sort of gambling device; legal providing the prize

For the first time, Younger's Special Beer was made available. Its immediate effect was to reduce the sales of 'Export'.

The Board agreed in March that Category I Golfers could be given full membership immediately at the discretion of the Board provided that they named Longniddry as their home club.

did not exceed 5/-) Research reveals that it was located in the back bar and that it ate sixpences. At the pull of a lever, one red and two white balls appeared which had to be manipulated adroitly in order to win a golf ball. Sadly the machine was put out of use a month or two later.

Five day Membership. 1966 concluded with two decisions: firstly to offer 5 day membership to the first 50 names on the waiting list at an annual subscription of £6.6/- and secondly, to arrange a display of Captains' photographs in the clubhouse.

1967. Some time between December 1966 and mid January 1967, a burglary took place in the clubhouse. Probably this was the occasion when entry was effected at the low level door under the terrace which gave access to a hatch behind the bar. The minutes of the 15th January 1967 express thanks to Gus McVey for the prompt manner in which the insurance claim had been settled.

The Club had won the Winter League, Mr McVey reported, and commemorative pennants would be awarded.

In the Board Minutes the intention of Tommy Hogg to retire on 5th August appears. He had been Head Greenkeeper before Duncan Herd arrived. Afterwards, he continued to work under Mr Herd. Even after a further retirement date he continued in the Club's employment on a part time basis. The state of the greens had been discussed with the Head Greenkeeper. He persuaded the Convener that watering in cold weather (i.e. when water was available) would not help in the long term.

Most generously, Mrs Douglas (Lady Captain) offered to give the Club a carpet for the lounge. Until then the clubhouse had been entirely uncarpeted.

Visitors. In order to control visitor numbers it was decided to limit individual visitors to two visits per month. The method to be adopted in implementing this is not clear, but Gordon Durward had been consulted. He must have felt confident that he would be able to identify over-frequent visitors.

Spoons and Medals. Since its inception, the club had been running 'spoon' competitions. The spoons which were awarded were attractive small silver spoons with Longniddry Golf Club engraved on them. They were prized as permanent keepsakes although it is possible that to the regularly successful competitor a proliferation of spoons could be an irritation. Possibly also there was a wish to improve the income of the Club's long-suffering professional, Gordon Durward. At any rate at the Board Meeting in May, 1967 without record of any prior discussion, it was decided that Spoons would not be awarded in the 1967 season. It is presumed that vouchers on the professional's shop were issued instead. Also recorded is the decision that Wednesday medals would be held in future although there would be no priority for members over visiting clubs.

Ladies Tuesday Mornings. At the same meeting, the decision was made to reserve the tee from 9.30 a.m. until 10.30 a.m. on Tuesdays for the Ladies Draw.

The Course. By June there was still concern about the state of the greens and aprons, although it is minuted that during the Open Tournament which had recently taken place there had been many complimentary remarks made about the condition of the course. Nevertheless it was decided that watering of the greens, tees and aprons was required. It is interesting that this time it was the Secretary who was instructed to see that this was done.

By the next month, the problem was the length of the rough. Apparently it had been agreed (but not minuted) that the length of the rough should be maintained at the same level as during the recent Open Competition. Mr Osborne must also have been charged to raise this with Mr Herd. Although the outcome of the watering demand is not recorded, Duncan's reply with regard to the rough is: he undertook to do his best but pointed out that the requirement would be extremely difficult to meet given the manpower available.

AGM. A proposal was made at the AGM in September that a concession be made to members who had reached retiring age and had been members for several years. Subsequently this was rejected by the Board on the grounds that the 5 day membership existed for this reason.

Sewer. Much of the business of the past year had been with the County Council's wish to lay another sewer through the course. The arrangements for this and consequences arising had been discussed frequently. The matter was handled for the Club by Greens Convener Bob Anderson. He had made careful stipulation as to the route of the sewer and he negotiated a significant compensation payment to the Club. His arrangements were as follows: Greenkeeping staff would remove turf and topsoil and reinstate on completion. Lines of sewers and manholes would be approved by the Club. Minimum damage was to be done to tree roots. The work was not to be done between the Spring and Autumn Meetings. The severe storm 15" overflow to the burn to be piped at least as far as the road culvert.

Longniddry Open Championship: The Durward Trophy. The Longniddry Open Championship had been running for many years. It was in existence in 1932 when Hilton's winning 69 was said to be two strokes above the record for the Course. In 1967 it was decided to present a trophy for the competition to commemorate Gordon and Gladys Durwards' outstanding

Children in the Clubhouse – Take 4. The problem of children in the Clubhouse which had rumbled on was raised once more with the need for better control the constant theme.

115

service to the Club. The first winner of the trophy proved to be worthy indeed, it was Bernard Gallacher.

1968. The first meeting of 1968 agreed upon significant increases in subscriptions: Males £17 instead of £13.13/- and the Ladies £10.10/- up from £8.8/-. Although the ladies fee did include the 10/- this does appear to be the beginning of the end of the old guinea charge. It was at this meeting too that the design of the club tie with a crest in the form of crossed golf clubs with a ball and a small letter 'L' was decided upon.

Within a month further improvements in the clubhouse were under discussion: heating for the dining room and Secretary's office, carpeting the entrance hall, a new lounge carpet (presumably gifted by Mrs Douglas), new lounge furnishings and finally a 'No Smoking' trial in the dining room.

British Summer Time was introduced or reintroduced to the country in the Spring of 1968. The Directors of Longniddry Golf Club were pleased to find that this did not affect the Artisans because they required only two starting times on Sunday mornings.

Two external competitions were held at Longniddry during the year: In the the Scottish Assistants Championship, N Wood of Turnberry carried off the first prize with a score of 139. The other competition was the Scottish Ladies County Championship when Ayrshire beat Angus in the final.

Arrangements for the men's dinner which were to be preserved through the next quarter century were finalised: men only, formal dress, and a guest speaker.

The dances were still very popular. Some concern was expressed about numbers - 'rather overcrowded' it was said. It turns out that there must have been about 200 attending the dances in the clubhouse and it was resolved to limit future numbers to 175. This still seems enormously high against dance numbers in the nineties of between 70 and 80, but of course standards, particularly to do with safety and ventilation, have changed very considerably in 25 years.

In December 1968 it was decided to purchase mats to be used at the 13th and 16th tees in winter in future.

Purchase of the Course Proposed. At its last meeting in 1968, the Board having agreed to proceed quickly with the improvement of the hot water supply, suddenly turned to the possibility of purchasing the course. It was resolved to approach the Estate with this in view since at that time the lease still had a considerable period to run.

Closure of Waiting List. In 1968, possibly for the first time in the Club's history, the waiting list was closed

1969. Notification that the Ladies' Home Internationals would be played at Longniddry in 1971 is one of the first recorded items of the year.

First Men's Dinner. Late in February the arrangements for the first men's dinner were discussed again. The response at that stage had not been very great, therefore each member would be allowed to bring two guests. Mr MacPhail was to be one of the speakers and it was hoped that Eric Brown would be the other. Duncan Herd would be invited as a guest.

On the Course. Duncan Allan was proving himself to be an active Greens Convener. In June he advised that young trees would be planted between the 7th and 10th fairways (This was where a gap had been torn in the pines by the storm in 1968.) The 8th and 10th tees were to be extended to the rear, and the 17th tee to the front. The use of pop up sprinklers was to be extended to the tees. Finally it was decided to dispense with the advice of the Bingley Sports Turf Research Institute for the next 3 years, although in the following month it was considered advisable to pay a fee of £6 per annum to maintain contact with the organisation.

SSS and Competitions. The argument about declaration of the SSS was settled by the decision that it would be declared by Gordon Durward on the morning of the competition.

Meantime the Invitation Foursomes Competition was not proving to be a success and consideration was given to replacing the event with a 'Mixed Open'.

Two external competitions were held at Longniddry: The final of the Lothians Championship was won by D F Campbell of the Royal Bank who beat J Mather 6 and 5 and the East of Scotland Professional Championship was won by A Fleck with a 143 total. Longniddry also hosted the second round of the 1969, Usher Vaux Tournament. An addition to the Club trophies was the presentation by Dr Forbes of a cup for the 'B' Championship.

Slacks Again. There is also in the October minutes evidence of a female reaction to the slacks appeal of March. By this time the terminology had changed slightly: 'A notice should be posted informing ladies that although they might enter the lounge in trousers to buy drinks to take upstairs, it was not otherwise permissible to wear trousers in the lounge'. (presumably the men were excluded from this last embargo and the change from 'undesirable' to 'not permissible' is noteworthy!! - Ed).

Metres. The introduction of the dreaded metre is recorded in October 1969. In future markers would carry the distance in metres as well as yards.

Purchase of the course. In November the Captain, Dr Ian Forbes, reported that negotiations for purchase or extended lease of the course would be taking place but the Earl of Wemyss had indicated that an early outcome was unlikely.

Heating and Slacks
By the end of March, a new boiler had been installed 'at cost' and it was decided but presumably unconnected that the ladies would be advised that the wearing of slacks in the main club rooms was undesirable. A notice to this effect was to be displayed.

Dress and Slacks once more. At the same time the Secretary was instructed to have a formal printed notice regarding the ban on ladies' trousers in the lounge and dining room (now a ban rather than 'not permissible'). Perhaps in compensation, it was decided at this meeting to grant the ladies the use of the Board Room for their meetings. It was also agreed that there be no relaxation regarding collars and ties for men. However at dances ladies should be allowed to wear trouser suits. More notices were to be posted to this effect.

John Segrott. At the last Board meeting of the year, the Earl's new factor, John Segrott attended for the first time. He was to prove a valuable source of wise counsel in the future.

1970. The records at the beginning of the year contemplate a redesign of the ladies quarters. Sketches were in preparation. The entrance to the men's quarters was also being considered and architects' proposals were to be obtained.

John Segrott

It appears from 1970 records that two alterations in Directors' Committee arrangements have become consolidated. Firstly, meetings are less frequent, perhaps 6 in the year whereas from '64 until '69 they were held at least once a month. The other change is that after April 1969 the day of the meeting moved from a Sunday to a weekday evening.

Children in Clubhouse – Take 5. The problem of young children in the lounge reappeared in April 1970 and the decision that no child under 7 years of age should be permitted, was made.

Throughout the Spring preparations were made for the Pringle Seniors and the Ladies Home Internationals. It was decided that the ladies would have the whole Club available for their use on that occasion and that the ladies quarters would be used by the men.

Waiting list. The waiting list was reopened in March 1970, two years after it had been closed.

Slacks Capitulation.

In September the slacks battlefield was abandoned by the Board. The minute says : ' it was decided to revoke the prohibition of slacks in the lounge'. An attempt to save face was made by adding 'for a period of 6 months'. Well we shall see!

George Ferguson's Tree. George Ferguson presented a tree to the Club at this time. It was planted between the 5th and 11th fairways.

Lease. Meantime discussions on the renewal of the lease in 1971 continued. The report of the meeting suggests that the possibility of buying the course outright had now dropped out of sight.

1970 Pringle Senior Professional Golf Championship. The Pringle Senior Professional Golf Championship was held from June 23rd until 25th 1970 at Longniddry. The published programme contained the following article from that popular sports writer, Norman Mair.

"LONGNIDDRY - The Perfect Venue. *by Norman Mair*

Ideal! was the defending champion's verdict on the choice of Longniddry for the 1970 Pringle of Scotland Senior Professional Championship. Nor was John Panton thinking of the fact that when the Scottish Professional

Championship returned to Longniddry in 1950 he had won the title for the third year in succession or even of his achievement of runner-up to Christie O'Connor in the lucrative Carling Caledonian Trophy on the self same East Lothian Links in 1961. Rather he was struck by the eminent suitability for senior golfers and their wives of a course within thirteen miles of Edinburgh whose questions are of exactly the right moderate severity.

Not of course that anyone in his right senses would underrate the calibre of those seniors still in Class A (50-54 years inclusive) or even Class B (55-59 years inclusive) since, after all, these two classes have, between them, provided the beaten finalist in each of the last three match play championships; namely the aforesaid John Panton and the ageless Dai Rees. Again, apart from the enduring example of Sam Snead on the other side of the Atlantic, it is a salutary thought that both Jack Cannon, the Scottish Amateur Champion, and Bill Hyndman, the American Walker Cup Player who lost to Michael Bonallack at Hoylake in the final of the 1969 Amateur would, were they mercenaries, qualify as seniors since 50 is held to represent the golfer's change of life in professional golf as opposed to 55 in amateur.

However, the field in the Pringle of Scotland senior championship stretches from Class A to Class F - the latter for youngsters of 75 years of age and over. Which is why a course such as Longniddry, which is largely flat where the fairways are relatively wide and the rough not especially punitive makes the perfect venue - since bunkers and an unusual number of trees for a seaside course are much less fatiguing hazards.

The professional record of 64 stands in the name of Tommy Haliburton and Bernard Hunt but since the course has been altered since the Carling Caledonian nine years ago, a new professional record is guaranteed this week. Longniddry now measures 6,301 yards with a par of 69.

The Professional at Longniddry is Gordon Durward who as a professional played for Scotland against Ireland in 1934 and against England in 1937 and who, for seventeen years was President of the Scottish PGA. Since the theme this week is of golfing longevity, it is worth observing in passing that one of the most faithful of Durward's pupils over the years has been the inimitable Mrs Charlotte Beddows who - for all her four Scottish titles - still turned up for her regular lessons when comfortably past her 80th birthday.

Among the Club's membership are such celebrities as Dick Smith who won the Scottish Amateur Championship in 1958 and Lawrie Reilly who, apart from his laudable habit in his heyday of popping an even larger ball than the 1.68 into the English net, is a neat technician on the golf course. Longniddry's most famous daughter must surely be Miss Nancy Jupp who at the tender age of 13 won the British Girls Championship at Stoke Poges in 1934 and who, after a career which embraced both golfing journalism and a global TV golf series emerged as Manager of the American Open.

Many a time and oft in the past decade such as John Panton, Dai Rees and Max Faulkner must have tempted the younger golfers of these islands to echo the historic exclamation of Harry Haddock, the Clyde and Scotland left back, as he ruefully congratulated Stanley Matthews at the end of yet another triumphant international for the English maestro: "Why don't you pick on someone your own age?"

This week on this charming Longniddry course - where every hole is within sight of the sea but the turf lush, almost inland - they will be doing just that to set all of us like Sir Bedivere, 'revolving many memories.'"

There was also an article in the programme by Gordon Durward:

"WE'LL TAKE THE SENIORS' ... says Gordon Durward, Professional at Longniddry Golf Club

Some 36 years ago, when I was a young professional stripling of 27, I had the good fortune - some said skill - to reach the final of the Scottish Match Play Championship. In the 36 holes battle I came up against the late Mark Seymour who many will remember was a half-brother of the great Abe Mitchell. I was beaten on the last green. Mark got £30 for his victory, and I was quite happy to take home the loser's cheque for £20 which after all in 1934 more than covered my expenses.

Our younger members of the Professional Golfers Association are this season playing for or being invited to play for the monumental sum of over £300,000. To say that the mind boggles is an understatement. And to say that one is tempted into wishing we were young pros. again is not to envy the British touring player at all. It is just a sobering thought that the biggest single sum I ever won in competition was a cheque for just under £200 in a Scottish Professional Championship soon after the war, though I recognised that most of my tournament playing was confined to Scotland.

On reflection I am not certain that I envy today's touring pros. at all. They are playing a different game from the one we knew in our heyday. Though the opportunities may be greater, the pressures are equally greater, and so must be the paths to ulcers and nervous exhaustion! You can leave us with our Pringle Seniors Championship. We love it and we are eternally grateful to Pringle of Scotland for not only continuing the sponsorship of a wonderful series of events, but also for staging it here in their own native Scotland for at least three years.

We are proud of our new Pringle Seniors tie and the Champion is prouder still to wear his light blue Pringle Seniors blazer.

The seniors you see is a great occasion. It is strictly for those who have turned 50. Take a look through the starting sheets and you can pick out a complete past Ryder Cup side - men who pioneered that same £300,000

The 4th green is one of the best protected with 7 bunkers cunningly placed, some on the approach and some on the perimeter.

From above the two-tiered 5th green looking down the fairway to the angle of the dog-leg.

pop-up sprinklers would be installed at the 1st, 2nd, 5th, and 11th tees.

British Seniors' Championship 1972. In June 1972 the British Seniors' Championship was played at Longniddry once again. It was won by ex-Royal Marine Ken Bousfield. Tom Scott writing in the 'Golf Illustrated' reports:

Ken Bousfield watches Sam Snead with his sideways anti-yip putting system on the 10th green.

"Ken Bousfield has played in this Championship three times, finishing third, second, and now first. That he is a worthy champion there is no doubt because in the run home he gained on and eventually passed Nagle and then went on to beat the cheerful Italian Alfonse Angelini at the first extra hole of the play-off.

Nagle was one up on Angelini and three up on Bousfield with three holes to play but he bunkered his tee shot at the short sixteenth, and after a fine bunker shot his usually reliable putter let him down from five feet. Bousfield birdied the hole to gain two strokes. Worse was to follow for Nagle: he missed from three feet at the seventeenth and after missing the green in two at the last he lost his title by chipping sadly short with a nine iron and taking three more to get down.

Bousfield therefore picked up four strokes on the last three holes to lead by one from Nagle and to tie with Angelini who was already in the Clubhouse and preparing to go home to Italy after three-putting the eighteenth, the last two putts coming from fifteen inches. So Angelini had to put his golf gear on again in order to contest the play-off with Bousfield.. But he was not kept at the Club much longer, because with a superb second with a three wood to the heart of the green at the first extra hole Bousfield guaranteed his four and when Angelini failed from nine feet after missing the green with a two iron it was all over......"

World Seniors' Title. The World Seniors' Title was at stake next day when Bousfield faced Sam Snead. This was the Tom Scott report:

Above: Sam Snead at the age of 60 attributed his still formidable golf to his suppleness. To demonstrate this he kicked his height for members in the lounge.

Above right: World Seniors Champion Sam Snead gives his winner's address from Longniddry's clubhouse terrace.

"If indeed Sam Snead was making his last tournament appearance in Britain at Longniddry in the Worlds' Seniors Championship he gave the large Scots crowd something to remember him by. His outward half of the afternoon round – he took only 32 strokes – was as fine an exhibition as the Old Master has ever given his British admirers. It also put paid to Ken Bousfield's ambition to take the title, for during Snead's devastating onslaught Bousfield lost five holes in a row and found himself three down. Of course nobody can win all that number of holes on the trot without the other man making his mistakes and Bousfield did make mistakes on the putting greens, the same putting greens on which in the morning he had holed everything in sight to burst into a two-hole lead, a lead which he increased to four at the fifteenth.

Snead's outward half in the afternoon gave him the title for the fourth time, but really the two crucial holes had come in the morning. These were the seventeenth and eighteenth which Bousfield lost and which made him only two up at lunch instead of being four up. The two holes were against the strong wind and one could not help wondering if this severe buffeting Ken Bousfield had taken throughout the week was to take its toll. One wonders too if his putting inspiration which had stood him in such good stead to counter moderate driving had started to go.

These fears alas were to prove well-founded, and the amazing Snead 60 years old, piled on the pressure and Bousfield could not find the answer until it was too late and thus Snead eventually took the title 3 and 2.

Snead is one of the most experienced players in the game and he quickly sensed that Bousfield was flagging, so he pulled out more and more as his opponent struggled. It is this sort of tactical play as well as power golf that has made him a legendary figure in the game. Modest man that he was Bousfield made no excuses. Although we had lunch together, I felt that he was anxious to get out on the course again as soon as possible. The long break might well have had something to do with his loss of concentration. Snead paid a tribute to his partner afterwards and went on to say "I have played against many British professionals in my time and have always found them to be gentlemen. This is a good deal more than I can say about some of my countrymen I have played against."

Only the fact that Snead failed to win the US Open Championship prevents him from being awarded the accolade as the greatest professional golfer of his generation."

Two other external events were held at Longniddry during the year: the Ladies Home Internationals and the Lothians Matchplay Championship. The Ladies Home International was won by England. A full report is given in the Ladies Section. The Lothians Matchplay Championship was won by R Bucher.

Ladies Accommodation or One of Our Conveners Failed to Return. A November Board minute has all the marks of one of history's great fighting retreats like Napoleon from Moscow or Ally McLeod from the Argentine:

The ladies had studied the proposal for their accommodation. Their reaction was somewhat adverse. It was too expensive; it would give them less locker room space than before; and there was a fire hazard. One of the Clubmaster's family was required to sleep in a room at the end of the Board room with no fire exit.

Well it had seemed a good idea at the time. Clearly the days of the smaller foot baths had gone. The Board's response was in the Dunkirk spirit: The whole Board room area would be included in the general plan giving the ladies more space and the steward more sleeping accommodation. The Board meetings would be held in the ladies lounge. Pax!

Car Park. One suspects that it was with relief that the Board turned to the car park and arranged for its resurfacing

1973. Men's Access. Is there just a faint trace of pique in the 1973 decision that the door exiting on to the terrace from the corridor should be for the use of males only? No females would be allowed beyond the mixed lounge except in special circumstances!

Improvements and Changes. The names of the holes on the course, proposed by Peter Barr were accepted and trees were planted on the north side of the 9th, 10th and 15th holes. Remeasurement of the course was carried out and the SGU confirmed that the SSS would remain at 70. The

Presentations.

Mr D H Teesdale presented a trophy in memory of his father, Jimmy Teesdale. Retiring employee R Burnside received a wallet of notes - £1 for every year of his 72 years service with the Club.

Winter League Team

Back row: J Gunn, A Harvey, W Bell, FA Hall, W Weston, T Porteous, TA Gass,

ladies 12th tee was to be moved away from the road. In the clubhouse the kitchen and dining room were renovated, and the alterations to the men's back bar completed. Stuart Laird took over Chairmanship of the Alterations Committee from Tom Porteous. The complications of Value Added Tax were encountered for the first time in November 1973.

Senior Open Amateur Championship. For the first time this Championship was held at Longniddry. It was won by J T Jones with a two round score of 142.

1974. The plan for the course toilets was accepted by Lord Wemyss with the Club bearing the full costs whilst the Estate took responsibility for the condition of the boundary fence. The ladies changed their minds about the 12th tee. Their 18th tee was moved back 5 yards to maintain the par 5. Duncan Herd advised against fertilising the fairways. Tree planting continued with 800 saplings being placed along the 12th, 14th and 15th holes.

Second row: JW Montgomery, JA McVey, WM Reekie, M Black, IB Jackson

Front row: TF Dickson, M Scoular, R Cunningham

Winter League. For the fourth year in succession, Longniddry won the Winter League. Longniddry also defeated Royal Musselburgh in the final of the County Championship.

New Lease. In December 1974 the terms of the new lease were finalised: The rent would be £3,250 per annum to be reviewed every 5 years. The

128

original furnishings were to be purchased for the sum of £500 to be paid over 5 years. The lease would be for a duration of 20 years and would include the clubhouse and all properties under the existing lease. The clubhouse was valued at that time at £120,000 and Links Cottage at £12,000. The rented dwellings were No. 4 John Knox Road, Fairway, and Links Cottage.

1975. With the lease problems resolved minds turned to other matters :

Dress. It was decided that the rules regarding men's dress in the lounge and dining room would be dropped for the period of the Seniors' Tournament but members were to be asked to maintain their normal high standards. Concern had been expressed about the declining numbers turning up to the annual dance in evening dress: it was decided to insist upon evening dress at this function.

The Granger Cup.

The minutes of the Board meeting in May 1975 record with justified pride that the Longniddry Ladies team of Mrs Jack, Mrs Lawrie and Miss MacNamara had won the Granger Cup at the Scottish Ladies Championship. A celebration took place in the mixed lounge later that month.

Gavel. A gavel and mallet was presented to the Club by Captain 'Jocky' Forbes.

Club Badge. An insignia for a Club badge was to be designed after consultation with the Earl of Wemyss' representatives. Badges of Office would be purchased.

A happy seventies group, Cristine Paxton, Dan Abbot, Gladys Durward, Reg Paxton, Celene Forbes, Gordon Durward, 'Jocky' Forbes, Chris Abbot, John Gunn, Dorothy Gunn

British Seniors' Championship. The National Seniors' Competition was held in June at Longniddry once again. The field included five past Open Champions, namely: Fred Daly, Kel Nagle, Bobby Locke, Max Faulkner and Roberto De Vicenzo.

Above right: The five Open Champions at Longniddry Fred Daly, Kel Nagle, Bobby Locke, Max Faulkner and Roberto De Vicenzo.

Peter Lowe caddied for Ken Bousfield whose playing partner was Kel Nagle. Peter says he felt privileged to be present; the golf was of the very highest class. Nagle shot 64 and 66 against Bousfield's 66 and 65. It seems likely that this was the occasion when George McIntosh was the official Police escort to the pair. The golf was amazing he recalls, and they behaved as gentlemen throughout with Ken Bousfield reprimanding some young spectators who laughed aloud when Nagle, for once, played a poor shot.

Nagle's first round 64 was a professional record for the newly lengthened course.

Starter Rules. It was agreed that 4-ball matches could be accepted on Wednesday Medal days up to 3.55 p.m. at the discretion of the starter. However no visitors would be allowed, even as guests of members, on Saturday medal days until after 5.00 p.m.

Kitchen. Renovation of the club kitchen at a cost of £5,500 was agreed upon.

Family Foursomes. It was decided to abandon the 3 club competition because support for it had seriously declined. At the instigation of Stuart Laird it was replaced by a Family Foursomes competition. In the following year a trophy called the Greenmantle Trophy (referring to their house beside the 17th fairway) was presented for this competition by Mr J D Sutherland and family.

1976. Archie Kerr. An early loss was the death of Archie Kerr who had been attendant in the men's dressing room for many years.

Central Heating. It was decided to install gas central heating in the clubhouse. The installation of a gas service pipe up the drive from Links Road would be required.

Gordon Durward OBE. One of the first items of business at the 1975 AGM was the announcement of Gordon Durward's well deserved OBE. A wine and cheese party was arranged for Gordon and Gladys to take place in November when the Earl of Wemyss would present them with an inscribed Edinburgh Crystal salad bowl.

Club Professional. Gordon Durward had decided to retire. The Board agreed to arrange a number of Invitation fixtures for both men and ladies in support of his retirement fund. It was suggested that the 18th hole be renamed 'Durward' (although later the 1st was considered more appropriate). With the willing help of George Gibson, ex managing director of the SGCA and Dai Rees, an exhibition match and golf clinic were arranged for the Sunday preceding the Seniors' Tournament, in 1977.

After Tom Milne had taken over the captaincy at the 1976 AGM, a sub-committee was formed to appoint a new professional. From 38 applications a short list of 6 was produced. W John Gray, a local man who had previously been assistant to Gordon Durward, was appointed from Chesterton Country Golf Club.

1977. Business Ladies. It was agreed that the Business Ladies should play their medal on the Saturday preceding the ladies medal. Where there was a clash with the men's programme they would play on the following Saturday.

Gordon and Gladys with all their friends.

Golf Ball Sweep.
John Gray began his golf ball sweep on men's medal days.

Retirement Dinner. A dinner in honour of Gordon and Gladys Durward was held in the clubhouse on 28th May. Gordon received a cheque for £3,100 (the final sum handed over was £5,621) and a colour TV. A pro-am tournament was planned in Gordon's honour.

Artisans. It was agreed that the Artisans' Club should be allowed use of the men's bar for an hour after their play at the weekends.

Dalmahoy Golf Club. The Board at its meeting in August 1977 considered with sympathy an appeal for accelerated membership for persons displaced from their membership of Dalmahoy Golf Club because of the changed constitution there. It was decided with regret that Longniddry could not provide assistance without adversely affecting the position of existing applicants on the waiting list.

The Secretary. John Gunn tendered his resignation as Secretary after 7 years in the job. Twenty-four applications were received for the vacancy. Of those 5 were interviewed and 3 invited to meet the Board. Captain Davies was chosen unanimously.

Retired Members. Following an appeal by George Ferguson at the AGM, the Board decided that reduced terms would be offered to members over 65 years of age who had over 15 years membership of the Club. The reduction in subscription for a full male member in December 1977 was fixed at £13, from £52. (The following year it would be £13 from £56).

1978. 1978 began with much housekeeping activity: The men's washroom was to be tiled, new carpeting was to be laid in the men's locker room and in the clubhouse passages, whilst a golf bag rack was to be installed inside the entrance hall. Cushions were to be purchased for the dining room chairs and, in the rented dwellings, central heating was to be installed by the Club.

The Winter League Team:

Back row: Willie Weston, Peter Lowe, Jim Issot, Fraser Hall

Second row: Willie Bell, Ian Jackson, Hugh McGilvray (Club Captain), Alex Harvey, Jim Johnston

Front row: Richard Blaikie, Mike Scoular

The 1977/78 Winter League Competition was once more won by Longniddry.

AGM 1978. The AGM took place in May. Mr T A Milne the retiring Captain, reported that the waiting list for membership was now 14 ladies and 95 men. He then advised the meeting of the Board's intention to proceed with a new sprinkler system for the greens and fairways concurrently with the obligatory replacement of the water supply system. The cost was to be £12,000. The plan received the full support of the meeting and it was recommended that the Board also consider extending the new system to include the tees.

Visitors. Under the chairmanship of the succeeding Captain, Hugh McGilvray, the meeting addressed the question of visitors. Members considered that too many visiting clubs were being allowed to play the course. Accordingly at the subsequent Board meeting in June it was decided that with effect from 1st January 1979, Friday would be a non-visitors day. That is to say on Fridays, no visiting societies or clubs would be accepted.

Applications for Membership. On 28th June 1978 an overhaul of the rules of application for membership was completed. In future applicants would require to be sponsored and seconded by persons who had been full members of the Club for a minimum of 5 years. A full statement of the new procedure was prepared.

Lounge Curtains. George Pearce was proving an active House Convener and he was authorised by the Board to proceed with the replacement of the curtains in the lounge at a cost of £900. He was also (it is whispered) responsible for the choice of the very dark wall paper in the fireplace recess which received a mixed reaction from members.

17th Tee and Greenkeeping Staff. Peter Lowe was Greens Convener at this time. At his instigation it was agreed that members of the greenkeeping staff should be allowed to become members of the Artisans section if they so desired irrespective of their postal address. Ken Archibald was appointed as a greenkeeper and Mr Scott indicated his wish to retire in 1979.

Paths. It was agreed on 20th September 1978 that all paths with the exception of the right of way would become an integral part of the course and that the Local Rules would be amended accordingly.

Suggestions Book Again. A Suggestions Book was to be placed in the lounge. Although the title and intention were more Director-friendly than the previous 'complaints book', its purpose was much the same. It was soon to be used with regard to the ladies 12th tee.

Ladies 12th Tee. On 20th September 1978, the lady Vice Captain Mrs Fisher, requested that the ladies' 12th tee be replaced in its original position. This was agreed upon. However at the Board meeting in November, an opposing suggestion made by Mrs Gentleman in the Suggestions Book was upheld. She had asked that the ladies 12th tee be moved in front of the men's tee.

1979. House Membership. It was decided that persons who had been on the waiting list for a period of 5 years or more would be offered House Membership.

Visitors. A comprehensive and definitive set of rules governing visitors was agreed by the Board in May 1979 as follows:

"Visiting parties of golfers will not be accepted on the following days:

Fridays, Saturdays and Sundays, or Wednesday afternoons
LGC Medal days, LLGC Medal days, Edinburgh and District Public Holidays,
Competition days i.e. Longniddry Open, Open Mixed Foursomes, Junior Open, RNLI Open, and any other competitions accepted by the Club.

The only exceptions to the above are:

Weir Pumps Ltd-	*may play on a Saturday outwith peak hours*
John Smith & Co.	*may play on the last Friday in April*
Airdrie Police	*now play on a Wednesday*

The maximum number to be accepted in visiting parties is to be 40. More than one visiting party may be accepted during one day, subject to the over-all figure not exceeding 40.

The first tee will be allotted to visiting parties as follows:

Parties of 25 or more - 9 a.m. and 2 p.m.
Parties of less than 25 - 9.30 a.m. and 2.30 p.m.
Members are requested to tee off either before or after visiting parties or use an alternative tee.

Casual visitors are not allowed to play during Saturday Medal days or PM Wednesday Medal days. Nor will they be allowed to play during ladies Medal days at times likely to interfere with play. Casual visitors will only be allowed times off tee when it does not inconvenience Club members. This applies equally to weekends or weekdays."

Practice. At the same time the board took the opportunity to declare the rules for practising:

"The practice ground must be used for all practice and under no circumstances will practice be allowed on the course itself. The only exception to this is: a single player may play a maximum of two balls if he/she wishes, but must ensure when doing so that he/she does not cause any inconvenience to other players."

1978/1979 Winter League. Once again the Longniddry team had won the Winter League Trophy.

1979 Lothians Championship. The match play stages of the Lothians Championship were played at Longniddry with Colin Christie emerging as the winner.

1980. As the Club entered the eighties some 'signs of the time' began to appear: A disco would take place, the ladies wanted handbag lockers and the reserve car park was completed

The review of the lease had been smoothly carried out with the figure agreed at £6,250 for the next five years from 2nd February 1980.

There was considerable clubhouse activity: The central heating system was upgraded by means of a control switchboard and circulatory pumps. A quotation of just under £3,000 was accepted for recarpeting the lounge. Tiling and painting was undertaken in the kitchen whilst the redecoration of the bar area was completed.

On the course a complete remeasurement was carried out by the Royal Engineers and two new bunkers were dug out at the left of the 17th fairway. The newly reintroduced system of handcutting the greens was judged a great success.

Members' Guests. Concern had been expressed about the number of times individual non-members were seen to be playing the course. Each time they seemed to be the guest of a different member. It was decided to tighten up:

Plant a Tree Scheme.
A consistent theme in
the minutes down
through the years is
the determination to
protect and renew
the woodlands of the
course. Tree planting
seems to have been
an almost perpetual
activity. In the
summer of 1980 the
Board announced its
'Plant a Tree
Scheme'. Members
could contribute to
the project by
purchasing trees for
planting or
subscribing to their
purchase.

From 1st May 1980 a member introducing a guest would be required to enter the guest's name in a book to be kept in the professional's shop. The same guest would in future be permitted to play as a member's guest only once per month irrespective of the number of members introducing him. Fine in principle as this arrangement was, it is always difficult to impose rules upon persons outside the organisation and the system placed considerable onus on the starter to be alert to transgressors.

Ladies Competitions. Possibly there had been some harassment, or perhaps only congestion, at any rate it was decided in the early summer of 1980 that in future prior to all ladies major competitions, the course would be closed 30 minutes before their first tee-off time.

Stuart Laird and his team – Duncan Herd, Gilbert Dempster, Stuart himself, John Kennedy and John Gray

AGM 1980. The AGM in 1980 seems to have gone smoothly. The R & A agronomist's advice had been carefully followed and an improvement to the tees and greens and indeed the course itself, had been noticed. Stuart Laird took over the captaincy from Hugh McGilvray and fielded questions about the terms afforded to the Army and the noise of the fruit machines.

Weekly Tickets and Advanced Bookings. At the Board Meeting following the AGM, it was decided to offer a weekly ticket for guests of members subject to the following conditions:

'The visitor should normally reside outwith 50 miles from Longniddry. The visitor must always play with the introducing member.'

This initiative does not seem to have been very successful. Perhaps the second condition was too onerous. After all, whilst the visitor might be on holiday it was quite likely that his host might not be.

However, the other change was much more enduring: A fee for advance club bookings was introduced at £1 per player. Not only did this survive, it had waxed to the extent of £10 in 1995.

Children on the Course. Perhaps the Board was comprised of more family men and women than in the past. Certainly their undernoted decision with regard to children on the golf course was wise, tolerant and quite brave: *'Members may bring a child aged under 11 to play golf after 7.30 p.m. any day free of charge provided that there is no interference with members or visitors playing the course. This arrangement would be limited to one child per member.'* - Conceivably this last stipulation was the cause of a few domestic disruptions.

Staff. On the staff side developments in the summer of 1980 included the award of membership to Duncan Herd, Head Greenkeeper and his assistant Ken Archibald, whilst Glyn Jenkins received a cheque for £50 from the Club on his departure from the post of Assistant Professional.

The Course. In September the ladies asked that the left hand bunker of the group of three strung across the fairway 160 yards in front of the 8th tee should be filled in. It is judged that the ladies (and some of the men) had suffered in silence at this hole for a long time. For those souls who cannot manage the carry over the bunkers, the gap which has to be found is still only 10 yards wide, and the ground profile is unkind. The left hand bunker was duly filled in and has remained so although the shape of the bunker is clearly to be seen and is still something of an impediment at this hole.

Catering. Rules were laid down to regulate private catering undertaken by the Clubmaster. Any applications would require to have the approval of the Secretary in the first instance. The Dining Room could be used by members outside normal opening hours as long as at least 50% of the party were Club members.

Bag Discs.
The introduction of membership bag discs at last - the possibility had been discussed over the years, was another sign perhaps that the old era had passed.

Discos. A disco arranged for November was unsuccessful. It had to be cancelled due to lack of response. A separate family disco had been run with some success. Even with this however, support was clearly tailing off and the 1980 one proved to be the last for several years.

George Mitchell, Vice-President. The minutes of November 1980 record the passing of George Mitchell, Vice-President of the Club for sixteen years. His sad departure seems to sever the connection with the very early days of the Club.

1981. Longniddry lost the Winter League to Gullane on a play-off but won the Winter League stroke play team event with the individual trophy secured by Keith Cunningham.

Fruit Machine Procedure. Prior to the meeting of the AGM the Board laid down in considerable detail the procedure which was to be followed with regard to cash involved with the one armed bandits. These rules are still in force today.

AGM 1981. Gordon Durward OBE was unanimously elected Honorary Vice-President of the Club. An appointment surely well deserved.

The admin. team from 1981-93 – Gilbert Dempster and Cristine Paxton.

Club Secretary. The Secretary Captain Davis had left the Club suddenly in the spring and on the 27th July, the Board appointed Gilbert Dempster as the new Club Secretary from the 18 candidates who applied for the job. He would take up the post in December and in the meantime John Gunn had kindly agreed to return.

Ladies 12th tee again. It transpires from the August minutes that in spite of previous indications to the contrary, the ladies 12th tee had not been moved. The ladies were still driving off with a version of a Silverstone motor race being conducted somewhere behind their right ear! This time protective posts were proposed.

Medal Round Duration. In August 1981 faced with a complaint about slow play, the Committee addressed one of the great imponderable questions of modern times. They decided that 3.5 hours was a reasonable time for a medal round - presumably for a three ball.

Professional's Day. Meantime the business ladies medal had run into trouble; John Gray with the support of the Board had decided to run his first Professional's Day on November 7th, a Saturday. This Saturday would normally have been used for the business ladies winter medal, which had to be somehow fitted into Sunday 8th November, without disturbing the Winter league match on that day. After the event which demonstrated that the Professional's Day was highly popular, it was decided that it should be held in June the following year.

Too much Bowing. It may be recalled that a visiting writer thought that it had been the 16th rather than the 15th green which had been modelled on the Road Hole at St. Andrews. A practical demonstration of how unlike the left hand bunker at the 16th is, to that of the St Andrews Road hole was given by Arthur Gimson. Arthur struck at his ball in the bunker in the accustomed manner. However, his is a very powerful right hand developed by years of sawing at his violincello. He skinned the ball out of the bunker (as he could never have done at the Road Hole) and it dislodged a roof tile on Ravelston about 100 yards away. The repair account for £7.71 was passed on to our musician member for settlement.

Mens' Games Night. Ian Watson organised and ran a very successful men's games night in December.

1982. The past year had been a dry one and the club had received a verbal warning from the District Council that if the recent rate of water usage were to continue, a restriction might have to be placed on supplies. Against this background the report received later in the year that the prospects of finding water by drilling, (George Ferguson had not been far wrong) were good, was particularly welcome.

On the social side, the programme for the year was being prepared by Rab Thorburn, House Convener. It was decided to have no more discos. Shortly afterwards 15 names in the Suggestion Book supported a proposal to relax men's dress rules in the lounge until 6.00 p.m. The Board rejected this and the ladies were requested to 'observe a change of attire after play'.

The preparations on the course for the PGA Seniors Tournament were progressing. Greens and tees were now being watered daily for 6 minutes. The reaction of the District Council is not recorded but possibly they had been consulted. Duncan Herd's opinion is not given either - perhaps the water supply had improved. But then perhaps not since a proposal to use burn water to irrigate the course was only thought better of after adverse advice by John Segrott, the factor.

PGA Seniors Tournament. The PGA Seniors Tournament took place early in June. It was won by Christie O'Connor with a total of 285. This was 21 years after his Carling victory at Longniddry and 16 strokes more. From comments received by the Board afterwards, the course seems to have been in excellent condition. Junior members were used as caddies but since some of them were engaged on this during school time, the Club were properly rebuked by local Headmaster (and member) David Allan.

New Members: Handicap. It had been brought to the attention of the Board that a new member had won a Club competition no less than 4 times during the year. His handicap had fallen from 21 to 6 in that period. It was resolved that the maximum handicap to be awarded to new members in future would be 18.

£80 Suit.

A golf ball was hit from the 18th fairway by a visitor through the window of the clubhouse lounge. The flying glass which it caused cut the suit of another visitor Alex Brown so badly that the Club had to pay £80 for a new one.

Professional Matters. Concern had previously been expressed about the Club's starting arrangements and the matter was raised with John Gray by the Captain. The pair agreed upon remedial action. Later in the year the Board were pleased to record that the required improvements had been accomplished. It was also decided that the professional's shop would stock confectionery for purchase by the Junior members only. The adult public, it was ruled would not be permitted access to this calorie-rich material!

Ladies. Lady Kincraig had taken over from Mrs BC Cooper as Lady Captain, to be faced with concern over the ladies 12th tee once more. This time it appears that they really meant it. A new tee was to be constructed. The Board asked that ladies should not play on men's medal days until after 6.00p.m.

The Winning Shot

Clubhouse. Redecoration of the dining room was decided upon. Changes to the back bar were also to take place. The serving hatch was to be widened and the partition between the back bar and the corridor from the lounge to the men's locker room removed. In the lounge itself cartoon prints presented by General Donald Young, G O C the Army in Scotland, were mounted. Nor was the back bar forgotten: a framed portrait of the 'Winning Shot' by Norman Orr was hung there. It was presented to the Club by the Artisans to celebrate their annual match with the main Club.

Trophies. A replacement cup for the John Adair Trophy which had been stolen was obtained. Unfortunately the list of previous winners recorded on the cup could not be retrieved. Lord Kincraig donated trophies for the Winter foursomes and Stuart Laird presented a pair of quaichs for the summer ones. Messrs W. McClure and W. Aitken both active Junior Conveners when on the Board, presented a trophy for the Junior Championship.

1983. An early decision in the New Year was to stock Southern Comfort in the bar. Shortly afterwards the Club was advised that Longniddry had been chosen to stage one of the final qualifying competitions for the Open Championship to be held at Muirfield in 1987. Play would take place on Sunday 12th and Monday 13th July with the course available to the competitors for practice on the previous two days.

AGM 1983. The 27th AGM took place early in March with the previous year's accounts to 30th November available. A plea was made from the floor by George Harkess for a modest relaxation of the men's dress requirements in the lounge. He suggested that no ties should be required, but that jackets should be retained. This was countered by George Ferguson dressed as usual in an impeccable sports jacket, who considered that not only should the standard of dress in the lounge be maintained, but that of some members required to be considerably improved. The Harkess motion was unsuccessful: another decade was to pass before dress requirements in the lounge were reduced.

Dr Rose Donaldson. In April members were saddened by the death of Dr Donaldson who had been such a prominent member of the Club and of the community. She had been Lady Vice-President since the passing of Charlotte Beddows. Dr Donaldson was succeeded as Lady Vice-President by Kath Rose (she of golf ball-in-the-bath family), the present incumbent.

Gender Matters. At mid term there seems to have been some disagreement between the sexes about weekend play. It is recorded that an understanding (not a rule) was reached that ladies would not play before 11.00 am (later changed to 10.30 a.m.) on either Saturdays or Sundays unless their competitions were in the fixture card.

About the same time a dilemma caused by the Club taboos regarding dress and gender was encountered. A male member complained that competitors in the Seniors versus Juniors fixtures were admitted to the back bar when they were found to be inadmissible to the lounge. His objection was that some of the Juniors turned out to be girls who, as females, were not supposed to be allowed in the male sanctum sanctorum of the back bar. Solution not recorded.

The Course. Problems with the sewer installed in 1967 were discovered in April 1983. Apparently there was danger of a partial collapse and corrective action was required. Eventually Lothian Region accepted the cost of 1000 square yards of new turf which was involved in the repair of the damage.

The search for underground water struck a happier note. The investigation had been entrusted to Engineers and members Alistair and Ian MacKay, in association with the Institute of Geological Sciences. The Institute's Mr Robins advised that there were favourable prospects of finding water. A test borehole at a cost of £2,000 was authorised. Wimpey were engaged for the work and an adequate supply of acceptable water was discovered at 9.2 metres depth. Outside the clubhouse, the Clubmaster's garden was sacrificed to provide a practice net whilst on the course the advice of the Earl of Wemyss was followed in the choice of additional trees.

The Club's enquiry about the farmland adjoining the 7th and 8th fairways proved disappointing. Mr A P Dale, the owner, had written advising that none of the land was available for sale nor likely to be in the near future. The Board decided to investigate the possibility of a leasing arrangement. Since the matter is not mentioned again, this must have been unsuccessful also.

1984. At the end of January what appears to have been the first 'Scots Night' was held in the Club. A mixture of Scottish songs and general entertainment by local artists, the occasion has turned out to be very popular. In contrast to the formal dances the 'Scots Night' appears to be an enduring item in the social programme.

On the playing side the new Handicapping Scheme 1983 was coming into effect with the first 4 months of 1984 in Scotland to be non-counting. The Club felt this to be unsatisfactory. The month of April at Longniddry normally saw the season in full swing and the Championship qualifying rounds were usually played in that month. The buffer zone had not been fixed and would not apply till 1st May.

Competitive play went ahead, the new handicap system notwithstanding. The winter league team had had mixed results: 5 wins, 4 losses and a draw. On the other hand later in the year, Michael McLaren became the first Longniddry player to win the Longniddry Open whilst Graham Sked lifted the handicap prize at the same event. In the Club competition, Stephen

Greenmantle Trophy.
The father and son partnership of Jim and Derek Ramage returned a net 55 (- a record breaking score) - to win for the third consecutive year. Second were Mr and Mrs S Gilmour 63 and third Stuart and Caroline MacKay, both juniors, with 65.

Thomson won both the Sawers Handicap Knock out and the Club Championship.

Meantime the ladies were more than doing their bit: Early in June Longniddry had hosted the Babe Zaharias Ladies Open Tournament. Participating were 16 American Ladies, some of them ex Curtis Cup players, travelling with the American Curtis Cup team. In the event, the Tournament was won by the Club's own Patricia Lees.

The men's senior members were getting organised and home and away matches were arranged with North Berwick, Gullane, Dunbar and Kilspindie.

1984 AGM. Dan Abbot took over the Captaincy from Ian Jackson.

Dr Donaldson's passing was already known but the AGM now learned also of the recent death of Gordon Durward OBE. The loss of these two popular and respected members left the Club without its two Vice-Presidents. Kath Rose had already been nominated for the ladies vacancy and Tom Porteous was now put forward for the other. Both nominees were elected unanimously.

The course had been remeasured. It was found necessary to move the medal tees back at the 4th and 6th holes to retain the SSS at 70 for the men and 73 for the ladies. The total distance gained was 19 yards.

Meantime negotiations had been proceeding through the year with the Estate. In the autumn, agreement was reached at a rent of £10,000 per annum.

1985. The second Board meeting of the year was marked by the attendance of the Club President, the Earl of Wemyss. The club had wished to extend the bottom car park. It had been considered that it might be necessary to tunnel the burn for three quarters of its length. The Earl was concerned about this prospect and although planning permission had been obtained, he wished time to consider the matter. Subsequently it was decided that there would be no tunnelling of the burn; the perimeter of the car park would be marked by the extension of the privet hedge.

The use of caddy cars was also clarified: it was agreed to permit the use of electrically powered caddy cars which were not suitable for some one to sit upon.

It was decided to rebuild the greenkeepers' sheds. By the Autumn, plans had been approved and quotations obtained. A price of £12,000 had been accepted. However, the Directors decided before proceeding with the expenditure, to consult the Estate on the position of the lease. The Estate were not at that time prepared to consider extending the lease, of which there were nine and a half years remaining. The Estate agreed that if at the end of that time the lease was not renewed, compensation to the members for the sheds expenditure would be made on the basis of one third of the original cost.

Meantime Mr J Arthur, the agronomist, had made his report on the course. It was very satisfactory.

As were the Winter League results, Longniddry had finished top. For the

Matthew Black JP with the Winter League Team 1984/85.

Backrow: K Cunningham, MS Robinson, C McNeill, R Burge, WJ Weston, PS Thomson, H Archibald MG McLaren.

Front Row: DC Hunter, N Elliot, A Harvey, M Black, IR Jackson, JA McVey, B McPhie, G Shed, ER Gray.

first time since its inception the Junior League included a Longniddry team. The first match against Royal Musselburgh was lost but nevertheless the team emerged runners up at the end of the season.

The Business Ladies Medals on Saturday mornings were not well supported. The tee had been reserved from 11.00 a.m. until 11.45 a.m. It was decided to change this to 11.00 a.m. until 11.30 a.m.

In the clubhouse, a supper dance in April had attracted a reduced attendance and in the Autumn a proposed dance was scrapped because of lack of support. The Police had been involved in the discussions concerning the Club's constitution and Bye Laws. It was concluded that the number of visitors to the clubhouse which could be introduced by a member should be limited to 3 on any one occasion.

The Professional. At a meeting with the Captain, the Professional had expressed unhappiness and this caused concern to the Directors. The Captain had a further meeting with the Professional and the minutes seem to indicate that the outcome was satisfactory to both parties. In view of later events, this was perhaps incorrect. In the meantime, David Yates, Assistant Professional left to join the Easter Moffat Club.

1986. With a vigorous Board of Directors in charge, chaired first by Dan Abbot and after the March AGM by new Club Captain Duncan Allan, the club seemed set to enjoy one of its most successful periods.

The new rental had been settled amicably. The condition of the course was good. The Club issued, free to members, metal plug forks to encourage repair of pitch marks on the greens. The construction of the new greenkeepers' shed/workshop was well under way and plans had been finalised for renovation of the old sheds for rest/washroom purposes. Estimates were in preparation for the extension of the Professional's shop and in the Secretary's office, a computer had been installed. To accord with the wishes of members the incidence of visiting clubs had been reduced.

On the playing side the results were excellent and held out high promise for the future. The Longniddry team had won the County Cup for the first time since 1974. Meanwhile at a younger level, Michael Stanton reached the 4th round of the Scottish Boys Championship. The Junior team competing for only their 2nd year won the East Lothian Junior league. At the final meeting, the team came second in the stroke play competition with Raymond Russell also second in the individual contest.

Ladies Senior Amateur Open. The British Ladies Senior Amateur Open

The Ladies Section received a bequest of £200 on the death of Miss Sophie McEwan. It was decided to run a senior ladies competition and to use the money to buy a suitable trophy. Patricia Lees meantime had brought the East Lothian Ladies Championship to Longniddry.

Captain Duncan Allan and Lady Captain Ethel Jack (4th from left, back row) with officials and winners of British Senior Ladies Golf Championship.

staged at Longniddry at the end of September was a 'tremendous success'. The winner with a 154 for two rounds was P. Riddiford. Following this the club had agreed jointly with Kilspindie to host the Scottish Youths Open Amateur Competition in 1989.

Small Clouds on the Horizon. In contrast to this picture of progressive activity and competitive success, there were two problems which were due to become more intractable:

Social Programme and Dress Standards. The first concerned the steadily falling attendance at social events. Only just enough tickets had been sold to enable the annual dance early in January to be run. At the other end of the year only 20 members turned up for the Men's Games Night. The clubmaster's income was being affected. It was admitted that new ideas were required. For example, the recently instituted Scots Night was proving highly popular. Some considered that the dress standards in the lounge were diverting members to more relaxed surroundings for their recreation.

The matter was debated at the AGM with George Ferguson fighting hard behind his entrenchments. It was decided nevertheless, that members should be balloted to discover whether a trial period of relaxed dress standards was favoured.

The ballot duly took place in June. The proposal was for a trial period when men would not be obliged to wear ties but jackets would be required. No proposed change for the ladies was recorded. Neither was the numerical outcome of the ballot declared. The minute states that the result was 'substantially in favour' of the suggested trial. It was therefore implemented during the months of July and August.

Observations during the trial period failed to detect any real increase in the usage of the Club's facilities. Bar turnover figures disclosed no improvement as far as the lounge was concerned. Perversely, Back Bar turnover had increased. It was decided to close the matter and intimate failure of the test to demonstrate any need for change of the dress regulations.

Starting Arrangements. The second problem concerned the control and administration of starting. The days of Starter Bob Himsworth were long gone. Starting was the responsibility of John Gray as it had been of Gordon Durward. The Professional was paid a sum for this called the 'starting allowance' in addition to his retainer. Although there had been expressions of dissatisfaction in the past by both the Professional on one side and the Board on the other, no serious differences appeared to exist.

In January 1986 the Captain received from the Professional a letter regarding conditions which the PGA recommended for the engagement of club professionals. It is not clear whether this letter was specific to Longniddry or whether it was a circular letter for general distribution. At any rate the Secretary took the matter up with the PGA and correspondence was exchanged on the exact circumstances applying at Longniddry.

In the meantime, Alistair Mackay, the House Convener, in preparing his forward programme was working on plans to extend the Professional's shop. His intention was to fill in the vacant corner between the shop and the Junior Clubroom to provide storage and office space for the Professional. A verbal price of £13,000 was quoted for the work.

In parallel with this, the Match and Handicap Committee, chaired by Billie McNeill were considering the starting arrangements at the Club. They were concerned to ensure that these were adequate against the background of the high incidence of visitors expected in 1987 when Longniddry would be one of the qualifying courses for the Open Championship. The Committee concluded that specialist starters should be engaged and should operate not from the Professional's shop but from the small summer lounge attached to the men's locker rooms. The Board authorised the Match and Handicap Committee to discuss the proposed new starting arrangements with the Professional.

By this time the proposals to extend the Professional's shop seemed to have been deferred. Detailed drawings had been put in hand but after July the idea is not mentioned in the record again. Possibly it was considered that if starting was not going to be conducted from the Professional's shop, an extension would not be required.

Ian Forbes.
A final sad note ended the year which had begun so well. Doctor Ian Forbes, Captain in 1968/69 and for several years a hard working Director of the Club, had died. Among many benefits with which he had endowed the Club was the 'B' Championship Trophy.

The appointment of specialist starters had of course important consequences for the Professional. Not only was his starting allowance affected, it was likely that because of reduced traffic to the shop, his sales opportunities would be diminished.

The negotiations with the Professional were not completed until February of the following year. It appears that some Directors had not been consulted at the final stages, whilst the Professional's acceptance seems to have been reluctant. At any rate it was understood that the matter had been settled and the appointment of three starters went ahead.

1987. At the Board meeting on 7th January it was noted that the new arrangements for starting were well in hand.

The AGM was fast approaching, and the new starting system, in its teething stages of course, was not proving universally popular. One problem was that not all of the starters were familiar with many of the individual members so that the old relaxed rapport and mutual trust appeared to have gone, at least temporarily.

The AGM took place on 28th February. Things proceeded reasonably smoothly until 'Any Other Business' when upon request the Captain gave an account of the negotiations with the Professional over the previous months and the details of the new starting arrangements. He advised the meeting of the additional costs of the new system. Against this it was judged that the previous starting system had been insufficiently formal and that a greater visitor volume was anticipated.

The arguments ranged back and forth chiefly between persons who had some knowledge of the circumstances. Other members attending the meeting however, may well have felt some bewilderment as they listened.

Three sticking points seemed to emerge. It was difficult to accept that the additional income could be achieved; there was an impression (certainly false) that the Board had rushed things through to present a 'fait accompli' to the AGM; and finally there was resentment that the Regulations of the Constitution prevented a petition on the matter, signed by 74 members, being accepted for discussion at the meeting.

Eventually without taking a vote the Captain agreed that an EGM would be convened to deal with the matter. It took place on Saturday 25th April, with the Captain in the chair.

EGM. First there was difficulty in approving the Minutes of the AGM. When this was resolved the Special Resolution was proposed by the Captain *"that the present starting arrangements as implemented by the Board of Directors should continue." It was seconded by the Vice Captain.*

A counter proposal was put forward by George Ferguson and seconded by Dick Burge to the effect that the starting arrangements should revert to the 'status quo'. The debate continued for some time, but eventually the Captain closed the discussion and asked the members to vote upon the Board's Special resolution.

When the counting had been completed, Mr Porteous advised the meeting that there had been 128 votes for the motion and 175 against. The Captain then stated that this had been a matter of confidence for the Board of Directors and that resignations would follow. He did not take the chair at Longniddry again.

Fortunately, Alex Harvey, the Club's highly respected Vice Captain, although signifying an intention to resign in support of the Captain agreed to soldier on until a new Board was in place. With the exception of John Barber who had resigned at the beginning of the year and Jim Johnston who now resigned for business reasons, the rest of the Board decided to follow the Vice Captain's example and continue in post meantime. To replace the vacant Green Convenership, Peter Lowe was co-opted to the Board.

A sub-committee was formed to address the question of the Professional and the matter of starting. It consisted of the Vice Captain, Mr Segrott and the Secretary. Its objective was to implement the EGM's decision that the 'status quo' should be restored. The first task of course was to determine exactly what the 'status quo' had been. Different perceptions appeared to exist.

Miscellany. In the meantime there had been the normal flow of events which had had to be dealt with 'hugger-mugger':

The conversion of the greenkeepers' sheds to a decent rest area had been completed. Leslie Davidson, a member of the green staff for 15 years had retired, and had been replaced by John Kay.

There had been a proposal, (not for the first time), that the ladies should have their own separate prize giving. After discussions it had been decided that in future the Lady Captain should present the ladies' prizes at the Club's Prize Giving Ceremony. This happy arrangement has continued successfully since.

Another event had been the election of Mrs Anna Barr to Honorary Life Membership. This had actually been accomplished at the EGM whilst the votes on the Special Resolution were being counted.

The Army in Scotland Officers' Golfing Society (ASOGS). The terms of the ASOGS visits to Longniddry were confirmed by the Club: The Society would bring a maximum of 40 members to their 12 outings. The Army in Scotland Officers' Golfing Society has a long history of association with Longniddry. Membership includes such senior officers as Nick Fleming, 'Tank' Nash, Julian Lancaster, Jack Wishart and many others, not forgetting Longniddry's own Gilbert Dempster. The annual match between the Society and the Club usually takes place in the Autumn and is amicably and keenly contested.

Martini Regional Final.

The Martini Regional Final held on 1st June at Longniddry for the first time had gone exceptionally well and letters of thanks had been received from Leisure Sports.

9th Hole. Dwelling. A matter which had particular relevance for 1994 arose in June 1987. An application had been raised for outline planning permission to build a house adjacent to the 9th tee. The house was to be a bungalow and ' should not present any serious obstacle to the view from the golf course', the minute says. Assurance had been given that no trees would be felled to make way for the new house. The Golf Club's consent would be subject to the understanding that any damage to the new building or its occupants from golf balls would not be the basis of any claim against the Club. It was not until 1994 that a dwelling was constructed on the site, presumably on the grounds of the 1987 planning permission.

Open Championship Qualifier. During July of course the 1987 Open Championship had taken place at Muirfield with Longniddry gaining some of the limelight as one of the qualifying courses. Afterwards a number of congratulatory letters had been received not only from the R & A but also from competitors including Bernard Gallacher. Bernard's scores for the four sets of nine holes were 36, 31, 31, and 36. He therefore completed Longniddry's 18 holes in 62 shots though having done them backwards in a manner of speaking he could not claim a record. It was generally accepted that the event had been most successful; the condition of the course and the organisation of the competition together with the arrangements in the clubhouse being highly satisfactory. The weather had been excellent. During the Qualifying Competition, the course record had been twice broken - the first time by an amateur, Christian Hardin from Sweden and the second by

an English Professional, Peter Harrison. Both had scored 63. The R & A member in charge at Longniddry, Mr John Boardman, had presented a plaque from the R & A in token of the competition. It is mounted in the lounge .

Club Competitions. Later in July the Invitation Fourball had been marred by extremely bad weather and slow play. In the afternoon the duration for a round was four and a half hours and flooding of the greens caused the abandonment of the competition. In the first of the Club mixed foursomes the cups had been withheld because a Junior, Derek Scott was recruited to complete the field and had won in partnership with Miss E C Phimister.

Back to the Starting Problem. Whilst all these events and incidents were in progress, the Board had been working to restore the starting arrangements and preparing for the appointment of a new Board of Directors.

A starting duties specification had been drawn up for discussion. The aim was to return to the 'status quo' by 1st June. Negotiations had continued with the possibility of the Professional employing a second Assistant considered. Unfortunately no agreement was reached.

The Directors concluded that it was necessary to convene another EGM to review the situation and appoint new Directors. Because of imminent heavy commitments however, particularly the qualifying round of the Open Championship, it was not practicable to hold this before September. The restoration of starting arrangements was therefore deferred. Nevertheless, discussions on starting duties continued through June and July and into August. On occasions in July Sandy Jones of the PGA was present. However by mid-August the Board concluded that agreement was not in sight and that there was no point in endeavouring to negotiate further. Resolution of the problem must await the new Board.

Towards the end of August Alex Harvey intimated his belief that the Board had lost the confidence of the members of the Club. He intended to resign from the position of Vice Captain in the hope that a new Captain with fresh ideas and the confidence of members would resolve the problem. In spite of persuasion to the contrary from the other officers of the Board and John Segrott, it was decided that all Directors except two Lady Directors would intimate their resignation before the EGM which had been arranged for 3rd October.

Twelve nominations for Directors were received before the EGM. None were submitted for the Captaincy but despite a last minute plea, Alex Harvey who clearly had borne a very heavy burden over the past months could not be persuaded to reconsider his decision to retire from the Board.

The voting at the EGM was as follows:

P D Lowe	198	A M Mackechnie	136
R W Fullard	189	A F M Fisher	131
T Edmond	165	J D Sutherland	110
G Bonnington	161	J J McKenzie	87
V J Barron	159	N Elliot	72
R B Thorburn	139	G Harkess	72

The Directors of the new Board joining Mrs R Lawrie, Lady Captain and Mrs S W Laird Lady Vice Captain, were, therefore: V J Barron, G Bonnington, T Edmond, R W Fullard, P D Lowe, A M Mackechnie and R B Thorburn. Of these only P D Lowe and R B Thorburn had served on the Board previously.

The first meeting of the new Board was held on 21st October. Due to illness the Vice-President could not attend. For the first time in the history of the Club, the Board meeting was chaired by a woman, the Lady Captain Netta Lawrie.

The first question was that of the Club Captaincy. The EGM had not addressed this. After debate the Board considered that it should act cautiously. It was agreed to ask Vice-President Tom Porteous to be Chairman of the Directors until a Captain was appointed. With regard to the starting problem, the Directors decided to take time to familiarise themselves with the history of the affair.

In the absence of the Vice-President the second meeting of the new Board was again chaired by Mrs Lawrie. An offer to be made to the Professional was worked out and a series of meetings with him took place ending just before the Board meeting on 8th December with the Professional's acceptance. In order to finalise matters a new contract would be prepared which combined the Professional and Starting Duties.

Prize Giving and Dress. In the meantime the Annual Prize Giving had to be organised. It was decided that the Vice-President would conduct it and that Mrs Lawrie would present the prizes.

The Board then went on to permit casual dress in the lounge until 11.00 a.m. when the bar opened. It was also agreed that dress regulations should be relaxed for the Men's Games Night. The effect of this seems to have been immediate with 38 members attending compared with 20 the year before.

With 20/20 Hindsight. So ended 1987, a year which had promised much for the Club but which had brought distress and dissension. A train of events started with the best of intentions had run into increasing difficulties. A Board which had been highly dedicated, efficient and active had felt collectively obliged to resign. A Vice Captain admired by all had been denied his rightful captaincy and an amicable Professional, knowledgeable and friendly had been distressed and aggrieved.

1988. The first meeting of the Board of Directors in 1988 had to decide upon which of the two candidates R B Thorburn or P D Lowe should be nominated to the forthcoming AGM for the captaincy of the Club. The Directors chose Mr Lowe. Ron Fullard was nominated for the Vice Captain's post.

Matters passed off smoothly at the AGM. Two additional Directors were appointed to replace Messrs Lowe and Fullard who had stepped up to become officers of the Club. The new Directors were Alex Fisher and Jim Forrest.

As the year progressed things began to return at least to the appearance of normality. A new Contract was agreed with John Gray which combined the Starter and Professional duties in one document.

Rules were changed concerning application for membership. In future both proposer and seconder would be required to have had knowledge of the applicant for at least 3 years and the deposit required from adults would be £20.

Open Disappointment. A letter from Mr Bonallack of the R & A caused general regret. He advised that the Championship Committee had decided to invite Dunbar Golf Club to accommodate the Final Qualifying event in the Open Championship in 1992. The initial reason given was that such changes had to be made from time to time. On further enquiry the Club was told that the nature of the Longniddry course being only partially links was not a completely fair test for those who were to compete a few days later on Muirfield; it being a links course entirely.

Friday Club.
Almost in passing the Board agreed to the proposal from Mr D R (Dougie) Gemmell that the bar would be opened experimentally on Friday evenings during October and November until 10.30 p.m. with the clubhouse closing at 11.00 p.m. This was the beginning of the Friday club which is still in vigorous life nine years later.

At the April meeting of the Board a suggestion submitted by Mr C M Grant was accepted. He had proposed that an indicating pole be erected in the rough between the 14th and 18th fairways to assist in determining the line of flight when seeking golf balls. Nine years later the post is still present.

The Board sadly turned its attention inward again and ruled that 18 minutes prior to any draw time in a ladies competition should be kept clear.

Junior Feats. The Juniors were particularly successful in 1988. Full details are given separately under Associated Clubs, but some achievements deserve particular emphasis:

Raymond Russell had been selected for full international honours and played in the Boys Home Internationals at Formby in August. On his return Raymond won the Longniddry Men's Open for the Durward Trophy. At the age of 16 he returned 133 – the lowest score ever recorded for the 36 hole event. One of his rounds played in very difficult conditions equalled the course record of 63. Last but not least Lindsey MacRaild had won her Scottish Schoolgirls Cap.

Jeanette Fiddler and Jim Scott receiving the Turnberry Cup from Lady Bader.

Adult Success. In the adult competitions the men's champion was Neil Davidson whilst Patricia Lees won the Ladies Championship for the 7th time. In the process she established a new Ladies Course Record of 72. Meanwhile at Turnberry Jeanette Fiddler and Jim Scott won the Turnberry Cup competition in aid of the Douglas Bader Foundation.

Back to Business. With the starter situation resolved the Board turned its attention to other matters.

Firstly the question of dress: It was concluded that no jeans, tee shirts or trainer shoes should be allowed on the golf course. This was consistent with the rules operating in other clubs and a suitable notice was mounted at the men's entrance to the clubhouse. The Newsletter of November 1988 declares:

1. Recognised golf shoes should be worn.
2. Tailored trousers, plus twos or plus fours should be worn.

Playing the short tree-girt 6th with its lovely Fife backdrop and its six lurking bunkers.

Late summer sunset over the Lomond Hills from the clubhouse verandah.

The prospect to the North East over the little peninsula of Fernie Ness to the far East Neuk of Fife across the Firth.

3. Collared sports shirts are preferable; non collared tee shirts should not be worn.

Then the matter of control of members' guests was tackled: It was agreed that from 1st April 1989 playing members would receive, upon paying their annual subscription, a total of 12 concessionary vouchers each year for visitors (The concessionary charge at the time was £2 during the week and £4 at the weekend.) This proposal was destined to run into difficulties at the AGM.

Qualification for Honorary Life Membership was re-examined. There had been a perception that Honorary Life Membership was automatic after 50 years of membership. When this recollection was challenged it was found to be invalid.

In the autumn contact was made with Professor Last, a world expert on terrestrial ecology. It was hoped that through the good offices of the Estate, Professor Last would carry out a survey of all the trees on the course. This was done in October. Professor Last was accompanied by Mr Bonnington, Mr Porteous and Mr Herd. It was obvious that a number of trees were affected by Dutch Elm disease and that about 7 or 8 of them would require to be felled immediately. A programme of further selective cutting and re-planting would need to be prepared.

In the clubhouse a substantial purchase of replacement crockery for the dining room was required. The lady Directors chose an attractive Grasmere ware pattern at a total cost of £1,700.

Losses and Injuries. Everyone was saddened when the Countess of Wemyss passed away in September 1988. She had been for many years Honorary President of the Ladies Section of the Club, displaying a keen and encouraging interest in its activities.

Earlier in the year the Board had learned with great regret of the passing of Bella Johnstone who had been a member of staff for many years. There was also concern and sympathy for Alex Harvey and Alice Tramp who had been seriously injured in car accidents.

Community Charge. Towards the end of the year the Directors began to contemplate the effect of the Community Charge or 'Poll Tax' as it came to be called (even by Mrs Thatcher on occasion). Its introduction was imminent. The Club had a number of employees whose terms of remuneration included rent and rate free accommodation. One of the deficiencies of the Community Charge precipitately introduced by Nicholas Ridley reputedly in contradiction of Kenneth Baker's original softly softly intention, was that the question of 'tied houses' was not addressed by the legislation. The Longniddry Board began to grapple with the problem of developing a compensation formula to offset the negated rates benefit.

Lockerbie.

This was the time of the Lockerbie disaster and the Club granted an extension in the men's' Winter Foursomes to accommodate a policeman member who had been called away to duty at the scene.

1989. The Earl of Wemyss kindly agreed to accept the Honorary Presidency of the Ladies Section in succession to his late wife.

A minute records that the Agronomist would no longer be visiting the course. The cause of this change is not apparent from the minute. A similar move had taken place in the past only for the independent Agronomist to be reappointed a few years later. It was agreed to accept modified membership of the Sports Turf Research Institute as a substitute.

Members' Guests. A written protest regarding the new system proposed for concessionary introduction of member's guests was received from Mr A M Thomson. Although the Board considered that the vouchers system which they had proposed was fair and reasonable at 12 vouchers per annum for full members and six for five day, it was decided to increase the number of vouchers for 5 day members to 9.

The 1989 AGM passed off quietly, debate being confined to the question of the rules for the introduction of visitors. Several members spoke against the new system which the Board proposed should be tried for a year. The Captain pointed out that the previous arrangement whereby visitors were limited in the number of times they could be introduced by a member, had not worked satisfactorily. When the Captain asked for those opposed to the new scheme to vote, 6 people showed. Members were promised that the situation would be carefully monitored and results advised through the newsletter.

Community Charge. By the middle of March the resolution of the Community Charge problem had been decided upon. Sums equivalent to two persons' Community Charge would be consolidated into the salaries of those employees occupying houses. This was reported as having been found to be acceptable to two of the employees concerned. A third had pointed out quite rightly that such an addition to salary would be taxable. However the Board considered that the responsibility for taxation was a matter between the individual concerned and the Inland Revenue. Interestingly John Segrott, with his customary prescience, advised the Board that they should make such compensatory arrangements provisional in view of the uncertainty of the future of the Charge.

The Ladies. The Ladies representation on the Board had routinely changed. At the Ladies AGM, Mrs Lawrie had retired by rotation with Mrs Laird stepping up to Captain and Mrs Reekie becoming Vice Captain.

Competitions. On the playing side, 1989 proved to be a busy season: A good start was provided by Peter Lowe when at Kilspindie towards the end of May, he won the East Lothian Hope Medal with a round of 67 gross, 62 net. He is thought to be the only Longniddry player to have won this prize.

On 21st July a match took place between Longniddry and the Britannia Club from the Cayman Islands. The result is not recorded. The PGA held their first Patrons Mixed Tournament at Longniddry. The Lothians Golf

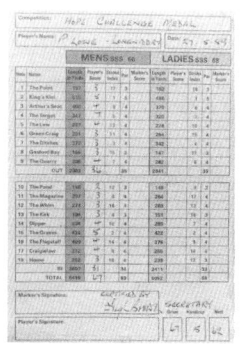
Peter's card

Association staged their Championship in which Raymond Russell – still a junior - reached the semi-final. The overall winner was Kevin Hastings of Broomieknowe. The Scotland Youths Championship was also run at Longniddry and was won by J McKenzie with 281.

The Club team reached the semi-final of the County Cup and Eric Mackay and Raymond Russell were both awarded caps in the Scottish Schools Team. Raymond was selected to represent Scotland against Sweden. He also won the Lothians Youth Championship whilst Roderick MacRaild won the Esso/Daily Express National Championship Regional Final and would be going to La Manga for the National Final in September.

Rent Review. Meantime, the last rent review under the current lease was to be effective from 1st February 1990. It was desirable that negotiations should begin shortly so that an expenditure figure would be available for the next budget. The Secretary was instructed to ask Mr Segrott (who though retired was acting as consultant to the Estate), for an early meeting. Most sadly the newly appointed Factor had died just after taking up his post and John Segrott had come out of retirement to fill the gap.

Two new trophies were presented to the Club. Peter Lowe donated the Merlinlee Trophy for the Ladies versus Gentlemen match, and Mrs Maisie Walls an Honorary Member kindly presented a trophy to be awarded to the lowest net scorer in the Ladies Summer Meeting.

Subsequently, Mr Bryan Marsh, Finance Convener, prepared a draft statement and letter with which he proposed to open negotiations with the Estate. It was agreed that the Club should seek to obtain a new lease for 20 years with a 4 yearly review.

By mid September the Secretary with Mr Segrott attending, pending the appointment of his successor, were able to inform the Board that agreement had been reached on renewal of the lease for a period of 20 years with reviews at 4 yearly intervals and a starting rent of £17,000. These proposals were to be referred to the Estate Trust.

Dress and Social Programme. The thorny subject of dress was debated at the end of the year. There were mixed views but it was decided in the end to maintain the established standards in the clubhouse and to amend the regulations for the course; to insist on golf shoes and to ban football and running shorts etc. At the same time, the possibility of a relaxation in the clubhouse in the future was recognised and recorded as a matter for a subsequent Board to consider.

There was still difficulty with the social programme: the Secretary was encountering increasing problems in finding suitable bands for dances planned. It was also noted that the piano borrowed by the Club from the British Legion might no longer be available.

Members' Guests. A sense of increasing dissatisfaction was being experienced with the new visitor voucher system. Introduced experimentally for a year and having encountered considerable opposition at the 1989 AGM, the perception was that if no change were made, serious objections would be raised at the forthcoming AGM. It was decided to abandon the voucher scheme and endeavour to achieve greater control through the price of the visitor ticket. Rates were proposed of £8 at weekends and £6 through the week.

1990. The start of the new decade was marked by the absolutely final appearance of John Segrott at the Board meeting. He had been Factor for 20 years. He expressed the opinion that in view of the rising rates of the cost of golf, the subscription fees at Longniddry were relatively low. Accompanying Mr Segrott was his successor Mr J J Hall who was made welcome.

AGM. At the AGM in February one of the first items was the display of a trophy from the Cayman Islands. This had resulted from the match against the archipelago the previous year. The trophy was, in fact, a turtle shell and it was decided that it would be presented annually to the member with the best 3 net scores in aggregate on Wednesday Medals.

Members' Guests Again. When Ron Fullard, who had taken over as Captain from Peter Lowe reached 'Any Other Business', he referred to letters received on the subject of the concessionary rate of green fees for visitors introduced by members. He invited Bob Anderson, one of the members who had written, to address the meeting. The matter was debated at some length with the Finance Convener pointing out that additional income was required, if not from this source, then from some other. The Captain promised that the subject would be considered again by the Board and the points raised borne in mind. At the first meeting of the Board afterwards, this promise was kept. The final decision was to leave the weekday rate unchanged at £4 but to reduce the weekend rate from £8 to £6. This arrangement would be subject to review at the end of the year. This reduction proved sufficient to contain the dissatisfaction at least until the 1991 AGM.

Junior Feet. By April the new dress regulations, so carefully prepared, were in trouble. Irate mothers had complained about the cost of golf shoes which children grew out of so rapidly. Unlike clothes bought large to be grown into, shoes had to fit. Eileen Dundas sent comments. The Board retreated and an amendment was made to accommodate Juniors' feet up to 15 years old. At the same time it was decided to hold a fresh survey to establish members' opinions on dress regulations.

Course Condition. Meanwhile, the Greens Committee were becoming increasingly concerned about the affects of low rainfall throughout the previous year and during the critical late winter/spring period of the current one. The Convener Mr A C Nicoll (Sandy) reiterated that the burns were very low and that the Canty Burn at the 7th tee was dry. It was decided to make enquiry of British Coal to discover whether their open cast mining

156

operations at Meadowmill were causing water to be diverted westwards. The Golf Club had invested over £4,000 on a second 12,000 gallon water storage tank. This would allow more water to be collected for distribution on the course during the hours of darkness and would allow fairways to be treated at the same time as tees and greens. Unfortunately delivery of the tank had been delayed. As the season advanced the shortage of rainfall continued and it was decided that the fairways should only be cut when absolutely necessary.

Future Projects. Looking to the future, the Finance Committee were asked to consider major projects for the development of the club including the possible purchase of the course upon termination of the lease. The possibility of financial support from the Scottish Tourist Board was to be investigated.

Dress Again. By June the results of the dress survey were to hand. 57.5% of members had voted and of these 37% wanted no change. This converted to 21.3% of the membership. Although the minute does not say so presumably 63% of those voting (36% of membership) did want change. It is also to be presumed that the 42.5% of the membership who did not vote could not have cared less. Having received this information the Board debated various options. In the end the 'status quo' was decided upon by the slimmest of margins. The unresolved problem of ladies carrying trays of drinks, coffees etc. up the stairs to their lounge remained.

The Clubhouse. The Captain, in consultation with Mr R Milligan (Bert), had arranged that two possible schemes be prepared for extension of the back bar and its complete refurbishment. In the main lounge of the clubhouse new curtains selected by the lady Directors were purchased and hung.

Ladies Successes. By August there was good news from the ladies. Hilary Monaghan had won the Connachan Cup and Joyce Hunnam had been selected to play for the county (which meant that unfortunately she had had to withdraw from the Club Championship). In addition, Mrs Quinn, who had suffered a long illness, was now on the road to recovery and had been appointed to the Ladies Golf Union with responsibility for training. She was also now Convener of the Scottish Ladies Golf Association. The donation of a memorial trophy for the Ladies Coronation Foursomes was received from the family of Mrs Iris Benson.

The Course. Back at Longniddry a section of the 3rd fairway was roped off. It had not recovered from the drought and returfing would be necessary. Work on the tees at the 15th, 10th, 11th and 13th had all been completed with the 14th still to be tackled. Six ball washers of the spiral type were to be purchased. Ken Archibald, the Assistant Head Greenkeeper had resigned to pursue a new career and advertisements for his replacement were

Course Rating. It was at this time that the Scottish Golf Union officially informed all clubs that Course Rating would be undertaken by teams trained by the SGU. The new rating system would not only take into account the length of the course, but also obstacles, difficulty factors, exposure to wind and many other conditions ignored in the past.

published. Subsequently, Raymond Russell also advised his intention to leave the green staff to compete as a full-time amateur.

Course furniture had been reviewed, particularly with regard to the tees. It was decided that the measurement of the course should be signified by a concrete block inserted in the ground at the tee, level with the turf, to mark the distance permanently. The concrete block would support a post of polished Oregon pine on which the distance and number of the hole would be carved.

Chiefly through the efforts of Mr J A M Mackenzie contacts with the Regional Authority about the sewers and drainage had borne some fruit. The drainage authority had examined the sewer behind the 1st green. There was evidence of obstruction which had contributed to the overflow experienced on the 5th fairway bunkers when storm conditions applied. Another obstruction between the 1st green manhole and the next one near the fairway bunker had been identified and cleared. The Region undertook to pay for the 4,000 gallons of the Club's water which they had used and to modify their equipment behind the 1st green as necessary.

The Clubhouse. In the house throughout the year there had been intermittent difficulty with the gas boilers. A revised quotation had been received for the back bar improvements and proposals for renovation of the entrance hallway and stairway to the ladies locker room were taking the costs of these projects beyond budget plans. At the same time provisional drawings for the men's locker room had been produced with a cost estimate of over £15,000. The idea (later abandonded) was to construct a Visitors Locker Room adjoining the existing men's locker room, utilising a financial grant from the Scottish Tourist Board and a loan from the R & A.

Special Reserve. At the beginning of December members were informed of proposals concerning the long term development of the Club. Although Mr Hall had advised that there was no indication of any possibility of the property being available for sale it was concluded that the long term situation should be put to members. Meetings were therefore held with the members in the clubhouse on the 18th, 20th and 21st December. The outcome of these discussions was that while many questions remained unanswered a large majority of the 170 members who had attended, were in favour of steps being taken to provide finance for the possible purchase of the course towards the end of the existing lease. A new fund to be called the Special Reserve would be established for the purpose.

1991. The year began with the appointment of Craig Hildersley to be Assistant Head Greenkeeper. He had been Head Greenkeeper at Turnhouse. The intention was that he would step up to Head Greenkeeper at Longniddry when Duncan Herd retired.

In the clubhouse the cost of refurbishment of the Entrance Hallway was met within normal budgeted repairs. However the back bar renovation was supported by a contribution of £6,000 from Scottish and Newcastle Brewers to be repaid over a period of 5 years. Mr J Forrest, House Convener, as well as nursing these Clubhouse projects, had produced a proposal for extension to the Professional's shop, which was to be costed. It will be recalled that this had previously been mooted by Alistair Mackay in 1987.

At the AGM on 23rd February 1991 the Captain, Mr Fullard, reported on the progress of the Special Reserve Fund. Donations were invited. Sub committees of the Board would consider the conditions of the Fund and the investment of its capital. It was agreed that the Entrance fee of new members should be increased by £20 beyond the figure already fixed at 150% of the annual subscription. These extra £20 sums would be transferred directly to the Special Reserve upon receipt.

Two Directors retired at the AGM: Alex Fisher and Jim Forrest. They had been respectively Match and Handicap and House Conveners. They had both worked very conscientiously on behalf of the Club and thanks were expressed to both gentlemen. Mr Alistair Thomson and Mr R O Smith (Bert) were elected in their place. Mrs Terry Reekie and Mrs Susan Hume, already Lady Captain and Lady Vice Captain respectively, were formally elected to the Board in the customary manner. Farewell was said to the Estate's factor Mr J J Hall who had resigned. Mr Richard Gledson was welcomed as his replacement. Another departure was the Club's long-standing auditor Mr St John Spence.

A special plea for support for the social functions was made by the Captain. At a recent dance only 40 members and friends had turned up and earlier in the year a disco had had to be cancelled altogether.

There would be no visitors on Saturdays and Sundays except those introduced and playing with members, and Fridays would be casual bookings only. It was hoped that by introducing 8 minute intervals for teeing off on Saturdays and Sundays the flow of play would be improved at the weekend. Unfortunately, this last move proved unsatisfactory and the gap between play was restored to six minutes at weekends except on Medal Days.

On the course tee boxes would be replaced by attractive sign posts. The winter programme had been dominated by restoration of the 3rd fairway. In all £3,000 had been spent on it including returfing and irrigation. Once again in the spring, the weather gave cause for concern. There were late frosts and May turned out to be a very dry month (perversely the Captain's day had to be postponed because of floods!). Fairways perforce were left uncut. The previous year, it was now recognised , there had been too much cutting done on fairways whilst growth had been poor.

Meantime in and around the clubhouse there had been several developments. The renovation of the back bar had been completed and extraction fans with remote controls had been installed in windows in the mixed lounge. Consideration was given to installing Sky TV but this was deferred. The overflow car park had been extended at a cost of £11,400. It also caused, according to ornithologist Mr Frank Hamilton, the loss of the rare Scottish warbler, the lesser Whitethroat, from the scrub which had edged the car park. The estimate for the extension of the Professional's shop at £16,500 had been received and was under consideration. Finally as far the clubhouse in 1991 was concerned, a complaint was received about the misalignment and inconsistency of the printing of the names on the Captain's board in the lounge.

The Special reserve had got a healthy send off with an allocation of £25,000 in its first year. Subject to agreement at the 1992 AGM (duly received) an alteration to the Articles of Association was made to ensure that the Fund could not be used for any other purpose than the purchase of the golf course.

1992. The AGM in February 1992 was comparatively straightforward. The amendment to the Articles of Association in respect of the Special reserve went through smoothly and the captaincy passed from Ron Fullard to Jim Mackenzie. Disappointment was expressed about the lack of success of the social programme.

At the first Board meeting afterwards it was agreed that the Professional's status would be converted to that of a self-employed person. There was also a change at Assistant Professional level: Paul Wardell assistant to John for two years was leaving for a job in Sussex and Derek Scott would take his place.

In May there were two matters of primary concern for the board meeting: first of all Duncan Herd, Head Greenkeeper would be retiring. It was decided that he could continue to occupy his cottage at 4 John Knox Road. The Board went on to appoint the Assistant Head Greenkeeper, Craig Hildersley as his successor.

The second question involved the golf course itself: A cheerful note was news that the extension of the existing water borehole had been successfully completed. The water supply from it was of good quality and the volume available had virtually doubled. However, a report from Mr Boocock the Agronomist expressed great concern. The condition of the course was rapidly deteriorating due, in his opinion, to gross overplay. His chief remedy was to reduce the amount of play not just from visitors but also from members. Faced with this most serious situation the Board advanced the verti-draining programme on the greens, adjusting competition completion dates accordingly, and planned to reduce play substantially over the winter period from October to April inclusive. Members' visitors would be limited to six in winter and twelve in the summer. A visitor control card to be stamped by the starter would be introduced. Subsequently the decision was taken to cancel all winter medals both men's and ladies for the 92/93 season.

Meantime the water supply was operating well with 18,000 gallons per day being used on the course. By June the volume was reported to be 40,000 gallons. However it was recognised that the sprinkler heads and pipe system were ageing. The Greens Convener Mr Sandy Nicoll reported that while greens and tees were in reasonable condition by virtue of the sprinkler system, fairways had been badly burned during the long dry spell. He pointed out that while the rainfall in East Lothian normally reached an average of 22 inches per annum; over the last three years the average had been 16.5. In the year in question, total rainfall so far up to August had been 10 inches but half of that had fallen in August itself. These figures highlighted the cause of many of the problems of the course. Sampling of the soil was to be undertaken as soon as possible on all tees, greens and fairways. The question of possible pollution from fall-out from the power station at Cockenzie was also being investigated. Five tee mats were purchased for use at the short holes, and wire netting installed at the east end of the course, to address the rabbit problem

The Ladies. The Ladies decided that at the prize-giving ceremony Mrs Terry Reekie the Lady Captain, would present Hilary Monaghan with a gold watch in recognition of her excellent golfing achievements. They also decided that a plaque received from the RNLI in recognition of all the work carried out by the ladies in fund-raising should be presented to Mrs Dora Sproul who had been so long associated with the RNLI competition. Increasingly girls were playing in Junior League matches. It was agreed that when this occurred at Longniddry, the teams would be accommodated for refreshments in the main lounge, dress regulations notwithstanding.

In the clubhouse painting and carpeting of the ladies powder room, toilets and corridors had been completed as had the new seating for the men's back bar. The social programme was obtaining a mixed reception and it was arranged that the Annual Prize-giving would be organised as a social evening with no dance

In November the ladies reported that Miss J J Smith (Bunty) who had been Secretary of the Ladies section for 7 years would be retiring from the post in which she had served so faithfully since taking over from Audrey Laird. Miss Smith was presented with a bouquet of flowers at the Club's annual prize-giving and in due course was elected to Life Honorary Membership of the Club. The office of secretary was then filled by Mrs June McEwan.

Trophies. Mr Charles Winter, a banker member presented a new trophy - the Enterprise Trophy - to the Club. It was won in that first year by Stuart Mackay. Later, George Taylor donated a trophy to be contested in the Men's Invitation Foursomes.

Raymond Russell won the 1992 Scottish Youth Championship and Steven Thomson, one of the Club's outstanding players got his handicap down to 1.

Presentations. At the prize-giving in November apart from the flowers to Miss Smith and the watch to Hilary Monaghan, presentations were made to Raymond Russell, Thelma Johnston and Duncan Herd. Thelma had just completed 20 years service with the club serving regularly behind the bar. Popular and helpful, she had been particularly valued by the members of the

As the year ended the Board were considering whether it would be possible to move the 11th tee back towards the greenkeepers sheds and so reduce the danger to players on the 4th green. The other long-term consideration giving food for thought was the declared intention of the Estate to build two new golf courses with two hotels and some dwellings within the Gosford Estate.

Towards the end of the year when the Club's finances were considered it was agreed to take up spaces which existed in the ladies authorised membership numbers. Hitherto the lady members numbers had stood at 175, although the constitution permitted 200. Membership was offered to 25 ladies on the waiting list, therefore.

Friday Club. Her willingness to attend the bar on Friday evenings had been a crucial factor in the establishment and continuation of the Friday Club. Duncan Herd had been Head Greenkeeper at Longniddry for 31 years by the end of 1992. He had originally come from Carnoustie where his brother was Head Greenkeeper at the championship course. Always his own man, Duncan's worth was appreciated by all at the Club. A Duncan Herd testimonial fund had been set up and at the Annual Prize-giving he received a cheque from it for the sum of £1,500. Further contributions were made and those he received at his retirement dinner held in his honour on his birthday, 16th December, attended by the Earl of Wemyss and several past Captains. At the AGM the following February, Duncan was elected to a well-deserved Honorary Life Membership.

1993. The year began with the change of lady officers. Mrs Terry Reekie having completed her two years of captaincy stepped down to be replaced by Mrs Susan Hume. The new Lady Vice Captain was Susan Bell. With Longniddry hosting the East Lothian Ladies Championship competition in 1995 and the Ladies Home Internationals in 1996 it was important to maintain the momentum on improvements to the ladies accommodation begun by Mrs Reekie and Bert Milligan. The Ladies Locker Room was badly in need of renovation and the furniture in the Ladies Lounge was no longer comfortable. On the playing side it was agreed that the ladies starting times for medals would be preceded by a gap of at least 15 minutes to ensure a reasonable clearance.

The House. Whilst first attention was to be directed to the ladies accommodation, other problems had to be addressed as well. The central heating boilers were misbehaving, the social programme was poorly supported and complaints about the Champions Board in the main lounge had been raised at the AGM in February. It had been pointed out that the gilt-painted list of Captains' names was irregular and out of alignment reflecting the different sign writers who had been employed down the years. Whilst these matters were given the necessary attention, the big decision affecting the Clubhouse was the relaxation of the dress rules in the mixed lounge. From 1st July, casual dress would be accepted in the main lounge until 6.00 p.m.

The Course. It proved impossible to reach agreement on the proposal to move the 11th tee back towards the greenkeepers sheds. As a compromise it was decided to fill in the bunker in the centre of the fairway and introduce another alongside the 5th tee. The other change to the course was the demolition of the old brick-built shed (the Home Guard storage place) in the trees near the 10th green. It had been subject to vandalism and it was decided to take it down. Members' opinions about the overall condition of the course seemed to be mixed. Comments were received in June expressing

162

approval of the condition of the course and offering congratulations to the Head Greenkeeper and his staff. They were supported by an encouraging agronomist's report confirming that the protective measures taken the previous winter had been successful and should be continued.

Competitions. The season started well with Raymond Russell registering two outright wins: the first in the Champion of Champions competition at Leven, and the second in the Open Tournament at Craigmillar Park. However the Longniddry team at 7th equal had not been very successful in the Winter League. Difficulties were encountered with the Invitation Greensomes competition for George Taylor's new trophy. The occasion was marred by slow play perhaps exacerbated by a large entry list. In future this would be a two-day event covering Saturday and Sunday.

Gilbert Dempster. Undoubtedly the most significant event of 1993 was the retiral of Gilbert Dempster from the post of Secretary/Treasurer of the Club. He had served in this position since 1981 and there was a sense of loss when in April 1993 he announced his intention to retire. For 12 years he had been an omnipresent figure at the Club devoted to its members' welfare. In his final year he had been Captain of the Golf Secretaries Organisation. A dinner was held in Mr and Mrs Dempsters' honour attended by the Earl of Wemyss, past Captains and Board members and a presentation from the Testimonial Fund was made at the annual prize-giving.

A total of 75 applications were received for the vacancy and Neil Robertson who had been Secretary at Thornton Golf Club, was appointed.

1994. By early January the drainage problem at the eighth had been resolved. Contractors using power jets had cleared the blockage.
In the clubhouse there had been difficulty with the central heating boilers over Christmas and it was decided to replace them as soon as practicable. A significant change at the instigation of Alistair Thomson the retiring Match and Handicap Convener was the substitution of wine for bottles of whisky on the tables at the men's dinner. In the clubhouse the cellar refrigeration for real ale had been installed and the contract for the installation of new central heating boilers awarded.

As Jim Mackenzie's Captaincy neared its end, review of the rental fell due. A letter from the factor proposing a significant increase was received by the Club. Associated with this was the suggested allocation of a proportion of tee times to a central booking system which was planned by the Estate for certain of its golf courses.

Against this background, the 1994 AGM was held. It proved to have some turbulent moments. The arithmetic of the report on the numbers of ladies was questioned. The condition of the course was criticised and the Champions Board deficiencies were raised again. The new Captain, Bill

Towards the end of the year a problem of flooding at the bunkers and fairways of the 8th hole arose. There appeared to be a blockage in the drains in the vicinity of the 10th tee, where there had been ponds in the twenties.

163

Thomson, undertook to address these matters

The situation with regard to VAT monies to be refunded was explained to members. Possible treatments of such refunds were described. The VAT refund finally settled at £85,000. The money would be devoted to improvement of the course and Clubhouse facilities.

One of the first matters addressed by the Directors after the AGM was the return of Paul Wardell from his post in the South. It was decided that he would be placed on attachment to the Club.

The Directors then considered the Head Greenkeeper's report. Greens had been top-dressed, the irrigation system made ready for the season and 150 trees planted, mainly pine and lodge pole pine.

To assist with the rent negotiations Mr Nigel Law of Montagu Evans had been appointed, and had attended meetings of the rent review sub-committee. Alternative offers were agreed upon to be made to the Estate depending on whether tee-times were conceded or not. The Board gave these proposals their support and they were communicated to the Estate together with notification that the Club hoped to discuss a new lease or extension of the existing one. These counter proposals did not find favour with the Estate. Firstly there was no intention to sell the course in the foreseeable future, and it was not timely to discuss the duration or renewal of the lease. In further response the Golf Club tendered an improved offer to the Estate. This was not accepted. Nor were counter proposals from the Estate considered acceptable by the Club. However early in October the Trustees of the Estate made a further proposal which the Board, after discussion and a vote, decided could be offered to the members for decision. A postal vote was arranged to be preceded by an explanatory meeting with interested members. The outcome was a substantial majority of members in favour of accepting the Trustees' final offer and the matter was concluded in early December.

Meantime much had been happening inside and outside the Clubhouse:

A formal Seniors' Section had been set up for members aged over 60. Hugo Galloway had accepted the task of Convener of this section.

In the Clubhouse the two new central heating boilers had been installed and were working smoothly. The ladies locker room had been refurbished and new furniture chosen for the ladies lounge and board room. The Captains board had been renovated at last, with a system of brass plates on top of the hardwood surface. Having reviewed the effects of the relaxation of the dress regulations in the previous year, the Board felt confident that a further relaxation could be accomplished without undesirable effects. Accordingly it was decided to relax standards for the whole day in the lounge and until 5.00 p.m. on weekdays in the Dining Room.

The more dramatic developments were outwith the clubhouse:

On the greens, the adverse weather conditions had persisted. Fertiliser application had had to be delayed due to cold weather and greens were bumpy because of slow growth. The battle to maintain the ageing sprinkler system in operation continued, buying new parts where available and cannibalising where not. Fairway sprinklers had been deprived of water in favour of tees and greens. In November the resignation of the Assistant Head Greenkeeper, John Kay was received. John had joined the greenstaff as a driver originally. His intelligence and application had taken him to Assistant Head of the greenkeeping staff and now he was leaving to take charge of the Musselburgh nine hole course, said to be the oldest course in the world still in regular play. Shortly afterwards Craig Hildersley announced that he too was resigning to take up a post with Hibernian Football Club. Suddenly the Golf Club was lacking both top greenkeeping men. It was decided that the Head Greenkeeper post would be filled first and advertisements were placed. Eleven applications were received. Meantime on the course, sub-airing of the summer tees had been completed, greens and aprons had been slit for the third time and fairways for the second. The fourth application of fungicide for fusarium had been applied. Work was about to start on the returfing of the 3rd tee and the ladies 12th and 14th tees. Detailed plans for replacement and upgrading of the irrigation system at a cost of £51,000 had been received from one contractor. An alternative quotation from another was awaited.

Back in April, the playing season had got off to a fine start when Gwen Smith won the East Lothian Girls competition which had been held at Longniddry. In the club Championship Steven Thomson came through again and David Wojtacha took the 'B' trophy. The Ladies Championship was won by Julia Denholm, whilst Gwen Smith triumphed again in the Girls. Donald Christian won the Boys Championship. In the Longniddry 36 hole Open Championship, J Noon of Musselburgh won with a 73 and an equal course record of 63. The Longniddry boys won the East Lothian Team Stroke Play Competition and came a creditable second in the League.

In the Clubhouse as the year advanced, the effects of the greater relaxation of the dress regulations began to be seen. Bar income and gaming machine takings rose. Attendance at social events improved and among other events organised by Social Convener, Stuart Hunter, a 60s/70s disco proved to be a great success. Further impetus was provided by the installation of Sky TV in the back bar.

In December, the Board noted with pleasure the appointment of Allen Davis as Junior Convener for East Lothian.

1995. Attention in the new year was immediately focused upon the greens and Greenkeeping staff situation. The first development was the appointment of Ken Anderson to the post of Head Greenkeeper. Ken had been Head Greenkeeper at Sheringham in Norfolk and prior to that had

Two new trophies were presented to the Club in 1994: Mrs Coldham and her sister donated a cup in memory of their father Dick Sproul. The cup was named the 'Dick Sproul Memorial Trophy' to be awarded for the Club Seniors best scratch score. The second new trophy was the Rose Bowl presented by Gilbert Dempster. His interest in the Juniors and encouragement of them had always been evident, and his gift reflected this. His Rosebowl Trophy was presented for the winners of the Adult/Junior Stableford Foursomes.

worked at Newmachar in Aberdeen. Philip Holmes, already on the Longniddry staff, was appointed Assistant Head Greenkeeper. Work was continuing on levelling and returfing the 5th and 7th tees. By mid February all the proposals for the new irrigation system were forward. The recommendation from the Green Committee which the Board ratified was to accept the proposals from Watermation at a cost of £65,000 plus VAT. Work would commence at the end of February.

AGM. At the AGM before the end of February, the Captain Bill Thomson gave details of the changes to greenkeeping staff and of the decision to replace the irrigation system. He drew attention to the fact that once again rainfall during the summer had been low (1/3 of the long-term average).

Mike Robinson and George Morgan stepped down at the AGM. Mike Robinson a very able golfer himself, had been Junior Convener for the previous two years. Under his tutelage the Juniors won two major events in 1994 and were runners up in the East Lothian Junior League. George Morgan had been House Convener during a period of exceptionally high financial activity. The VAT changes, the rent negotiations, the introduction of the new Club Secretary and the appointment of new Auditors had all occurred during his period of office. The Club had been fortunate to have had his advice and counsel during these changes. The new Directors were Malcolm Graham, Norman Elliot and Douglas Gemmell. Unfortunately, shortly afterwards, like Stuart Hunter, Douglas Gemmell was obliged to resign because of his business commitments. His place on the Board was taken by Andrew Glasgow. Susan Hume had retired after a most effective two years as Lady Captain and Susan Bell replaced her with Eileen Dundas becoming Lady Vice Captain. Subsequently Robert MacKay succeeded Hugo Galloway as Senior Convener.

The Course. As the spring approached members began to detect a significant improvement in the course. In particular the greens began to play true and fast. The report from the STRI was circulated. It pointed out that on the fairways rooting was still poor and continuation of aeration and verti-draining was necessary. Nevertheless, the course was improving. At the end of April members were given the opportunity to comment on the course at the finish of their medal round. The general view was that members were mostly very satisfied with the condition of the greens particularly for the time of year. Some months later wild orchids were seen growing again in the little dell beside the 12th fairway after an absence of some years.

The Clubhouse. In the clubhouse plans were prepared for improved ventilation in the kitchen and renovation of the men's toilets. A special working party directed by the Captain was set up to progress the layout and selection of materials for the new toilets. After competitive quotations had been considered the contract was placed with local builders Reywood. Work was programmed to begin early in January 1996. In the ladies lounge, Sky TV was installed.

The Social Side.   There were some novelties on the social side, where Andrew Glasgow had taken over from Dougie Gemmell. A pub quiz night run expertly by Allen Davis was held in March and proved to be very successful. Telescopes were hired to view the Tall Ships Race in July. The clubhouse was an excellent vantage point but the morning was overcast and windless. Persistence paid off because after the delayed start, a clearance occurred and the ships, although far across to the north side of the Forth, made a brave showing. In early November the Gilbert and Sullivan Society of Edinburgh entertained members in the course of publicising their forthcoming Iolanthe production at the King's Theatre. Through the year two dances and two discos had been held. All were successful particularly the one featuring the Club's own Danny Gillan. There had also been the provision of background piano music by various local young music students.

Competitions.   Early in the year administration of the men's medals was greatly eased by the introduction of a computer-based score input system which had been tried out the previous year. The competitive season got off to a fine start with Hilary Monaghan winning the East Lothian Championship at North Berwick. She followed this up by winning the Scottish Ladies Amateur Championship at Portpatrick. The first Longniddry winner since Doris Park in 1936, she came home to an ad hoc champagne reception in the clubhouse. But the ladies were not done yet. Joyce Hunnam and Caroline Hunter won the National Playing Fields Scottish Foursomes and with Hilary were selected to play for the East Lothian County Team. Susan Bell the Lady Captain, subsequently presented Hilary with an engraved crystal bowl. Finally on the female performances, Lesley Nicholson of Haddington broke the ladies course record with a scratch 69. Meantime the ladies course had been remeasured and an SSS of 73 confirmed with a corresponding winter figure of 72.

The Club Championship finished with Donald G R Hunter the winner for the men and Susan Bell for the ladies. Not since 1929 had the current Lady Captain won the Ladies Championship. The men's 'B' winner was Robin Sharp and the Boys', Jamie Peacocke. The winner of the Girls Championship (played late in the season) was Heather Robb. Three juniors were nominated for extra tuition during the year: G Harris, S Kerr and J Blackwood. On the Mixed front, Sandy and Wilma Gilmour got to the Regional Final of the Benson and Hedges Mixed Foursomes Competition. A new trophy was presented to the Club by Mrs Ray McVey in memory of her husband, past captain, Gus. The trophy was presented to the best net score in the men's Handicap Open, won in this first year by David Robson, a

In the course of the year some important anniversaries and a retirement were recognised. John and Jean Kennedy celebrated 30 years with the Club at the beginning of March. The Captain made a presentation of crystal to them. A little later in the year Cristine Paxton completed 25 years service and a presentation was made to her at the Annual Prize-giving. Isobel Munro had also completed 30 years service and this achieved, she decided to retire. A presentation was made to her by the Captain and she and Mr Munro were guests at a celebratory lunch afterwards in the clubhouse.

member of the Club's greenstaff.

Artisans. Towards the end of the year it began to appear that it would be possible for the Artisans to be fully incorporated within the club. A joint working party directed by Allen Davis had devised a formula whereby Artisan members would be accepted into the main Club but persons already on the waiting list would not wait longer in consequence. The Artisan Club would remain in existence within the main Club.

Raymond Russell. A final pleasing note was that Raymond Russell who turned professional in 1994, had secured his tour card. He gained 19th place out of a total of 40 with the following scores: 70, 73, 71, 76, 71 and 72, total 433. Raymond had also come equal second in the Scottish PGA Masters on 275 one stroke behind P Lawrie.

End of Term. Bill Thomson completed his term of office as Captain at the AGM in February 1996, the beginning of the Club's Jubilee Year. He could look back on an eventful and successful period of office. It had begun with a new Club Secretary in place and continued with important and difficult rent review negotiations. These were conducted with skill and patience and the outcome found general acceptance with the membership. Significant Clubhouse improvements had been carried out culminating in the renovation of the men's toilets by Reywood Ltd which provided four individual shower cubicles. In parallel with this the final relaxation of dress regulations for the lounge encouraged healthy attendances throughout an enhanced social programme. The most outstanding achievements however were in the undoubted improvement in the condition of the course, the new irrigation contract, and the appointment of Ken Anderson as Head Greenkeeper.

As Gordon Bonnington the incoming Captain acknowledged the two years of Bill Thomson's Captaincy had seen significant advances on all fronts: Course, Clubhouse and staff. The Club was in good shape on the brink of its 75th year.

From the 17th fairway looking over one of Bob Anderson's plantations to Port Seton and Edinburgh under Arthur's Seat. The clubhouse and course from below the 15th tee in an Autumn evening.

The 18th green against the backdrop of sea buckthorn and the loom of Fife beyond.

CHAPTER VII

ASSOCIATED CLUBS

1. The Ladies Club

The records of the Ladies Club are more complete than those of the main Club. They display right down the years to the present day a wealth of really excellent lady golfers. The Longniddry Ladies Club was formally convened on 10th September 1923.

Inaugural Meeting. Mr Connor took the chair at this first meeting; there were 16 members present.

Ethel Jupp was elected to be first Captain. The Jupps had just moved to Longniddry that year from Edinburgh, following a post-war stint in London. Miss Emma H Sawers who lived at Longniddry House was elected Honorary Secretary, a post which she was to hold for 30 years. In October 1925, two years after this first meeting, the Ladies Club agreed to join the Ladies Golf Union.

It has already been suggested that the outstanding lady golfer Charlotte Stevenson (Mrs J B Watson, Mrs E C Beddows) was one of the earliest members of the Club. The details of her golfing career are given later. Also of formidable golfing stature though their affiliation dates may have been slightly later were the cousins Doris and 'Katie' Park. They came of a high golfing pedigree:

The Parks of Musselburgh. The following account is taken from 'Who's Who' in the 1971 edition of the "Golfers' Handbook".

"The Parks are famous in the annals of Golf for the numerous money matches they played - the two brothers, Willie and Mungo, and a son of the former – Willie Junior. ...... The Parks have been associated with Musselburgh for over 400 years and old Willie Park had the distinction of winning the Open Championship in the first year of its institution – 1860, and he won it again in 1863, 1866 and 1875. His brother Mungo won it in 1874. For twenty years old Willie Park had a standing challenge in "Bell's Life" London to play any man in the world for £100 a side, and he was always ready to defend his challenge. ...... Willie Park Junior won the Open Championship in 1887 and 1889. ...... Willie Park Junior was perhaps the deadliest putter the game has ever known. He reckoned himself stone dead at two yards. ...... The third generation of this great golfing family has sustained a prominent golf association by Miss Doris Park (Mrs Aylmer Porter) a daughter of Willie Park who has a distinguished record in ladies international and championship golf."

The Ladies at the first meeting were:
Mrs Banks
Mrs J R Alexander
Miss J Park
Miss Denholm
Mrs H Alexander
Mrs Mungo Park
Mrs Mather
Mrs Wright
Mrs G Jupp
Mrs J E Dods
Mrs Fernie
Mrs J Shields
Miss K J Wishart
Miss Kellie
Miss E H Sawers
Miss Inglis

The Golfers
Handbook's entry for
Doris reads:
*"Clubs: Worplesdon,
Gullane, Longniddry.
Scottish Ladies
Champion 1936,
runner-up 1929,30,31.
Midlothian Ladies
Champion 1928, 29,
30, 31 and 33. East of
Scotland Ladies
Champion 1933.
Runner-up 1931 and
38. British Ladies: won
Qualifying
Competition 1933,
runner-up 1937. Played
for Scotland on 13
occasions. Played for
Great Britain against
USA 1932. Played for
Great Britain against
France 1932, 33 and
38."*

The Golfers Handbook
for 1971 gives Katie's
CV as follows:
*"b. Edinburgh 7.7.07
Clubs: Gullane,
Longniddry, Kilspindie
Midlothian Ladies
Championship:
Winner 1933, 34, 35,
36, 38, 47, 48, 51, 53,
56, 58. Runner-up East
of Scotland Ladies
1933, 48, 52.
Semi-Finalist 1931, 34,
47. Scottish Ladies
Runner-up 1939.
Semi-Finalist 1947, 48,
58. In last eight 1935,
37, 51. British Ladies
Championship
Last eight 1937.
Scottish Internationalist
1939, 47, 48, 51, 53.
Hon. Member
Midlothian County
Ladies Golf
Association"*

Doris Park. It is not certain that Doris Park was a founder member of Longniddry Golf Club. She lived in one of the cottages south of the railway at Canty Hall. Her name is absent from the list of those who attended the inaugural meeting of the ladies club in September 1923. Whilst Doris may not have been a founder member she certainly joined the Club at an early stage because she was Ladies Captain in 1929 and champion the same year. This feat was not repeated until Susan Bell's success in 1995.

Miss Katie Park (Mrs W C Ritchie). Miss 'Katie' Park was Doris' cousin. Like Doris her name is not included in the attendance list of that first meeting of the Ladies Club. She was elected Captain as late as 1960, 31 years after Doris although having been born in 1907, she must have been contemporaneous with her. She was a full Scottish International. She lived in Haddington.

Ladies Competitions. The first Ladies Spring Meeting was held on 2nd May 1924. At this time the SSS for the ladies was 80. The award for the first prize, a challenge bowl was gifted by Emma's brother, Bailie Tom Sawers. The trophy is now called the Emma Sawers Cup. In that first year it was won by Miss F J Wishart, who was to become Lady Captain in 1928. It seems that at that time, at their Spring, Summer and Autumn meetings the Ladies, after a medal round in the morning, played foursomes in the afternoon.

Although these various meetings had begun in 1924, and a hole and hole competition was introduced in 1927, there appears to have been no ladies championship as such until 1929. In that year a championship competition was held for a new trophy presented by Stuart Forsyth . It was won by Miss Doris Park who was to take the trophy a further three times, namely 1936, 1938 and 1946. Another cousin, Miss I M V Park won in 1934.

The first Ladies versus Gents match took place in July 1931. All played off the men's tees. The normal rule of 3/4 of the difference in handicaps applied, but the ladies received 6 shots in addition. The Board minute discreetly stops there, and the ladies records do not refer to the event. However, the Haddingtonshire Courier in an act of betrayal reveals that the ladies won by 91/2 matches to 51/2!

In 1931 the final of the Midlothian Women's Championship was fought out at Dalmahoy in miserable conditions, between Doris and 'Katie' Park. Doris won. Subsequently at Longniddry Doris was beaten in her turn in the final of the East of Scotland Ladies Championships by Mrs J B Watson (Charlotte Beddows of course). Doris won the Scottish Ladies Championship in 1936 having been runner-up in 1929, 1930 and 1931.

Royal National Lifeboat Institution. In the autumn of 1931 the Longniddry Ladies held what appears to be their first open meeting in aid of the RNLI.

The Haddingtonshire Courier of 25th September 1931 reports as follows:"*A Ladies Open Meeting consisting of a medal round in the morning, and a flag foursomes competition in the afternoon was carried through by courtesy of Longniddry Golf Club on Tuesday. Mrs Gore-Greenshields, and Miss E H Sawers, Secretary of the Longniddry Ladies Club, were responsible for the arrangements. 24 couples left the tee among whom were some leading Scottish women players. The weather was cold and the prizes went to Miss Doris Park along with Mrs J B Watson (Mrs Beddows) and Mrs R Wallace Williamson, whose 85 was the best scratch score. Mrs JN Duncan returned an 86. Better known as Miss Mary Wood who in the previous 2 years had won the ladies Open Championship of India, this was her first appearance since returning from abroad.*"

The tradition of Lifeboat Day in the Longniddry Ladies section has continued for 65 years only interrupted by the Second World War. It is still a very important event in the ladies calendar, with contributions to the Lifeboat Fund steadily rising year by year. The men get involved too with such as Dan Abbot, Alex Livingstone and David Smart assisting in administering the competitions. Proudly displayed in the ladies lounge is a RNLI scroll presented in recognition of the contribution to the Fund of Longniddry's lady golfers.

Below left: May 1973: Mrs AD Sproull accepting the Certificate from the RNLI.

Below right: Lifeboat Day 1981: Miss MS Smith, Mrs NC Osborne, Mr SW Laird (Captain), Mrs BC Cooper (Lady Captain), Miss K Rose, Mrs R B Cadzow, Mrs M Smart, Mrs F Morgan, Mrs T Porteous.

The Curtis and Vagliano Cups. The 1931 Daily Telegraph report is of particular interest:

'*Years of scheming and planning by Margaret Curtis bore fruit when the USGA and Britain's LGU agreed to play biennial matches. The French were to join in when they were able. Andre Vagliano presented the silver Vagliano Cup for annual competition between England (sic) and France. Sir Ernest Holderness, the former Amateur Champion opposed such matches. He said that a married woman with young children could not be expected to win titles. "It would be grounds for divorce".*

In 1932 Doris Park partnered by Stuart Forsyth reached the final round of the National Mixed Foursomes Competition at Worplesdon, Surrey. They were defeated at this last hurdle by Miss Joyce (What train?) Wethered - later to become Lady Heathcote - Amory - and the Honourable Michael Scott of St George's Hall.

Early in 1932 Doris Park was picked by the LGU to play against America at Wentworth in May. In June of the following year Doris partnered by Miss Graham played for Britain versus France at Weybridge. They won their match on the 15th green. *'Their golf being much too steady for their opponents'* says the Haddingtonshire Courier.

Also in 1933 Longniddry held what now seems an unusual mixed foursomes event. Each player was allowed one club only. The clubs were however interchangeable between partners. It is recorded that most couples favoured a 2 iron and a mashie and that Mrs Banks and Mr Gibbs won with an 84. Whether a putter was allowed in addition is not said – probably not.

There were of course occasional debates, even arguments perhaps, with authority in the form of Mr Connor or the LGU: The ladies minutes of 16th May 1929 for example record Mr Connor's refusal to increase the grant from the main Club to the ladies. Not only did he refuse to increase it from £15, he reduced it to £10 in 1936 just before his death. (His successor at the Estate Office Hunter Murray did the decent thing in 1937 and agreed to a grant of £20.)

And there was the matter of procedure: The ladies minute of 11th August 1931 is justifiably indignant: Mr Connor had, on his own initiative admitted 2 ladies without reference to the ladies committee on the grounds that the entrants were wives of members. The ladies committee understandably were not amused. They declared that all applications for lady membership should come through them.

Dealings with the LGU were chiefly to do with the SSS for the course. In 1930 the SSS was established at 80 but if a proposal to move the 9th tee were to be adopted (presumably to enable ladies to carry the fearsome cross fairway bunker off the tee) it would reduce to 79. By 1934 the LGU were stating that their Scratch Score Committee had fixed the Longniddry SSS to be 78 as from the 1st July 1935. By August 1935 the LGU had reduced it once more to 77 in spite of the new 6th hole being 40 yards longer than the old one. The Longniddry ladies committee challenged the LGU to come and play the course and see for themselves. However the LGU refused to budge at least at first: they added another stroke a year later.

It was a proud moment in 1934 when Nancy Jupp from Elcho Road won the British Girls Championship at the age of 13 both the youngest and smallest ever champion at that time. She is described as a tiny figure beside her clubs. She had gone to the Championship intending to caddy for her sister Rhoda, and decided to enter at the last moment.

A formidable mixed foursomes pair who played at Longniddry were Mr and Mrs G Seymour Noon who defeated their opponents in the 1932 Club Championship by 9 and 8 with the third hole halved.

Of course the Longniddry Ladies were not unanimous about SSS themselves. The minute of 12th August 1930 refers to a letter from Mrs Wallace Williamson which says "Mrs J B Watson, Mrs Holm and Miss Purvis Russell Montgomery all thought that the 14th hole (576 yards at this time) should be a bogey 5. I have told the LGU this. I said I thought it a very hard 5, but as these three champions thought it should not be more, I felt I had to tell them so. We may lose one off the SSS".

Kath Rose, now Vice-President of the Ladies Club, and Marjorie Douglas remember being in the guard of honour who met Nancy at Drem station on her return and held their golf clubs above her head as she alighted (Page 88). Others in the reception committee were Douglas Teesdale, Norman Campbell and Andrew Purdon. According to Duncan Herd the lone tree in the grass triangle at the top of Links Road, which carries the lights at Christmas, was planted to commemorate Nancy's win.

Nancy went on to become a leading golf journalist, operating from Oklahoma, where she took up tournament management. At the peak of her career she was hired by various clubs to conduct their championships - setting up the committees, organising ticket sales, advertising and recruiting and training on each occasion up to 1500 volunteer workers. She is now a lifetime guest of the golf club in Tulsa, playing off a handicap of 16.

Nancy Jupp a Mary Erskine pupil amazed the golfing experts. She was described as a 'prodigy' and 'wizard'. 'The impossible happened' said RH Montmorency the international golfer who refereed the Girls Championship Final.

In mid 1935 the Ladies SSS for Longniddry was reduced to 77, and Stuart Forsyth got to the finals of the National Mixed foursomes at Worplesdon once more. On this occasion his partner was Jean Hamilton. For the second time though, Stuart's team was defeated. The year also saw the Scottish Ladies Amateur Championship won by Doris Park. She defeated Miss P R Montgomery at the 19th hole at Turnberry. Doris was presented with a commemorative pearl and diamond brooch by Longniddry Ladies and shortly afterwards she and Charlotte Watson (Beddows) were selected to play for Great Britain in the Curtis Cup.

At the outbreak of the war in 1939 an emergency committee of the Lady Captain, Mrs J J Latta and of course the Secretary, Emma Sawers was formed, to look after affairs for the duration of the conflict. Two competitions were held both in 1940. One was for the RNLI as in the past, and the other was in support of the Red Cross.

On 16th February 1946 the first Post war AGM of the Ladies Club was held. At that time only 15 holes were in play, so the 18 were made up by playing the 1st and 2nd and the 15th a second time. At this meeting the ladies adopted a new constitution. Miss S M L Millar was elected Captain and the Countess of Wemyss kindly accepted the Honorary Presidency of the Club, a position she held until her death in 1989.

In 1938 the first girls International match against England was held. Nancy Jupp captained Scotland. Her sister Rhoda was also in the team. The match was played at Stoke Poges, Slough and at one stage a thunder storm swept the course reducing the number of holes played. Scotland won. Meantime back at Longniddry, Doris Park was beaten 4 and 2 by Jessie Anderson in the final of the East of Scotland Ladies Championship.

Ladies Open Golf Championship. In June 1947 the Ladies Open Golf Championship was held at Gullane. The format was knock-out match-play. Longniddry players took the opportunity to compete but were not too successful that year:

Annice Latta lost 3 and 2 to Mrs Bolton of Royal Portrush.
Mrs Beddows was beaten by Mrs Wyllie of Lee-on-Solent, and
Nancy Jupp was beaten by Miss R Woodeward of the USA.

The final was won by 'Babe' Zaharias, the first occasion the trophy had been taken by a transatlantic player.

The Longniddry Ladies SSS was reduced to 76 in 1948. Presumably this reflects the reconstruction of the course and its return to 18 holes. A year later it is recorded that there were three evening meetings arranged between the men's and ladies' Clubs each year. An open meeting was also held by Longniddry Ladies in aid of the Scottish Ladies Golfing Association International Match. The final took place on a Tuesday. There were 126 entries but half of them scratched because of the exceptionally heavy rain on that day.

In 1953 after 30 years of devoted service as Secretary and Treasurer Miss Emma Sawers resigned and was elected to Honorary Membership. To replace her Mrs A Arnot was appointed Honorary Secretary with Mrs R B Cadzow as Honorary Treasurer. At this time also the annual RNLI event which had been suspended after 1940 was resumed.In 1964 the format of mixed foursomes play at the Club was established. Men would tee off at the odd holes and the ladies at the even.

The Ladies SSS was further reduced to 74 in 1969.

Two years later, Longniddry hosted the Ladies Home International, when England won. The proceedings are described in the Golf Illustrated of 16th September 1971. Although Longniddry's Nancy Jupp reported frequently in the publication, the article was by the regular writer, Enid Wilson. She seems, from the tone of her report given below, to have got out of bed on the wrong side that morning: *The real winners of the Home Internationals were the greens at Longniddry. Only twice during the three days did I see chips end close enough to the hole to be 'gimmies'. And as for the putting, some of that had to be witnessed to be believed. Admittedly the greens were full of borrows, and each morning covered with dew that dried out in the sunshine, so they were constantly changing pace. But golfers who have been considered good enough to represent their countries should have met such conditions frequently enough to have some idea of dealing with them. I could find no excuse for the former champion who left herself ten yards short of a green, had to chip uphill, and went so boldly for the pin, her ball came to rest on the back edge of the putting surface. She had played that hole at least eight times during the week. Nor does one expect to see yet another former champion on a green for one, following a good tee shot to within twelve feet of the pin, by putting fifteen feet past it.*

What the Curtis Cup selectors who were there, thought of such goings on, they will doubtless keep strictly private, but their hearts can hardly have been filled with gladness by the overall performances of the players within fifty yards of the hole.

With six conspicuous absentees, Michelle Walker, the British champion,

The East of Scotland Ladies Championship was held at Longniddry in 1949. Jean Donald beat Mrs Beddows in the final. The championship returned again in 1952. This time Jean Donald lost at the 21st to Mrs R T Peel.

A further East of Scotland Championship was held at Longniddry in 1967. This was won by Mrs McIntosh.

Abroad, Nancy Jupp gained the Women's Amateur Championship of Norway in 1953 with a 12 and 10 victory over Mrs Annie Berg.

Dinah Oxley the English champion, and Mary Everard kept out of the English team owing to their impending departure for the Commonwealth Tournament in New Zealand, and Belle Robertson the Scottish Champion, Joan Lawrence and Jillian Hutton, of Scotland also prevented from playing for the same reason, there was a golden opportunity for some of the lesser lights to assert themselves, and in particular for Ireland to take the scalps of the other countries, but, in all my experience of Home Internationals, going back not far short of fifty years, I have never known such a lack of atmosphere. There was none of the tension normally associated with this event.

England were further weakened by the absence of Sally Barber, and the Scots for some inexplicable reason decided to do without Marjorie Fowler, finalist in their championship this year. Next to Belle Robertson she is their most experienced golfer, and it would not be unreasonable to suggest that her omission from their side cost them the championship.

Continuing in critical vein, once more we saw the accustomed messing about for the first five or six holes of every game in the mornings, when all were like vintage motor cars on a cold and frosty morning. The first twelve drives, on ample, wide open fairways in calm conditions were pathetic, only one out of the dozen ending on the middle of the course.

And as an epilogue to this catalogue of indifference, an observation on some states of minds, was unconsciously summed up by one player who got home on the last green, and then remarked, "I was determined to win." That is what they were all there to do, but from the absence of sharpness in the golf, it was problematical if this has registered with all concerned.

England were defending the International Shield, and they retained it by defeating Wales by eight games to one, Scotland by six games to three, and Ireland by six and a half games to two and a half. Scotland finished second, they beat Ireland by eight games to one, and Wales by seven games to two. Ireland again relegated Wales to last place by defeating them by five and a half games to three and a half............"

Mrs Beddows. Mrs E C Beddows died in 1976 after a wonderful career in ladies golf. Originally as Charlotte Stevenson and then as Mrs J B Watson she had been elected Honorary Member of Longniddry Golf Club in 1950 and Honorary Vice-President in 1963. She was a member of the 1932 Curtis Cup Team and Scottish Ladies Champion in 1920, 1921, 1922 and 1929. At Longniddry in 1931 she beat Doris Park 3 and 1 in the final of the East Lothian Ladies Championship and she won the Longniddry Ladies Championship on six occasions between 1949 and 1962. Her career demonstrates so well the difficulty of following ladies through the years of tournaments and marriage. Originally she was Charlotte Stevenson whose family owned a drapers shop in Princes Street at the corner of Hanover

Of course Enid Wilson was a character. According to the Daily Telegraph she had deliberately got herself thrown out of school in 1927 for swearing so that she could get down to serious golf right away. She wore trousers (1931), smoked cigarettes, was very much her own woman at all times, and remained firmly of the opinion that their war service and not the suffragette movement had won votes for women.

The Granger Cup.
The Granger Cup Competition is held in association with the Scottish Ladies Championship. In order to compete at least three ladies from the Club must enter the Championship. In May 1975 the Longniddry team consisting of Mrs P G Jack, Mrs R Lawrie and Miss S MacNamara won the trophy for the first time.

Right: Mrs E C Beddows.

Far right: Mrs E C Beddows being congratulated by Club Captain Tom Porteous having won the Frank Morran Trophy in 1964. Others in the photograph from left to right are: Frank Morran, Mrs Babs Thomson, Gordon Durward, Norman Osborne, Joe Sykes.

For some time there had been increasing concern about the proximity of the ladies 12th tee to the fast traffic of the shore road. There was considerable debate and some indecision. Eventually in September 1978 the tee was moved in front of the men's.

In 1980 the ladies succeeded in having the left hand fairway bunker at the 8th hole filled in.

Street. Then she became Mrs J B Watson having married Jamie Watson who owned an optician's business (possibly what is now Lizars) in Shandwick Place. After his decease she married Brigadier Beddows, thus becoming Mrs E C Beddows. In the latter capacity she would arrive at the course in her chauffeur-driven limousine and the chauffeur would then convert himself into a caddy for the occasion. Her golfing CV is presented by the "Golfers' Handbook" as follows:

Mrs Charlotte Beddows, formerly Mrs J B Watson
b. Edinburgh 22.10.1887
Clubs: Hon. Member St. Rule, Murrayfield, Craigmillar Park, North Berwick, Longniddry, Gullane Ladies and Grim's Dyke.
Won Scottish Ladies Championship 1920, 21, 22, 29. Runner-up 1923, 50.
Bronze Medallist 1905, 13, 27, 30, 31. East of Scotland Champion 1931,32.Runner-up 1936, 49.
Won Ladies Veterans Championship 1947, 49, 50, 51.
Represented Scottish Ladies in Home International Matches 1913, 14, 21, 22, 23, 27, 29, 30, 31, 32, 33, 34, 35, 36, 37, 39, 47, 48, 49, 50, 51.
Great Britain v France 1931, 32. Great Britain v USA 1932 Captain
Great Britain v France 1939.
Captained Scottish Team 1921, 22, 23, 30, 31.
Won Gibson Cup 1911.
Hon. Vice-President Edinburgh and District Professional Golfing Association.
Has played County Golf 1909-1966.
Awarded Frank Moran Trophy 1964.
Other sports: played hockey for Scotland 1905, 1912."

It was in 1976 that it was agreed that the Business Ladies should play their medal on the Saturday preceding the Ladies Medal.

In 1980 to ensure that players in the ladies major competitions suffered no harassment it was decided that the tee would be closed 30 minutes before the ladies first tee time. Subsequently in 1993 it was agreed that the ladies starting times for medals would be preceded by a gap of at least 15 minutes to ensure a reasonable clearance.

Dr Rose Donaldson. In 1983, Rose Donaldson passed away. She had succeeded Charlotte Beddows as Honorary Vice-President. Rose's record in the Longniddry Ladies Championships was even better than Charlotte's. Rose won the Championship in 1961 and again in 1963 and thereafter on 8 successive occasions until 1971. Kath Rose succeeded Dr Donaldson as Honorary Vice-President.

Patricia Lees. So far, the only other person to approach Rose Donaldson's performance has been Miss Patricia Lees who won the Ladies Club Championship first in 1972 and then again on 8 occasions between 1979 and 1990. Patricia had two other important victories between these dates, both at Longniddry. She won the Babe Zaharias Ladies Open with a net 73 (handicap 4) in 1984 in front of sixteen American ladies travelling with the Curtis Cup Team, some of them past Curtis Cup players themselves. Patricia followed this by winning the East Lothian Women's Championship in 1986. Incidentally in 1952 it was Patricia's father who broke the Longniddry course record by 3 strokes with a round of 65 including a brilliant inward half of 30, in the Lothian's Teams Tournament.

In 1986, Longniddry hosted the British Seniors Ladies Championship. The winner Mrs P Riddiford of Royal Ashdown Forest stayed with Kath Rose during the competition. Mrs P Riddiford won with a total of 154 for two rounds. It was this year also that the Ladies Section received a bequest of £200 on the sad death of Miss Sophie McEwan. It was decided to dedicate the money to a suitable trophy.

1989. Lady Captain Audrey Laird and Lady Vice Captain Terry Reeckie with John and Jean Kennedy and Cristine Paxton.

Countess of Wemyss. On the sad death in 1989 of the Countess of Wemyss who had supported the Ladies section so steadfastly for many years, Lord Wemyss himself took over the presidency of the Club.

1992 saw the beginning of the renovation of the ladies accommodation with the painting and carpeting of the ladies powder room and toilets.

1995 was a remarkable year for the Ladies Club: On the 9th May Lesley Nicolson of Haddington established a new Ladies Course record of 69.

Hilary Monaghan the 1995 Scottish Match Play and Under 21 Stroke Play Champion

The summer of 1990 brought good news. Joyce Hunnam had been selected to play for the County and Hilary Monaghan had won the Connachan Cup. Mrs Quinn (Miss S Macnamara) having recovered from illness had been made Convener of the Scottish Ladies Golf Association and had been appointed to the Ladies Golf Union with responsibility for training.

Lesley Nicolson's score card reads:
Out 4, 5, 4, 3, 4, 2, 5, 4, 3 – 34
In 4, 4, 4, 3, 4, 5, 3, 4, 4 – 35 Total 69

Hilary Monaghan. In that year also Club member Hilary Monaghan accomplished a succession of triumphs. She won the East Lothian County Championship at North Berwick beating three other international caps on the way. She was the 1995 winner of the Ness Open 36 hole event at Inverness. The Laing Jeweller Order of Merit 1995 was topped by Hilary, whilst at Lanark she returned a 68 to secure the Ladies course record at 6 under. Hilary was capped for Scotland playing in the 1995 European Ladies Team Championship in Milan where Scotland came second. She won the Scottish Ladies 1995 Match Play Championship at Portpatrick at the same time picking up the under 21 stroke play championship run concurrently.

The following year Hilary represented Scotland in the 1996 Ladies Home Internationals played at Longniddry. An account of the match is given in Chapter VIII The Jubilee Year.

This concludes a brief account of the Longniddry Ladies Club down the years. It is noticeable that the level of ability is at least as good in 1996 as in 1921. The Club began with a Scottish Ladies Champion in their ranks: 75 years later they have another. There is also still to tell the story of the Ladies Artisans, however the Male Artisans Club was established some years before the Ladies and claims chronological precedence.

2. The Longniddry Artisans Golf Club *by W. Carroll*

The Longniddry Artisans Club was founded in 1923 and although information from its very earliest days is scant there are full records from 1930 which show it has always been a healthy and active golf club. Membership in the early years was, as today, made up of two categories: Full Artisans who qualified for membership because of residency in the postal district of Longniddry and who also had an appropriate occupation. Plus Associates to the club who resided in the village and who were already members of Longniddry Golf Club.

The number in each category varied: in 1930 it was 25 full members and 5 associates and just before the outbreak of war there were 35 and 5. The numbers have been constant since 1956 until present with 40 and 10.

After the war Longniddry Golf Club allowed places to be kept for members who had served in the armed forces. These returning Service men caused a peak of 60 Artisan members which gradually dropped to 40 and 10 in 1956. Numbers have remained constant at that level since.

In 1930 the Annual green fee paid to Longniddry Golf Club was 10 shillings and this remained unchanged until 1957 when it increased to 21/-. The Artisan's subscriptions never appeared in the minute book but early cash books showed that the annual increases in subscriptions were because of internal running costs. The occasional extra six pence had to be added to assist with prize funds or to pay for transport to golf outings.

The Artisan Club raised funds by organising whist drives which eventually became a weekly feature of village life. They were run every Monday night in either the Recreation hall or the New School. During the war years funds raised were distributed to East Lothian District Nursing Association and to a Comfort Fund for members of the Artisan Club serving in the armed services.

The list of Office Bearers in 1930 was interesting as the newly appointed Captain of the club Mr. P. Allen remained in that office until 1963 with only three years gap in the late 1940's. The Artisan Golf Club owes a great deal to the Allen family as not only was Peter captain for 30 years but the use of his home at the Orchard Gardens was the regular venue for Committee meetings well into the 1960's. Mrs. Allen even appeared in the Office Bearers list as Honorary Vice-President from 1940 until 1963.

The Artisans in 1930 played 12 competitions with prizes of 10/- for the winner and 5/- for the runner up of each.

In years that followed prizes were also donated by Commander Purdon, Major Stevens and Major Hilton. Mr. G. A. Connor the Factor for the Earl of Wemyss continued close interest in the club until his death in 1936.

Probably the finest trophy was the challenge cup presented by Councillor T. Sawers O.B.E. in 1936. In 1953 the present Championship Cup was donated by Mr. and Mrs. P. Allen. The Jubilee Cup presented by Mr. R. Wilkinson in 1973 and the Dalrymple Trophy first played for in 1986 complete the silverware contested to date. Probably the most unusual trophy played for was the golf ball belonging to Jack Nicklaus which he autographed after his win in the Open Championship at Muirfield in the 1960's. The ball mounted on miniature golf clubs was damaged a few years ago and is no longer contested.

A boys' section was started in 1949 and Mr. Morris the Club professional ran classes for the prospective young members. The boys' section disappeared in the late 50's as most lads with an interest in golf in the village joined the 'Big Club'.

The Artisans operated their own handicapping system until 1954 when they fell into line with the National Guidelines. Each season before competition

The season 1931 winners were as follows:

May Medal
Charles Tawse
Club Prize
James Bathgate
Mr J. White's Prize
(local professional)
George Thomson
June Medal
James Smith
Captain's Prize
(Peter Allen) ?
Spring Medal
James Cormack
Baillie's Prize ?
July Medal
Andrew Bathgate
President's Prize
(G A Connor)
Andrew Thomson
Summer Medal
James Duncan
Merchant's Prize
Charles Tawse
August Medal
James Cormack

Artisan competitions are now played on Sunday mornings with a 7 a.m. draw but Friday was the competition day until 1947 when there was a shift to Monday then back to Friday in 1960. These were evening competitions with tee off at 6.15 p.m.

In 1947 a 'Haddingtonshire Courier' report records that Bob Burnside returned a 68 to win the Artisan Medal on 1st August. His round included only 22 putts.

During war years the Artisan Golf Club and the Ladies Artisan Golf Club drew closer together in fund raising events such as whist drives and dances but the two golf sections never merged.

began the Committee would meet to review each member's handicap. Up until 1939 a scratch score of 75 was the yardstick. This was then reduced to 72 because of course alterations and in 1954 it was further reduced to the present S.S.S. 70. That year each member had two strokes added to his handicap.

In the 1930's to ensure members returned cards after a stroke competition a new rule was introduced which said "irrespective of how many holes completed a card must be signed and handed in. Failure to do so will result in the penalty of one stroke being deducted from the offending member's handicap".

Also in 1936, "Any member winning two competitions will have their handicap revised."

Outings were a feature of the Artisan Club from the very earliest days and most other golf courses in the area were visited, three outings each season being the norm. In more recent times with transport easier, outings have gone much further afield. One never-to-be forgotten was the 1978 visit to Dougalston at Milngavie. Participants were warned that the new course might cost a few lost balls and that is the way it proved. A calculation after the two rounds put the total at 196 balls lost. Mr. George Gillan to this day will not speak of his personal losses but it was a fact that if you missed a fairway your ball was likely to be lost.

The Aberlady Artisan's Golf Club have provided Longniddry Artisans with home and away fixtures since the very beginning; there was only a gap during the war years. We also look forward to the annual challenge with the main Club. The drawing entitled 'The Winning Shot' by artist Norman Orr in the back bar of the clubhouse was presented by the Artisans to the main Club to commemorate this annual event.

The Artisans Club has thrived since its inception. Reading the early minute books illustrates the central position the club had in village life with regular dances, whist drives and charitable fund raising events.
The integration of the club into Longniddry Golf Club in 1996 should not prevent the Artisans from enjoying many years of success to come.

3. Longniddry Women's Artisans Golf Club

At 7.00 p.m. on Friday 17th April 1936, a public meeting was held in the Reading Room at Longniddry. Its attendance consisted of 15 or possibly 16 females - Miss E C Sawers of Longniddry House presided. The full minute of this important meeting is as follows :-

"MINUTE of MEETING of the LONGNIDDRY WOMEN'S ARTISAN GOLF CLUB, held in the Reading Room Longniddry, on Friday, 17th April, 1936 at 7 p.m.

Present: Miss Sawers (presiding), Mrs Lawrie, Miss Herkess, Miss Swan, Miss Bell, Mrs Gordon, Mrs Mason, Miss Aitken, Miss Anderson, Miss Burnside, Miss C. Chirnside, Miss M. Chirnside, Mrs McLeod, Miss M. White, Miss I. White.

Miss Sawers submitted and read a letter from Mr G. A. Connor intimating that the approval of Longniddry Golf Club had been given to the formation of a Women's Artisan Golf Club in Longniddry. Miss Sawers thereafter read the Constitution and Club Rules which had been enclosed in Mr Connor's letter. These were noted and approved. The names of intending members were then taken and in addition to the above list it was noted that five other persons were desirous of becoming members, namely Miss Gillies, Miss Lyle, Mrs Taylor, Miss Taylor and Miss Paterson, which makes a total of 19 (sic) members.

The meeting thereafter proceeded to appoint office-bearers. It was unanimously agreed to appoint Miss Sawers, Longniddry house, Longniddry, President of the Club and Miss Nancy Sawers, Woodburn, Longniddry, Vice-President. The following members were appointed to be members of the Committee:

Captain	*Mrs Lawrie (proposed by Miss Sawers and seconded by Mrs McLeod)*
Vice-Captain	*Mrs McLeod (proposed by Miss Herkess, seconded by Miss Swan)*
Hon, Secretary/ Treasurer	*Miss Bell (proposed by Mrs Lawrie, seconded by Miss Herkess)*
Miss Herkess	*(proposed by Miss Bell, seconded by Mrs Gordon)*
Miss Swan	*(proposed by Miss Herkess and seconded by Mrs Lawrie)*
Mrs Gordon	*(proposed by Miss Sawers, seconded by Miss Swan)*
Miss Burnside	*(proposed by Miss Swan and seconded by Miss Bell)*

It was agreed that the Secretary should arrange to have the "Constitution and Rules) printed, a copy of which should be given to each member. On the suggestion of having a Club badge Mrs Lawrie offered to make arrangements to get a selection of designs and prices. The meeting approved. The meeting noted that the subscription of 10/- to be paid to the Golf Club was to be in the hands of Mr Connor by 2nd May in any year. It was agreed that a subscription of 2/6d should be made towards the Club's own funds. The Secretary was asked to write to Mr Connor sending a list of members and asking when the Club would be allowed to commence play. All notices to be posted in Longniddry Post Office by the Secretary.

A vote of thanks was given to Miss Sawers for presiding."

Strangely, and perhaps accidentally, the name of Miss Nancy Sawers of Woodburn who was elected Vice-President at the meeting is not mentioned.

She is not on the attendance list, nor is she included with the absentees who were known to wish to join.

The day following the meeting the Honorary Secretary and Treasurer, Miss Mary A Bell, who lived at 3 John Knox Road wrote to Mr Connor to advise him of the outcome and ask when the Club could commence play. His reply was received three days later. They could play at once. On Saturdays they must start before 9.30 a.m. or after 5.30 p.m. (The 5 day working week was not established in Britain until the early 1960's). No woman Artisan was allowed to play on a Sunday at any time. Women Artisans were required to give precedence on the tee to members of the main Club at all times.

In September of that year Mr Connor died suddenly. The Women Artisans' Secretary sent a message of sympathy to Mrs Connor. The notice from the Earl of Wemyss Estate's office notifying the appointment of Mr Connor's replacement has been preserved in the papers of the Women's Artisans Club. It is reproduced in Chapter VI.

An intriguing aspect is the use of the word 'women'. It is not clear whether this was the decision of the members themselves in modest unpretentiousness or whether it was foisted upon them by the main club. Whereas properly the terms 'lady' and 'gentleman' relate to standards of behaviour, in the past they were often perceived as specifying social class. In 1936, therefore, it may have been considered that the phrase Lady Artisans was an impossible contradiction in terms.

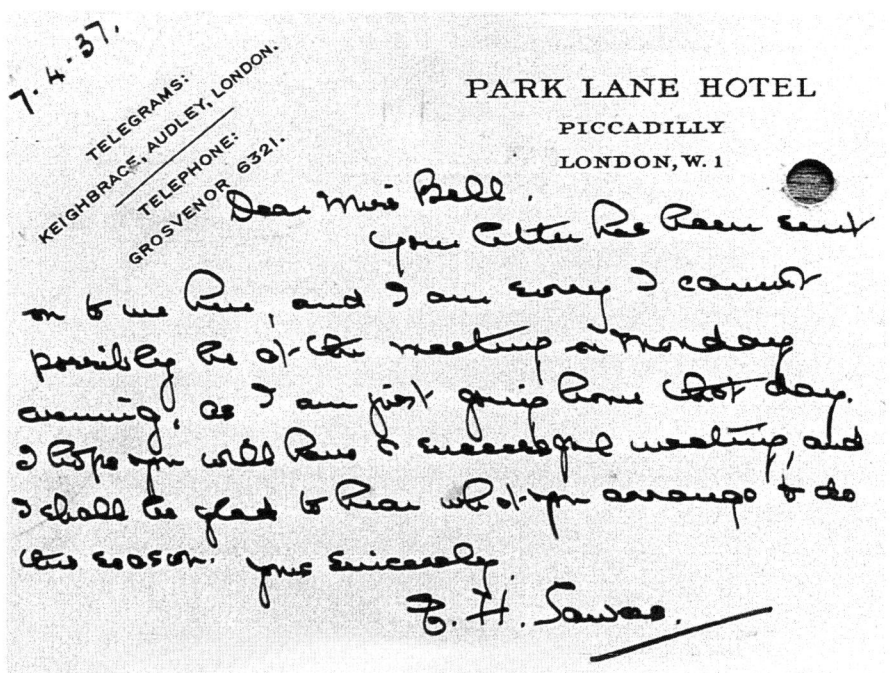

At the first AGM following establishment of the Club, held on 12th April 1937, Miss Sawers the Honorary President could not be present. Her postcard of apology is of interest (shown above).

During 1937, the business of fixing handicaps was begun. It was done on a 14-hole basis with a maximum of 36. Several competitions were introduced.

In each of the six summer months a Ball competition was held. Miss Burnside was the first winner. A President's Prize was presented by Miss EC Sawers and won in that first year by Miss White. There was also a Hole and Hole competition. Mrs Mason was the inaugural winner. Two mixed foursomes events with the Men's Artisans Club proved very successful. Tea was taken after the game on both occasions. In the Winter of 1937/38 a small whist drive and social evening were held.

It seems likely that since its establishment, the officials and members of the Women Artisans had been quietly working to influence favourably the members of the main Club. One suspects from later evidence that Miss Mary Bell had been particularly persuasive.

At any rate by 1938 the attitude of the main Club had begun to soften towards the 'Women'. On application by Miss Bell, Mr Cutter wrote to advise that the Women's Artisans were to be given permission to play on Sunday evenings. This overturned a decision advised two years before by Mr Connor. Almost at the same time, again after application by Miss Bell, the main Club granted permission to the Women Artisans to introduce friends to the course at the usual green fee. In effect the 'Women' now had obtained the conditions which the male Artisans had enjoyed for some years.

1938 was of course the year of the Empire Exhibition in Glasgow. The ripples which it caused even reached to the Longniddry Women's Artisans. They sent two representatives Miss Burnside and Miss Gillies to a meeting with the WRI to discuss an Empire Exhibition Ball. Unfortunately nothing further is recorded.

Whatever the personal language however, written communication was still very formal: On 1st May 1939 Roy Cutter acknowledged receipt of the annual subscription from the Women's Artisans Club by writing to Mary Bell:-

"Dear Madam

Thank you for your money order. Herewith official receipt."

Clearly there was more work to be done. And it must have been, because the tone of the communication on the same occasion in 1941 is very different:

"Dear Miss Bell

Many thanks for the subscription. Official receipt herewith. But why didn't you bring it yourself? It is a long time since you have been to see us, and if you aren't careful the sherry will all be finished.. Certainly your members may play on Saturdays and Sundays for the period of the war at any rate."

From these early beginnings the Women's Artisans Club has continued successfully for sixty years. At some stage whether through a formal decision or from recognition of the good manners and courtesy of its members, the name became the Lady Artisans.

By 1996 only a handful of Lady Artisans remained and in parallel with the male artisans they were incorporated as full members of the main Club.

The activities down the years included matches against the staff of the County Council, regular outings to Gifford, and matches with the men's club. A particular feature in later years was a regular match with Torphin Hill. There seems to have been a warm friendship between Florence Bathgate, Secretary in the '60's and Jess Foote, Honorary Secretary at Torphin.

Whilst not all the records are to hand, some of the Officers of the Lady Artisans Club down the years can be listed:

Secretaries
Miss Mary Bell
Miss Isa White
Mrs T Porteous
Mrs J McDougall
Mrs Margaret Hunter

Captains
Mrs Lawrie
Mrs Mason
Mrs Gordon
Miss Burnside
Mrs Porteous
Mrs Bathgate
Mrs McDougall

Nevertheless it will still be possible for their Artisan identity to be preserved as an associate club within the main one.

Mrs Elizabeth Robb became President in 1967.

4. Longniddry Wednesday Club *by Jack Little*

First records of the Wednesday Club date from the early 1960's and members, guests and friends have been enjoying its particular brand of relaxed amiable competition and lively social activities for an unbroken period of over thirty years. The founder members were mainly shopkeepers and others who benefited from the local Wednesday "half day" and felt the golf course provided a better arena for displaying their talents than the kitchen or the garden! More recently stalwarts have tended to come from the ranks of the retired and the self-employed which, according to some, amounts to much the same thing.

The main focus of the club is of course the Wednesday round and, while competition had always been secondary to companionship, a number of trophies have been donated over the years and are contested on the basis of the club's own handicapping system. Another regular feature of Wednesday Club activities has been the organising of day outings to Muirfield, Rosemount and Gleneagles among others and of weekend trips to Banff Springs, Rosemount, Turnberry etc. A number of very popular annual trips have also been arranged to Northern Ireland, Majorca and the Spanish mainland where it is rumoured a couple of members once accidentally found themselves within an easy 5 iron of a golf course.

Longniddry Wednesday Golf Club.

Back row standing, left to right: Walter McAinsh, Bert Smith, Ken Kinnear, Alex Thomson, Jim Mason, Alan Butler, Robin Cameron, Gordon Fyffe, Jim Little.

Front row sitting, left to right: Bill Gordon, Jack Little, Bill Little, Grant Malcolm, George Arbuthnott.

On a social level, the members' Christmas Outing has always been most enjoyable while the highlight of the calendar is our January 2nd event when, after a round of golf, we are joined by the ladies for dinner in the clubhouse followed by a party. Despite years of tireless effort on the accordion, Jackie Little has failed to dampen the enthusiasm for this occasion.

The Wednesday Club is proud of its friendly approach to the game of golf and has always happily accommodated any member of Longniddry Golf Club in search of a game who is willing to participate in the "sweep" and accept the club's "social rules" approach to the laws of the game.

The Wednesday Club is very grateful for all the courtesy, assistance and good service it has received from John and Jean Kennedy and all the clubhouse staff over the years; John Gray and his assistants, and of course from the Golf Club itself for the facilities and other support.

5. Saturday Sweep /MAO Trophy *by Peter D. Lowe*

During the winter of 1974/75 a group of members decided to have a sweep every Saturday morning at 8.30. The object was to allow members to turn up without having arranged to do so and get a game (in those days pre-arranged 4-balls were the rule). This was possible as at that time the tee could not be pre-booked until 9 a.m. To ensure that players mixed, a "draw" was conducted each Saturday. The rules were simple - strokeplay with short putts given to speed up play. The stake was a top grade golf ball - winner takes all except those who were second had their ball returned. In the event of a tie the balls were shared. During the main season (1st October to 31st March) an ad hoc handicapping system was used - First and ties cut 2 if the winning score equalled or bettered a scratch score of 68 and cut 1 if the score was 69 or higher. Handicaps could not go lower than +2.

In the summer months Club competitions and other commitments prevented regular attendance and while the sweep was played each week (except on competition days) the handicapping system was suspended.

The Saturday Sweep retains the above format to this day except that the weekly stake is £1.50 (sweep of £1 and 50p for two's). It also retains the rule that any member can join as the social aspect is very important. The "crack" in the back bar is considered as important as the golf that precedes it!!!!!

It is impossible to recall the names of those who played on that first Saturday but those who took part in the first day's outing (described below) could be considered the founding members of the Sweep:- Alex Harvey, Gordon Watt, George (the machine) Harkess (so called because one Saturday he claimed to be playing like a machine - a sadly rare occurrence), Peter Lowe, Ian Jackson , Jim (Araldite) Mackenzie (so called because no matter the strength of the wind his hair never moved), Tom Porteous, Hugh McGilvray, Roger Laidlaw, Gil Gass, Alf Ware and Bob Anderson.

At the start of the 1975/76 winter season it was decided that each member should put aside 50p per week to fund a day at Gleneagles in March. The £12 saved was to cover bus hire, green fees (an amazing £4.75 for 36 holes over the Kings and Queens courses) and an evening meal in nearby Auchterarder. The chosen March Monday dawned grey and 12 intrepid

Over the years the Wednesday Club has enjoyed the company of a remarkable number of professional footballers including Bobby Parker (Hearts), Jimmy Miller and Ralph Brand (both of Rangers), John Hunter (Motherwell) and George "Josie" Samuel (Aberdeen). Golfing talent has not been entirely absent with John McLean of Bathgate, a regular winner of the Lothian Champion of Champions, being a frequent attender while few who have seen Kenny Kinnear's swing can fail to have been moved.

golfers set off from Longniddry. Surprisingly it started snowing and by the time we had reached Dollar it was obvious that there would be no golf at Gleneagles. Two phone calls later our day was cancelled and we returned to Longniddry where our return to the Club caused Dave Taylor to panic when he thought that a group of visitors had arrived to take the 1st tee. Past Captain Gil Gass suggested that we phone Muirfield to see if we could play there. John Gunn phoned on our behalf to discover that Paddy Hamner was on holiday and that the deputy secretary Mr Stewart was agreeable on John Gunn's assurance that we were all "scratch" golfers. On the way to Muirfield we arranged to eat at the Golf Hotel, Gullane, in the evening and Maxine McGilvray (Hugh's wife) agreed to supplement our packed lunches between rounds. A 36 hole stableford competition was played and was won by Alf Ware. Thus the Muirfield Annual Outing (MAO) was born. The 1977 outing saw Bob Anderson present the MAO Trophy with its Little Red Book containing a golfing version of Chairman MAO's thoughts.

The MAO Trophy is contested each year to this date and the Club's Jubilee Year will see the 21st competition. Unfortunately costs and other factors mean that it is no longer played for at Muirfield but the format is unchanged. As can be imagined such an outing and the characters involved throw up a myriad of golfing and other memories for which there is no space. A feel for such events is obtained when it is learned that George Harkess got the sack as Treasurer when we ran out of money and what monies we had were found on the floor of the bar in the Golf Hotel. Also the occasion when Willie Weston (who had booked the bus) received an irate letter from the bus company about failure to settle the account. Intense investigation revealed that the last man off the bus (Fraser Hall) could not understand where the £25 in his jacket pocket had come from - all was settled. Settling the account at Muirfield was equally hazardous. On one occasion we received a refund when Captain Hamner adjudged our tip to be over-generous and a rather pointed suggestion on another occasion when we forgot to leave a tip that one should be paid (which was hastily sent with profuse apologies). It would be untrue to suggest that this outing is a teetotal affair!

Other stalwarts of the Saturday Sweep/MAO Trophy competition include Andrew King, Peter Stanton, John Montgomery, Douglas Hally, Alistair & Ian Mackay, Bill Laidlaw, Jim Walshe, Robin Sharp, Jim (Airport taxi) Little, Davie (Pog) Donaldson, Robert (Bobo) Pow and Tom Edmond and a large number of members who have made only occasional appearances. So much for the "scratch" golfer tag given to the group in 1976.

6. Longniddry Friday Section (also known as The Friday Night Club)
by Allen Davis

The ethos of the Longniddry Friday Section, formed in 1987 is clearly expressed in this extract from the minutes of the first meeting: *"The Section*

should provide an opportunity to unwind at the end of the week, and to enjoy the game of golf in friendly company."

Membership of the Club is always open and complete anonymity is guaranteed. There are no rules specific to the Club and in addition, the Rules of Golf are loosely interpreted. From late March until the end of September each Friday evening from 5.30 p.m. members meet for a sweep over 13 holes. Pairings are by lot and handicaps are controlled.

The Spring Cup and Autumn Trophy are keenly contested on outings. The Singles Cup is played on a matchplay knock-out basis throughout the season. In May the Stapleford Trophy is played for at Longniddry over 18 holes. During the remainder of the year the Club meets in the back bar to participate in the game of dominoes, an activity which gives members an advantage in the Annual Games Night where Longniddry Friday Section members figure consistently on the prize list.

7. The Lochend Club

One of the long established clubs originating from Craigentinny Golf Course is the Lochend Club. Many of its members also play at Longniddry appearing particularly on Saturday mornings about 11 a.m. Their annual

The Lochend Group, left to right:

Keith Baillie, Charles Forbes, Gil Wallace, Tom Galloway, Derick Naughton, Jimmy Mason, Geo Thornburn, Alan Devlin, Tom Jardine, Bert Milligan, Rab Thornburn, Bert Smith.

A valued member of
Longniddry Golf
Club for many years
was international
sprinter George
McNeil's father,
George Snr, who for
a time was Provost
of Tranent. Also in
athletics in Andrew
King, the Club has a
British Athletics
Association Board
senior coach for
middle distance.

dinner is a very pleasurable affair conducted at Longniddry with the current Captain of Longniddry as an honoured guest. The present members are: Rab Thornburn, Derek Naughton, Keith Baillie, Charlie Forbes, Alan Butler, Gilbert Wallace, Tom Jardine, Jim Mason, Bert Milligan, Tom Galloway, Alan Devlin, Bert Smith, Archie Johnston and Alan Richardson.

8. Other Sporting Connections

Longniddry Golf Club is a broad church. Many predilections are tolerated especially where sport is concerned. This is particularly demonstrated during the men's games night when expertise at darts and dominoes is of value. Throughout the year besides golf itself, football commands the greatest attention. There are other keen interests though: bowls - indoor and outdoor - is highly popular and cricket is well represented - Alex Dudgeon, Gordon Bonnington and the late Pat Gracie spring to mind.

A large number of members are devoted to Rugby Union. Not a few of these are or were Heriot's Old Boys like Bill McClure and Gus McVey, and there are a few who were schooled at Ross High. Euan Kennedy who scored the winning try against England in 1984 is a Tranent man. He learned his golf as a junior member of Longniddry Golf Club. In George and Rena Morgan, Longniddry Golf Club has the parents of Scotland scrum half and Rugby Coach Douglas Morgan. The greatest number though are Preston Lodge FPs. Matt Bilsland is a past President of Preston Lodge FP Rugby Club. Then of course several of the males of the Allan family were involved including Headmaster David himself, Duncan, David Jr. and Roderick. Pride of place must go to prop forward R F (Bobby) Cunningham who was capped for Scotland. His senior rugby club was Gala, but he was a Preston Lodge FP and although living in Elgin now, he is still a Longniddry Golf Club member. Another Scottish cap (under 18 schoolboy) was Gordon Guiney- full back and three quarter. Brian Smith was another strong and safe fullback in his day, and Stuart Mackay a fast winger. 'Kipps' Clifford another PL Rugby Club President, and Derek Ramage are further examples of the three-quarter line whilst in the forwards 'Rab' Dickson was a fast and aggressive predator (though a nicer chap off the park you couldn't wish to meet). 'Podge' Paterson was another prop forward whilst last but not least was the illusive probing flanker Danny Gillan who packed at zero altitude till they changed the rules.

There is even a
Musselburgh Rugby
Club man: Norman
Elliot confesses to
playing for them at
scrum half, or more
usually stand-off
until about aged 28
when his father Alex
finally persuaded him
to concentrate on
golf, "I wasn't much
good at stand-off
anyway" admits
Norman, "I would
never pass the ball to
anyone."

It must be admitted though, that for general interest apart from golf, football takes pride of place. Randomly scattered through the membership there are odd personalities like Dick Morris or Dougie McIntyre whose football loyalties lie with clubs in the far west. There is even the odd maverick who might confess to a weakness for say, Stenhousemuir (George Armstrong) or Queen of the South (Allen Davis). Apart from those eccentrics the abiding interest is with the big Edinburgh Clubs Hearts and Hibs.

According to Eddie Turnbull, Hearts and Hibs team members regularly played challenge matches at Longniddry in the past. The story goes (per Alan Anderson) that if you didn't play you still had to walk round. The matches seem to have involved some peculiar practices because a 1971 Longniddry Golf Club Board Minute records that a specimen of the boots used by Hearts players at their outing was inspected and passed by the Board as acceptable. Nevertheless, the Secretary was instructed to write to both Hearts and Hibs Managers regarding the dress rules of the Golf Club and advising that football boots must not be worn on the golf course. Some sort of strange goings-on are indicated.

Heart of Midlothian. One of the most outstanding Hearts personalities to belong to Longniddry Golf Club has been John Harvey. In 1956 Hearts won the Scottish cup, beating Celtic 3 – 1 at Hampden before 132, 840 spectators. John Harvey was trainer at that time and right through the great times of the fifties going on to become manager when Tommy Walker retired in the autumn of 1966. A most parfait gentil knight, he was a most popular member of the Golf Club. His succeeding dynasty is still well represented unto the third generation by son Alex and grandson John.

On the playing side, as Jack Little points out, Bobby Parker the Hearts full back was a Longniddry Club member for many years. Bobby Parker came to Hearts in 1949 from Patrick Thistle in a swap deal that took Heart's favourite Tommy Walker to Firhill. Bobby was right back when Hearts began their great era of the 1950's with a 4 – 2 win over Motherwell in the League Cup Final of 1954. Kirk replaced Bobby in Heart's Scottish cup winning team two years later. Parker went on to coach before joining the Heart of Midlothian Board, becoming Director and then finally Chairman.

No other Heart of Midlothian player has been unearthed among the Longniddry Golf Club membership. This is perhaps understandable for with their location at Tynecastle it is natural for Hearts to look to the west side of the city. It seems that their favoured course has been Ratho Park where Alfie Conn has many friends.

Hibernian Football Club. Perhaps because Hibs are based on the east side of Edinburgh their staff and playing representation at Longniddry is much stronger than that of Hearts. The first Hibs player to join Longniddry Golf Club was Gordon Smith. Gordon of course played for both Hibs and Hearts. He remains the only player to have won three Scottish Championship League Medals with three different clubs – not one of them from Glasgow: that is Hibernian, Hearts and Dundee. Gordon moved to North Berwick Golf Club after a time but he was followed to Longniddry by many more Hibernian players including Eddie Turnbull and Lawrie Reilly. Names of some of the current members are: Willie McFarlane, Jock Buchanan, Jimmy Thomson, Willie Clerk, Jimmy Kerr, Gordon Marshall

The Craiglong Trophy. *The Craiglong Trophy was presented by the Harvey family in memory of their father. The Trophy is played for annually between Craigmillar Golf Club where John's son George is a member and Longniddry where John's other son Alex is of course a past Vice Captain and six times Club champion. 1997 is the 21st anniversary of these keenly fought matches with the scores exactly even.*

and of course Cecil Graham ex-secretary of Hibernian Football Club itself.

There exists within the Golf Club at Longniddry a Hibernian Former Players Club. For years its members played Dundee ex-footballers on a home and home basis. Dundee played their home matches at Rosemount. Johnny Pattillo put up a trophy for the contest in 1975 and the Hibernian men won it every time up to 1983 when the contest lapsed. The Hibs FP Club has continued however and several trophies are contested. There is the Bob Powrie Tankard, the Bill Harrower Trophy, another beautiful trophy donated by Tom Hart and last but not least a second Pattillo trophy incorporating two wooden golfing figures. The Captain of Longniddry Golf Club is made an Honorary Member of the Hibs FP Club for the duration of his office. Tommy Younger was the first President and he has been followed by Alex Harkess, Tommy Preston, and Sinclair Mackie.

There can be no more dedicated Hibs supporter in the Golf Club company than Ronald Jardine Herkes, ex Royal Bank of Scotland Investment Manager. More importantly during National Service he performed (he claims) as a tricky left-winger somewhere in Germany. Ron recalls some years ago playing a foursome tie against Johnny Harvey of Hearts and his partner. The outcome of the match is forgotten now (which probably means that Ron lost) but he remembers that when they all retired to the back bar, they found already ensconced there, larger than life behind an enormous cheroot, Tommy Younger Esquire. He was on a high. He had just won the Hibernian FP's Golf Championship and he was ready to lavish his hospitality and the tale of his triumph on a suitable audience.

Tommy's expansive arms akimbo on either side of his cigar, he directed the Harvey – Herkes foursome to his table and furnished all with generous refreshments. After a time the golf was disposed of and the football talk waxed interesting and eloquent. As a goalkeeper Tommy's preoccupation was with defensive strategy. Ron remembers that he talked of how he and Don Revie organised the back six at Leeds. "Always remember" he said, "You've already got one point when you run onto the park. The first job is not to lose it."

9. The Junior Section

The first recorded references to Junior members at Longniddry are found in the minutes of the Ladies Club. They are there because the Ladies Committee of the day found itself in disagreement with the Club Secretary/Treasurer Mr G A Connor. The Ladies Committee had been insistent that all admissions to membership of the Ladies club should be subject to their approval. Mr Connor had transgressed this stipulation when he admitted two ladies in August 1931 without consultation. His justification that the ladies concerned were the wives of members of the main Club did not wash with the Ladies Committee.

There seems to have been no further difficulty until 1935 when the procedures which affect the Juniors were written. Then a note came from Mr Connor to the Ladies Committee advising that the Committee of the main Club had decided "to admit Junior Members to full membership at 16 instead of 18 as formerly if they so desired." This received a dusty reply. The Ladies Committee considering this action to diminish their authority replied with a declaration that 16 or 18 notwithstanding, the admission of lady members required the sanction of their Committee. In consequence of this, Nancy Jupp's entry to full membership was deferred.

After this episode in 1935 the surviving Longniddry Club records are silent about Junior members for a long period. It is 30 years later when a Board Minute records that it had been recognised that a concession which had been afforded for years to Loretto Boys gave them playing rights beyond those of the Club's own Juniors.

In 1965 Tom Porteous was Club Captain; his immediate successors were Joe Sykes followed by Ian Forbes. All three were particularly interested in encouraging young players and a momentum to develop the Juniors Section established at that time has been maintained through the years. What had happened regarding the Juniors beforehand is largely lost to us, although we do have Willie Carroll's remarks about the Artisans Boys Section which existed for ten years from 1949. Certainly there can be no doubt of the main Club's commitment to young players from the early sixties onwards. It is reckoned to have been about 1962 when the Club began to offer free tuition to young prospective golfers. No stipulation of Club membership was required. Professional Gordon Durward and his assistants provided tuition to all young persons turning up. Several of today's category 1 golfers can look back to the excellent start that they got at that time: Willie Weston, Alastair Barr and David Baillie, among others. Longniddry was one of the first clubs in the Lothians to adopt this generous and far-seeing initiative. The practice has continued until the present day with John Gray continuing from Gordon Durward. The consequence has been that Longniddry has produced a long line of exceptionally good young players both male and female, from the 1970's onwards. Raymond Russell and Hilary Monaghan are obvious examples and there are many more: Steven Thomson, Mike Mclaren, Paul Wardell, Derick Scott, Neil Davidson, Patricia Lees, Heather Robb and Gwen Smith to name a few. Peter Lowe and his brother David are another two.

Peter remembers the early days of the Russel Patrick competition. The trophy had been presented by Molly Patrick about 1958 for competition on a handicap basis among Junior members. In those days there were no Junior handicaps and some of the Juniors were quite young. It was decided therefore to limit the contest to nine holes only: the first to the sixth and the

Chiefly from Nancy Jupp's account, it is possible to list some of the names of the Junior members of the Club in the 1930's. There would be Nancy herself and her sister Rhoda, together with Kath and Betty Rose. There were also Douglas Teesdale and Nancy Sawers. Presumably Andrew Purden and Ruth and Isobel Nash would be among the others.

The Sykes Trophy.
A further step in the
development of the
Longniddry Juniors
Section was taken by
Joe Sykes,
Headmaster of
Preston Lodge High
School. Joe was
Captain during
1966/67. At the end
of his Captaincy he
donated the Sykes
Trophy to the Club
for annual open
competition by
Juniors on a
handicap basis. It
was to be a few years
though before it was
won by a
Longniddry player.

eleventh to the thirteenth. These were called 'the competition nine'. Before competing in the Russel Patrick the youngsters had to get handicaps. They were required to submit two scores on the 'competition nine.' This they did. Peter was awarded a handicap of 35 and he says that Graham Gitchen was given 55. He remembers this because in the competition proper, he returned a net score of 19, while Graham's net score was 17. These are Peter's recollections: he is surprised to be told that the first name on the Russel Patrick trophy is not Graham Gitchen, but Michael Walls. Goodness only knows what Michael's score must have been.

Nowadays of course an organised handicap system exists and the competition for the Russel Patrick trophy is knock-out match play over 18 holes.

Reading down the list of winners after Michael Walls, names jump out which are familiar now in the Club's Winter League or County Cup Teams: Charles Passmore and Alastair Barr for example. Some names represent the old established Longniddry families such as M C Douglas or the Sked brothers and some, the more newly arrived, such as Eric McKay and Roderick MacRaild.

In 1974 the Board decided that the number of Junior members should be limited to 100 with 11 the minimum age. This decision probably reflects the substantial increase in the population of Longniddry brought about by the development of the Glassel Park and Douglas Road areas of the village from the mid-sixties. The following year, the East Lothian Junior League was established. Longniddry decided not to participate because of the League's intention to play matches on a Sunday.

This decision contrasts with Longniddry's early reputation of permitting Sunday golf when other courses were closed.

Billie McNeill. Towards the end of the seventies, Billie McNeill was appointed Junior Convener. Billie was an enormously popular person. A very gifted school teacher and a skilled and committed sportsman, he endeared himself to a wide range of people: pupils, friends, colleagues and golfers young and old. Sadly, Billie passed away in 1996. It is certain that in his spell as Junior Convener, he offered great encouragement and demonstrated standards of sporting ability, dress and behaviour which stood as an example to all Longniddry Juniors under his influence. Not least, Billie generated among these young people a healthy enthusiasm for the game and for Longniddry Golf Club.

In 1981 under Bill McClure's Convenership, the Board gave consideration to housing the Juniors in separate accommodation outside the Clubhouse. It was decided to renovate the building behind the Professional's shop at a cost of £1,200. Fresh thought was also given to the question of the Club participating in the East Lothian Junior League. The Sykes trophy competition had been running for 13 years and now it was won for the first time by a Longniddry Junior – Michael Mclaren, with a gross 69.

The following year, 1982, Neil Davidson, offspring of Club members Jim and Morag, won an Open Junior Tournament at Newbattle. Back at Longniddry the Board decided that during the school holidays, Juniors should have priority on the tee between 11.00 and 11.45 a.m.

It appears that not only had Junior girl members become a thing of the past, their very existence may have been forgotten, because when in August 1982 it was decided to establish a Ladies Junior Section, it was said that this was the first time there had been such a thing in the Club. The more likely interpretation is that whilst there had been girl Junior Members before, this was the first time there had been a Junior Girls Section as such. At any rate, there was to be a maximum of 20 girls and their handicaps would be administered by the Ladies Section. The girls would be able to play in Junior medals.

Junior Championship. Still in 1982 Bill McClure and his succeeding Junior Convener Bill Aitken combined to present a trophy for the Junior Championship. It was won in this, its first year, by Michael Mclaren just 12 months after he had won the Sykes trophy. Like Billie McNeill and Bill McClure before him, Bill Aitken was an active and conscientious Junior Convener, encouraging and supporting the young players at every opportunity. He was succeeded in his turn by another enthusiast, Willie Weston.

East Lothian Junior League. During 1984 it was decided Sunday play notwithstanding, that Longniddry should enter a team in the East Lothian Junior League in the 1985 season. In the first match played, the team lost to the neighbours, Royal Musselburgh. Willie Weston remembers that the boys took a little time to become accustomed to the formality of a match – opposing pairs joining up to make a foursome when the pace of play ahead was particularly slow, for example. After this first match there was much more success and the team in its first year of competition, finished runner-up at the end of the season.

Meantime, upon the recommendation of the Professional, three Juniors who had shown particular promise were afforded extra tuition by the Club in addition to that already funded by the Golf Foundation. They were: Eric McKay, John Hunnam and Lindsey McRaild. A little later further tuition was authorised for Elliot Gray, Michael Stanton and Caroline Mackay.

1986 began to show the benefits of all the hard work: Michael Stanton reached the 4th round of the British Boys and the Junior team won the League on this its second year of trying. At the final meeting of the League the Longniddry team came second in the stroke play competition with

Sweet Toothed Grown-ups. Perhaps in line with the priority tee-time decision for the Juniors, it was also declared that the Professional's shop would stock confectionery for purchase by Junior members only. This stipulation appears to have become undermined somewhat with passing years and grown-up first tee appetites.

Promotion to Full Membership. What the previous arrangement had been is not recorded – perhaps there had been no change since Mr Connor's 1935 note – but in 1982 it was decided that full membership should be offered to each Junior upon his or her 18th birthday. There would be no obligation upon the Junior to take up the offer until the start of the next subscription year.

Raymond Russell also second in the individual contest.

The Longniddry Junior League team repeated their success in 1987, winning their final match against Tantallon. The team had also won the 1987 Junior League Team Strokeplay with Eric McKay's performance the best. In those second and third years in which the team had been engaged in the competition only two points had been lost.

The Club continued the practice of providing extra tuition where there was seen to be promise, and Derek Scott and Colin Sinclair benefited in this way. Later in 1987 Raymond Russell was selected for special tuition by the Scottish Golf Union and Andrew Whitelaw by Lothians. Andrew had played in Spain that year in the Daily Express Esso Tournament and he had won the Golf Foundation Schools Tournament.

Meantime the Longniddry Board gave consideration to the financial difficulty facing young people when they were required to step up to full membership. It was decided that as from 1988 the entrance fee for Juniors going to Seniors would be on a scale rising from nil for those who had joined at 11 to 100% for those who joined at 17.

Still in 1988 Raymond Russell was selected for full International Honours and played in the Boys Home Internationals at Formby in August. On his return he won the Longniddry Men's Open for the Durward Trophy. At the age of 16 Raymond returned the lowest score ever recorded for the two rounds of the event. His first round equalled the course record of 63. This was all the more meritorious in that it was accomplished in wet and windy weather – contrasting with the balmy conditions of 1987 when the record

In 1988 half of the Lothians team to meet the Borders consisted of Longniddry Juniors. At the annual stroke play event at Gullane No. 2, the winners were the Longniddry team of Raymond Russell, Paul Wardell, Eric McKay and Justin Fiddler. Eric McKay took the best individual prize.

In June 1988, a 6-round Golf Junior Marathon was played in aid of Cancer Research. The photograph shows with Peter Lowe: Michael Stanton, Lindsey MacRaild, John Donaldson, and Fiona Stanton handing over the cheque for £1,706.54. The others who participated were Caroline Mackay, Joyce Hunnam, Kate Kennedy, David Allan and Neil Davidson of 63 was established.

While Raymond was enjoying this success for the boys, Lindsey McRaild, daughter of Club members Edith and Ian, was awarded her Scottish Schoolgirls Cap. Another three boys were selected for additional lessons at the cost of the Club: Alistair Rennie, Calum White and Derick Scott.

In the following year, 1989, the Lothians Golf Association held their Tournament at Longniddry. Raymond Russell reached the semi-final. Both Raymond and Eric McKay were awarded Scottish Schools Team Caps and Raymond played for Scotland against Sweden. He also won the Lothian Youth Championship. Meantime, Lindsey's brother Roderick McRaild had won the Esso Daily Express national Championship regional Final.

In October 1990 Vince Barron, the dedicated Junior Convener following Willie Weston, submitted his report. The East Lothian Junior League had finished in a tie that year between Longniddry and Kilspindie. The play-off was drawn, so it was decided to share the trophy. The County Stroke Play event was won by Raymond Russell with Calum White coming second equal. The team entry won once again. The special coaching for promising youngsters was sustained with Hilary Monaghan, Simon Mees and Andrew Hall the latest trio chosen.

In July 1991 Hilary Monaghan won the East of Scotland Girls Championship and was awarded her Scottish Cap. She was also appointed to be the first Captain of the Girls Section of the Club.

Raymond Russell had now left the Junior ranks and the following year at the age of 20, he won the Scottish Youth Championship.

Promising girl golfers with their tutors.

Back row: Joyce Hunnam, Betty Monaghan (Thomson), Eileen Dundas, Lorraine Robb.
Second row: Susan Bell, Janet Wake, Margaret Stewart, Rena Morgan.
Middle row: Jennifer Morgan, Margaret Smith, Terry Reekie.
Seated: Katy Gracie, Hilary Monaghan.
Front row: Susan Dundas, Morag Anne McNeill, Heather Robb, Nicola Robb, Julie Weston, Sarah Hardy.

Junior County Cup.

The 1994 Junior County Cup was played at Winterfield and Longniddry's team of Donald Christian, Steven Burton, John Gray, Heriot Smith and Jamie Peacocke won it. This performance was not quite sustained in the two following years – runners-up 1995 and semi-finalists in 1996 – but the golfing standards of the Longniddry Juniors continued to be remarkably high.

1993 saw a downturn in Longniddry performance when a comparatively inexperienced team came 6th in the League. The extra tuition continued with Stuart Letchford and Michael Robinson selected this time. The 1993 setback was only temporary because the following year saw the Longniddry team win the East Lothian Stroke Play contest and come second in the League. At about the same time Gwen Smith won the East Lothian Girls Championship at Longniddry.

Reflecting at the end of the Jubilee year on the truly exceptional string of excellent golfers emerging from the Junior ranks at Longniddry, it is clear that great credit is due to all concerned. It bears repeating that Longniddry was one of the first clubs in the Lothians to provide free tuition to all aspiring young golfers. This, having begun in Gordon Durward's day, has continued under John Gray and his assistants and the results speak volumes for the quality of instruction provided. They also bear testament to the dedication of the various Junior Conveners down the years: Billie McNeill, Bill McClure, Bill Aitken, Willie Weston, Vince Barron, Bill Thomson, Mike Robinson and Allen Davis.

Similarly in the Ladies Section there has been continuing effort and dedication to introduce young girls to the game and to support and encourage them as their ability developed. Many ladies have been involved, but probably none more so than Jeanette Fiddler, Joyce Hunnam, Eileen Dundas and Isobel Massie.

Nor should Gilbert Dempster be forgotten. Throughout his twelve years as Secretary, he took an unfailing interest in the welfare and progress of the young persons in the Club.

Above everyone however, stand Tom Porteous and Kath Rose. For many years they have nursed Longniddry's Junior development scheme and taken a personal interest in all young golfers, making themselves available to give advice and encouragement whenever required.

Raymond Russell's CV up to and including 1994 is as follows:

1991. Winner of Toxandria International Youths Championship
Scottish Youths Six-Man and Eleven-Man Teams

1992. Scottish Youths Six-Man and Eleven-Man Teams
Great Britain and Ireland Youth Team
Winner of Scottish Youth Stroke Play Championship
Fourth European Mens Championship
Fifth British Youths Championship
British 'Nineteen Year Old' Champion
Second Toxandria International Youths Championship
Fourth Scottish Mens Stroke Play Championship

1993. Walker Cup Team
Scottish Six-Man Team (Europe)
Scottish Youth Team
Great Britain and Ireland Youth Team
Scottish Eleven-Man Team Home Internationals
Winning Scottish Three-Man Team Spanish Nations Cup
Runner-up in Scottish Order of Merit
Runner-up Scottish Amateur Championship
Third in Scottish Stroke Play Championship
Winner of Cameron Corbett Vase (National Competition)
Semi-Finalist in British Amateur Championship
Winner of Craigmillar Park Open
Winner of Scottish Champion of Champions
Winner Toxandria International Youths Championship
Most Improved Golfer Longniddry Golf Club Limited

1994. Played for a European Tour Cards in the Autumn. Pre-qualified at
Pals, Spain for the final qualifying school at Montpelier, France.
Achieved the half-way cut and consequently was invited to compete
in a limited number (5/10) European Tour Events and all Challenge
Tour Events (restricted 'satellite' European Tour) plus the South
African Tour Events.

Other Scottish Boys Team 1988, 89, 90.
Runner-up in Scottish Boys Stroke Play 1989
Quarter-finalist British Boys Championship 1989
Great Britain and Ireland Boys Team 1989
Winner of Scottish Boys 'Under Sixteens' 1988.

CHAPTER VIII

JUBILEE JOURNAL

by Neil Robertson

"A sub-committee comprising, the Captain, Vice-Captain, Lady Captain, House Convenor and Mr A Glasgow, was formed to formulate ideas for the Club's 75th anniversary in 1996." It was minuted that 'A history of the Golf Club is in preparation.'

The first formal indication of the decision to celebrate 75 years of the Club's existence is contained in the Minutes of the Board Meeting held on September 4th 1995.

It was considered appropriate that momentos of the year featuring a Jubilee Logo should be acquired, for distribution by the Club or for sale through the ProShop. The momentos would include Edinburgh Crystal and gift-packs containing golf balls, tees, pitch mark repairer or ball marker.

Sponsorship. No less than 21 companies with whom the Club did regular business elected to contribute to the cost of the Jubilee activities, either by making a cash gift or by providing prize materials. Leading the field was Abercromby Motors who through Alistair Gibson donated £500. Members helped too. Ian Rolland consented to the reproduction of one of his water colours on the front cover of the new score card, and the Club's past Captains jointly funded the first prize of the Jubilee Day competition.

Events

The Mens' Dinner. With the Mens' Annual Dinner being the first social event in the Club's calendar, it seemed natural to have this declared a Jubilee Mens' Dinner. Captain Bill Thomson had negotiated a strong team of guest speakers, including Ian Wood, Sandy Anderson, Hugh McGilvray and David Allan. With John Kennedy producing, as usual, a splendid dinner, the occasion was a great success. One of the highlights of the evening was the presentation and toast to David 'Cubby' Cuthbertson who was called out from the bar to acknowledge the tribute from the assembled company upon his 75 years which duplicated the age of the Golf Club.

The Annual General Meeting and EGM. There were a number of unusual items for consideration. Firstly, the Directors wished to nominate Alastair Mackechnie as Vice Captain, but Alastair was due to 'retire by rotation'. There was reason to believe that this nomination might be interpreted by the members as contravening the 'Constitution Rules and Bylaws' and the issue was referred to the Club's solicitors for clarification. After protracted correspondence it was considered advisable to hold an Extraordinary General Meeting immediately prior to the AGM to pass a Special Resolution *"That the Articles of Association of the Club be and are hereby altered by adding at the end of the second sentence of Regulation 40 the following words:*
"provided always that (i) the retiring Vice-Captain shall be eligible for election as Captain...."

In retrospect it seems sensible that a deserving Board member, who would otherwise be required to retire by rotation, should be allowed to stand for election as Vice-captain.

The second issue to be discussed at the AGM was the proposal to incorporate the Artisan Membership into the Club. It was evident that qualification for membership as an artisan was increasingly difficult to justify, and, additionally, Artisan Membership could be an unfair fast track to gaining playing rights over the course.

The EGM and AGM proceeded smoothly. Sadly, due to a family bereavement, Gordon Bonnington was unable to attend and was elected Club Captain in absentia. Alastair Mackechnie deputised as appropriate. Hilary Monaghan was awarded Honorary Membership, in recognition of her golfing achievements and this received universal acclaim. Bill Thomson, retiring Captain, stood down; Alastair Mackechnie was elected Vice-Captain; the Artisans would be incorporated. Some items were referred to the Board for consideration, including the prevention of unauthorised play on the course.

The Playing Season. The golfing season commenced with an Alternate Day Medal for the Ladies on Saturday 23rd of March. By this date the Seniors Open, to be held in August was already over-subscribed despite the qualifying age having been raised from 55 to 57. The men's golfing season began on Saturday 13th of April with a Medal in aid of 'Help the Aged'. The course conditions at this time of year were not ideal and the event was

The Board of Longniddry Golf Club Ltd 1996 Jubilee Year.

Back row: Malcolm Graham, Tom Edmond, Andrew Glasgow, Allen Davis, Norman Elliot, Alan Murray, Neil Robertson (secretary), Ian Robertson

Front row: Alastair Mackechnie *Vice Captain*, Gordon Bonnington *Captain*, Susan Bell *Lady Captain*, Eileen Dundas *Lady Vice Captain*.

The Pub Quiz Night, held prior to the start of the playing season, and compered by Allen Davis, was highly successful.

declared non-counting. Stephen Burton, with a net 65, qualified to compete at Rosemount in August in the 'Help the Aged' Regional Qualifier. The last medal of the year, won by D E Allan with a 69, was held on October 13th.

Raymond Russell in his first year on the European Tour won the Monaco Open at Cannes and went on to qualify for the Scottish Dunhill Cup Team. Scotland lost all three matches, but with scores of 69, 71 and 72, Raymond won two of his three matches and in doing so beat Nick Price on the final day. There was strong support from the Club at the event and some well-kent faces were seen drinking Raymond's health in The Jigger after the matches.

The County Cup.

Mike Stanton, Steven Thomson, Donald Hunter and Stuart Mackay won the County Cup for Longniddry at Muirfield in July. Here they are with Gordon Bonnington receiving the trophy.

Captain's Day on May 11th. The format was a 'Texas Scramble', followed by a dance with the ever-popular Dan's Band. The prize giving - scheduled for 7.30pm, with sponsored prizes arranged by the Captain - was delayed due to the large number of entrants and there was some difficulty in persuading the band to stop to allow the presentation to go ahead! The winning team comprised Murray Laird, Stuart Mackay and Derek Ramage with a gross 56 (best ball) strokes.

Invitation Foursomes, Friday 31st May. All 15 East Lothian Clubs were invited to send their Captain and Vice Captain to take part in a Foursomes Match against members of Longniddry. Guests convened at 2pm for a glass of wine in the Clubhouse and play commenced at 2.30pm. On a bright blustery day, the result was close enough to call a tie and was followed by dinner at 7.30pm. For Gordon Bonnington, as host and Captain, it proved gratifying to receive so many favourable comments on the event, and perhaps more importantly, on the condition of the course itself. It was apparent that Ken Anderson and his greens staff were getting things right. The greens were particularly praised.

Jubilee Day, Sat 20th July. This was the main event in the Jubilee Calendar, with a fourball best ball team event, open to all members and invited sponsors, followed by an evening barbecue, complete with "Oompah" band. Andrew Glasgow, as Social Convenor, must be given due recognition for his efforts to ensure the evening's success, particularly his choice of entertainment. Tables and chairs were hired, staff organised, and - just in case - a marquee had been erected by the Longniddry Scout Group. The weather was perfect - hot dry and sunny during the day, a cooling breeze in the afternoon followed by a warm, still, sunny evening. The prize-list was long and varied, with no outright winners. Four teams tied on 58 with a further seven teams one shot behind. Gillian Watt, with a deft touch, selected her green-keeping husband's team card from six others for the fifth prize.

On the night John and Jean Kennedy, with relentless efficiency and admirably assisted by family and staff, produced and distributed food and drink for 160 people, with 200 people attending in total. That the irrigation system sprang to life at 11.30pm was as comical as it was unexpected, particularly for the many people sitting on or near the first tee, but with hindsight this proved a fitting end to the day.

The Captain and the Professional entered the Volvo Pro-Am at Gullane and, in winning, qualified for the national final at Wentworth. This had been John Gray's first competitive round of golf for some years and his stated objective (certainly achieved) was not to disgrace himself. Winning was as unexpected as it was welcome.

Jubilee Day: The evening barbecue seen from one of the lurking sprinkler heads.

Gents v Ladies Jubilee Match, Sunday 18th August. This incorporated the annual challenge between Gents & Ladies for the Merlinlee Trophy. Matches commenced at 2pm and were followed by a wine reception and buffet. Fifty people took part, the Ladies won, the meal was superb.

Jubilee Dance, Saturday 24th August. The final event in the Jubilee calendar was held in the village Community Centre. This venue resulted from the Directors' wish to invite all staff and their partners as guests of the Club, something which would not be possible if using the Clubhouse.

Alistair Harkess beat George Morgan in the final of the newly inaugurated Seniors Summer Matchplay, one of several new competitions introduced by an active seniors section during the year.

Catering and bar were provided by Nita Ramage and Kilspindie House Hotel respectively and with the Portobello Celidh Band providing the dance music, all proceeded smoothly. There were no formalities or awards on the night, but if there had been, greens staff would have been in contention, particularly Kenny Mason, in full highland regalia, for Best Dressed Man.

The Ladies Home Internationals September 11th -13th September. It was an added bonus to hold this tournament during the Jubilee year, particularly with Hilary Monaghan, selected for the Scottish Team.

The first planning meeting was held in November 1995 and included Mrs Geraldine Turner, Chairman of the Ladies Golf Union, Sally Hepburn, LGU Tournament Secretary, the Club Secretary and June McEwan, the Ladies Honorary Secretary. During the preparations, Julie Hall took over from Sally Hepburn as LGU Tournament Secretary.

In due course, Tuesday 10th September, the day of the first practice rounds had arrived, with the competition proper only hours away and everything in place except flagpoles! In the afternoon the competitors and the LGU officials met the Longniddry Golf Club President Lord Wemyss and the Countess together with the members of the Board at a most pleasant and friendly reception in the Clubhouse. Hostilities began next day. Scotland played Wales and England met Ireland.

During the week the weather played its part, changing from warm and sunny to cold, windy and overcast, then back to warm and sunny on the final day. With a round-robin format, foursomes in the morning and singles in the afternoon, all the girls competed with good humour, determination and incredible skill. All the teams enjoyed considerable support and who among us could not fail to be impressed by their distance off the tee. On the final day it was between Scotland and England for honours. England won a very close match 5-4.

Club Captains Gordon Bonnington and Susan Bell with the winning team and officials.

In retrospect, the organisation and effort put in by Club members proved one of the deciding factors in ensuring the success of the competition. From floral arrangements in team colours in the newly decorated dining room to the supply of fruit and bottled water in the locker rooms, nothing had been over-looked. Team hostesses, trolley pullers, marshals, car-parking and locker-room attendants, locker volunteers and the piper at the prize-giving, all deserve credit. (No one person should be singled out for praise, but if there was an E for Effort, Joyce Hunnam would surely merit it.)

1996 in the Clubhouse. During the year the routine and not so routine activities continued. Bill Thomson and Alastair Mackechnie had been instrumental in progressing the renewal of the men's toilets and showers. Work commenced on January 3rd by local builders Reywood. On February 9th the toilets were re-opened, if not completed. The decision to provide a toilet near the door of the men's locker room enabled spikes to be prohibited on the new quarry tiles of the renovated toilet area.

Not surprisingly, once the toilet and shower area had been renovated the adjacent locker room appeared by contrast somewhat worn and shabby. A decision to not to revamp the locker-room until the following year was reviewed and the work was brought forward.

By mid summer, with much of the planned decoration and refurbishment completed, including the lounge ceiling, the dining room was repainted, with lights and new curtains. The existing carpet and furniture were retained. It is only a slight exaggeration to state that this work was completed only hours before the Dining Room was given over to the teams and officials of the Ladies Home Internationals.

1996 – on the Course. During the winter the greens staff implemented the first phase of bunker refurbishment. This proved to be a drawn-out process and for a while, with an ever-increasing number of dug-out bunkers, it appeared that staff had attempted too much. The problem lay with the lack of availability of materials. 'Tay sand', ordered well in advance, was unavailable because the dredger was laid up in dry dock. Secondly, the long dry summer of 1995 had resulted in a severe shortage of turf for re-vetting. Staff were obliged to use turf from the edge of fairways, with the difference in quality evident all summer, particularly at the 12th and 16th greenside bunkers. The winter and early spring also proved a bad year for disease on the greens - fusarium, again - a common problem elsewhere in early 1996, but this was little consolation.

If murmurs of discontent were being heard, they were soon to be replaced by a growing appreciation among the membership on the improvement in the putting surfaces.

Despite the difficulties with another dry summer and the ravages of the

It is a pleasure to report on minutiae. The birth of a son, Hamish Alexander in February to the Secretary and his wife Belinda, the wedding of Bruce and Pauline Kennedy in the Clubhouse in June, also the month of Iain and Gillian Watt's wedding, the Captain's Silver Wedding Anniversary in July, a grandson for the Finance Convenor George Morgan in September, the marriage of Stephen Thomson and Betty Monaghan in October.

These gains could not have been achieved without the green-keeping skills of Ken Anderson, the Head Greenkeeper and his staff. However, the commitment from the Directors for continued investment in capital items must also be recognised. By and large, Ken was given a free hand to choose the equipment he thought necessary for the job and over £100,000 of new equipment had been acquired over three years, excluding £65,000 spent in 1995 on a new irrigation system.

rabbits from the bents, the staff produced true and fast putting surfaces. At last! Better than Luffness ? better than Muirfield ? best in East Lothian ? (move over Jim King – Ed.) Perhaps an exaggeration, but that summer there was evident pride amongst staff and members in what had been achieved in a relatively short time. By mid-September, during the Home Internationals, the greens were being cut three times a day to ensure consistency but they were also being watered at night to 'slow them down'. The stimp-meter was 10 or better. This treatment could not be sustained indefinitely, and given the scores on the Saturday Medal, CSS +1, during perfect golfing weather, it is perhaps just as well! Not everyone can putt on fast greens.

During the season Ken Anderson also ensured that all the other essential operations were being attended to: fairways were reshaped (sometimes, it has been muttered, to suit the game of those doing the re-shaping); trees were planted or removed where appropriate; gorse and buckthorn were cut back to encourage regeneration; ditches were dug out; worn areas were re-turfed, bridges were re-newed - business as usual.

By October the second phase of bunker renovation was under way and fairways had been scarified. Fairway verti-draining and the implementation of 'winter play' was imminent.

And all the while, as this is being written, the Secretary's Office continues as a hive of activity. Most of us would expect that the summer would be the busy period, but in fact the reverse is true. July and August are the quiet months. Everything which should have been done to ensure a successful season either has been done or it won't be. In September things are starting to hot up, with thoughts of the financial year end at 30th November, the need to track current year finances against estimates, detect trends, and start the process of budgeting - with the impact on subscriptions. By October, trophies are being recalled in readiness for engraving and the prize-giving in November. Expected changes in the membership profiles are being examined, with Juniors reaching 18 years to be advised of options. Handicaps to be reviewed, fixture list confirmed, provisional bookings from visitors confirmed. Auditors are due in the first week of December, just after the year end and the annual report is to be written, to go to the printers immediately following Christmas. AGM Report to be agreed, issues resolved, subscription notices to be sent out, with newsletter, and AGM Report in January. Subscriptions recorded, resignations, renewals and new memberships processed, hold AGM, arrange Men's Dinner in February. And so it goes on, until, hopefully by June, after the Club Championships, it all calms down for a bit.

All in all, 1996, our Jubilee, has been a successful year. Perhaps even a vintage one. Here's to the next 75.

ACKNOWLEDGEMENTS

There are numerous acknowledgements to be made: many people have helped in the research and preparation of this book.

Firstly, I must all thank the members of my immediate family and my friends who not only helped me directly (obtaining photographs, offering comment, searching library records etc) but who have had to put up with all the abstractions, absences and preoccupations of an inexpert author.

Then I must also say 'thank you' to the several writers and professional persons whose participation has been so crucial. In this category not only did the Earl of Wemyss kindly agree to provide the Foreword, he carried out significant research and and afforded valuable comment and advice which was much appreciated. The contributions of the six other writers were also most gratefully received. Frank Hamilton was the first to be asked, and he responded almost immediately. His enthusiasm was typical of the responses of the others, and it can only be refreshing for the reader to encounter articles in the book from other members: Willie Carrol, Jack Little, Peter Lowe, Allen Davis and Neil Robertson . The whole credit for the attractive design and layout of the book must go to 'Chico' Ramos and his typesetting friend Dave Hall. Chico as a Club member offered his professional services at an early stage.

Grateful acknowledgement must also be made to two other Club members, Frank Latimer of 'Say Cheez' who took many of the photographs and Douglas McIntyre who prepared all the illustrations and text for reproduction in the book. Finally in this category are two essential persons – typists Belinda Robertson who saw the beginning of the project and Marilyn Young who took it up, organised and finished it for me in such fine style. I found that the accuracy of these ladies and their enduring patience with my revisions and changes were vital to the whole process, and I am greatly indebted to them both.

The illustrations of the holes of Longniddry Golf Course in chapter I are taken from the course planner published by Birdie Golf Productions. A special 'thank you' is therefore expressed to Directors Brian Short and David Howden for the ready and helpful response which they gave to my request to reproduce their excellent diagrams in the book.

Several publications have been consulted. Of them the History of Longniddry Village by local historian David Robertson must have first mention. His book is an essential starting point for anyone who wishes to learn about Longniddry and its surroundings. A difficulty was the temptation to include much fascinating information contained in David's account which was not relevant to the golf course story. I offer my grateful thanks to David for his permission to use so much of his material. Other publications and authors to whom I am indebted are: The Scotsman, The Daily Telegraph, The Observer, The Golfer's Handbook – various editions, publishers Macmillan 'The Pillars of the Temple' – a History of Duddingston Golf Club by Norman Mair, 'An Illustrated History of Golf' by Robert Green, publishers Harper-Collins, 'Scotland's Golf Courses' by Robert Price, publishers Aberdeen University Press D & J Croal of Market Street, Haddington, for permission to reproduce the text of their 1928 booklet 'Longniddry District and its Golf Course' Thanks are also due to Pringle of Scotland for permission to reproduce the articles by Norman Mair and Gordon Durward originally written for the 1970 Pringle Senior Professional Golf Championship, and to 'Golf Illustrated' for its report on the outcome. Two years later the 'Golf Illustrated'carried articles by Tom Scott describing the 1972 British Seniors at Longniddry and the World Seniors which followed it. Thanks once again to the publication for permission for the use of this material. Acknowledgement and thanks must be expressed for some other articles: The Illustrated London News for permission to reproduce the MEL cartoons and commentary from the Tatler, the Evening Dispatch representatives for the report of R M Lees' record round for permission to print exracts from their programme for the 1961 Carling Caledonian Tournament. Penultimately in this category is the article by Ian Stuart given in the Introduction and which was originally published in Scotland's Magazine. I am most grateful to The Scottish Tourist Board for permission to quote from their publication.

Lastly one of the greatest debts which must be acknowledged is that to the East Lothian Courier (previously the Haddingtonshire Courier) and to Director Ken Whitson, Editor Elaine Holt and her deputy Ian Metcalfe and their staff. I was most generously given access to their records and I experienced nothing but kindness, help and encouragement from all the staff of the paper. At the printing/publishing stage Allan Doyle was particularly helpful and encouraging. I am most appreciative.

There may be omissions in the above list. Best efforts have been made to trace copyright holders concerned, but should it transpire that a copyright has been infringed, this has been inadvertent. In such circumstances if the matter is reported to the Secretary of the club he will ensure that subsequent editions of the text are corrected.

Finally, at the end of this long reckoning, comes the most important 'thank you' of all. That is to all the persons in the Club who offered me information and put up with my enquiries, interviews and 'phone calls. Of these pride of place must go to Nancy Jupp who took the trouble to write to me from Oklahoma. Later she sent her full scrapbook which arrived just as we were going to press so that there was only time to include a few items from it. Her early letter came when I was at a low ebb, having great difficulty in getting the story going. The information about the course and personalities of the early days which she furnished gave me an excellent start and high momentum for the rest of the journey I only hope that having inspected the outcome readers will consider it to have been worthwhile. I did endeavour to keep a note of everyone I had seen or talked to, or whose writings I had used. However there were so many that it is possible that some have been omitted from the following list. If so I offer my apologies.

Dan Abbot
Betty Adams
Peter Allis
Bob Anderson
Duncan Ayton
Andrew Bathgate
Malcolm Balfour-Melville
Susan Bell
George Bonnar
Gordon Bonnington
Dick Burge
Peter Burt
Joan Campbell
Linda Conroy
Matthew Cunningham
David Cuthbertson
Gilbert Dempster
Marjory Douglas
Eileen Dundas
Maurice Dunleavy
Gordon Durward
Peter Dobereiner
Allan Doyle
Mary Elliot
Victor Elliot
Norman Elliot
Rt Hon Earl of Wemyss
George Ferguson
John Gray
Dorothy Geddie
Alex Good
John Gunn

The Hayward family
George Harkess
Alastair Harkess
Alex Harvey
Ron Herkes
Duncan Herd
Angus Hunter
David Huish
Bob Jackson
Archie Johnston
Thelma Johnston
Nancy Jupp
Ted Justin
Peter Lowe
John Kennedy
Jean Kennedy
Euan Kennedy
Louise Lees
Patricia Lees
Stuart Laird
Audrey Laird
Jean Mackechnie
Alan Mackechnie
Colin Mackechnie
Bob McInnes
June McEwan
Dougie McIntyre
Nancy Hay
Jimmy Hume
Jim Hunnam
James McKay
Alistair Mackay

Norman Osborne
Cristine Paxton
Robina Paxton
(Ruby Bell)
Tom Porteous
Bella Porteous
Bob Powe
Dorothy Rennie
Mrs Russell
Bill Reekie
Lawrie Reilly
Kath Rose
Neil Robertson
Ian Robertson
Hilda Smith
Bunty Smith
Jim Scott
Eddie Turnbull
George Taylor
Bill Thomson
Jenny Morrison
Mrs F Morgan
Ian McRaild
Archie Moore
Gavin Boyd
Michael Walls
Ella Vlandy
Maisie Walls
Willie Weston
Sandy Williamson
John Wood (LGA)
Peter Wood

HONORARY PRESIDENTS OF LONGNIDDRY GOLF CLUB

1921 - 37	Hugo Richard Charteris	1937 - Present	Francis David Charteris
	11th Earl of Wemyss and March		*12th Earl of Wemyss and March*

HONORARY VICE-PRESIDENTS OF LONGNIDDRY GOLF CLUB

1936 - 45	Sir David Kinloch, Baronet	1964 - 80	George Mitchell
1946 - 52	Bailie T Sawers	1981 - 83	Gordon Durward OBE
1952 - 64	Maurice F Yorke	1984 - Present	Tom Porteous

HONORARY PRESIDENTS OF LONGNIDDRY LADIES GOLF CLUB

1946 - 88	The Countess of Wemyss	1988 - Present	Francis David Charteris
	and March		*12th Earl of Wemyss and March*

HONORARY VICE-PRESIDENTS OF LONGNIDDRY LADIES GOLF CLUB

There is no record before Mrs Beddows

? - 76	Mrs E. C. Beddows
1976 - 83	Dr. R. Donaldson
1983 - Present	Miss K. Rose

HONORARY SECRETARIES OF LONGNIDDRY LADIES GOLF CLUB

1923 - 1954	Emma H. Sawers, J.P.	1974 – 1982	Elaine Osborne
1955 - 1966	Jenny Arnot	1982 – 1987	Audrey Laird
1966 - 1968	Mary Lawrence	1987 – 1992	Bunty Smith
1968 – 1974	Dora Sproul	1992 – present	June McEwan

CAPTAINS OF LONGNIDDRY GOLF CLUB

Until 1935 Lord Wemyss was both President and Captain of the Club

1935 – S. Forsyth   A very good golfer. Proprietor of prestige retailers in Glasgow and Edinburgh, R. W. Forsyth, Stuart lived at 'Jock's Lodge' on the edge of first fairway. He donated the Ladies Championship Cup and the trophy for the best scratch score in the Autumn Meeting.

1936 – A. F. Simpson   Quantity Surveyor. First class golfer, reached final in British Amateur in 1926 when he was beaten by Jesse Sweetzer USA. Champion of the Club three times. Arthur's drawing of the original course dated 1930 is highly valued by the Club. He was also Captain of Lothianburn and Royal Burgess.

1937 – J. McCredie   An Edinburgh Car Sales Executive associated with Sloan's Garage beside the Dean Bridge. Distinction of holing his tee shots at the 6th both just before and just after the hole had been changed. John was Club champion in 1936 the year before his Captaincy.

1938/39 – J. C. (Tim) Rose   A banker with the Royal Bank of Scotland. Tim was twice Club Champion of Duddingston Golf Club. Lived at 'Shalimar' at the bend of the 17th fairway. Sadly, died in second year of his Captaincy. His daughter Kath is Lady Vice-President.

1940/46 – T. Sawers   An Edinburgh Bailie. Tom was a member of the Sawers family which was active and supportive to Longniddry Golf Club. Captain of the Club throughout the Second World War. Lived at 'Woodburn' at the bottom of Lyars Road. Donated the Emma Sawers Cup for the Ladies Spring Meeting and the Sawers Cup for the Mens Summer Handicap Singles Competition.

1947/48 – V. B. Hilton   Major Hilton (Vernon) became Captain in 1946. He lived in 'Divot' in

Gosford Road. It was under his Captaincy that the Mackenzie Ross changes to the course were made. In September 1947 Major Hilton was able to report to the AGM that Longniddry Golf Club had an 18 hole course once again.

1949/50 – I. M. Buchanan Ian Buchanan was a very good golfer. In his profession he was a Marketing Executive with the Dunlop Rubber Company. He proved himself to be a very active and conscientious Captain.

1951/54 – A. Dudgeon A Haddington Seedsman. His first love was cricket. Alex had captained Haddington Cricket Club and turned to golf on his retirement. Was one of the chief negotiators for the Club when the new Constitution was agreed with the Estate in 1956.

1955/57 – J. A. (Gus) McVey An Insurance Executive, 'Gus' was an excellent golfer and dedicated Captain. A Heriot's FP, he was chiefly responsible for the establishment of the East Lothian Winter League Competition.

1958 – R. Patrick Russel Patrick was a senior partner of Patrick and James WS which had been founded by his father. Russel lived at 'Hilden' in Links Road and had been educated at Viewforth School and Edinburgh Academy. He held a commission in the Royal Horse Artillery during the First World War. He joined the Golf Club in 1937. He was Platoon Commander of the local Home Guard during World War II and he presented the Boy's Championship Trophy to the Club. Most sadly, he died only three months after being elected Captain of the Club.

1959/60 – P. Barr A Royal Bank of Scotland man. Formidable golfer with a deadly short game. He defeated Bob Anderson in the final of the Club Championship in 1947. Peter's son Alastair is also an excellent golfer and is coach nowadays to the English Ladies Golf Union.

1961 – A. McLellan Archie McLellan was another Banker. He lived beside the first fairway in 'Blackness' the house later occupied by Dr. Ian Forbes.

1962/63 – J. M. Adair John Adair was a draper. He was an old Heriot's man like Gus McVey. His shop was in Leith Street. Like Alex Dudgeon, his first love was cricket. John captained the Heriots FP Cricket Club for some years.

1964/65 – T. Porteous Tom Porteous is a Quantity Surveyor. His career started with Richard Baillie and he moved on and upwards until he retired from Scottish Special Housing Association. An extremely good golfer, characterised by the unusually high wooden tees which he uses. He lost to Alex Harvey in the final of the Club Championship in 1978. He has been a dedicated supporter of Longniddry Golf Club all his life. Tom remains the youngest person ever to have been elected Captain of Longniddry Golf Club. He has always been interested in young players and has contributed enormously in their management and development. Tom was responsible for extensive and significant improvements to the Club during his Captaincy. As Honorary Vice-President he attends Board meetings with consistent regularity giving valuable advice to the Officers and Directors of the day. For a time he was President of the Lothian's Golf Association and represented Lothians on the Scottish Golf Union.

1966/67 – J. Sykes The Headmaster for several years of Preston Lodge High School Joe gifted the Sykes trophy. Joe had an artificial leg. One day he slipped coming off the 4th green and could not continue. He had to sit in the hut at the 4th hole, the story goes, until his wife arrived with a replacement leg.

1968/69 – I. A. Forbes Doctor Ian Forbes was a Senior Executive of Scottish Distillers and a dedicated Director and Captain of the Club. He lived at 'Blackness' beside the first fairway. He donated the 'B' Championship trophy to the Club in 1969. He was also a member of Muirfield. Ian took a particularly keen interest in the young players of the Club.

1970/71 – T. C. (Gil) Gass A category 1 golfer, and ex Navy man, Gil was a Civil Servant with the Scottish Office before his retirement. Gil, a tall well built chap, is a formidable match player, and was Club Champion in two consecutive years.

1972/73 – W. M. (Billie) Reekie A very level-headed and competent Captain, Billie is a strong player with a short powerful swing. He is a local fishmonger, and one of the longest playing members , having joined in 1947. It is said that in his younger days his swing was much fuller.

1974/75 – J. W. M. (Jocky) Forbes Jocky Forbes of fond memory was of diminutive stature but perpetually cheerful and self deprecatory. He would tell the story about being dismissed from the Scots Guards 'after they found out that he had lied about his height.' Jocky donated the mallet and gavel used at formal meetings of the Club.

1976/77 – T. A. Milne Tom Milne was a National Coal Board Officer before his retirement. He had had a notable war record and if pressed could tell how, with the vehicles in his charge, he managed to transport a contingent of the Royal Greenjackets to the Channel coast when France fell. A dedicated business-like and hard working Captain of the Club.

1978/79 – H. M. McGilvray Another naval man with Arctic Convoy experience it is whispered. Hugh McGilvray is tall and friendly with a polished courteous manner. A gifted public speaker and excellent golfer, Hugh organised a comprehensive overhaul of the Club's rules of membership, entry application, and control of visitors.

1980/81 – S. W. Laird Stuart Laird is a Consulting Engineer. His Captaincy was a highly successful one. One of his Club projects was the irrigation system. Refurbishment and re-furnishing of the lounge was another. It was he who persuaded Gilbert Dempster to accept the post of Secretary to the Club.

1982/83 – I. B. Jackson Although of short stature, Ian Jackson was extremely strong and in his heyday he was one of the longest drivers in the Club. An Insurance Executive with Scottish Widows, he had in his youth played professional football - described as 'a fast winger'. Ian's nephew Graham Parkinson is also a Club member and a formidable golfer himself. He tells us that Ian played in the Stirling Albion Team which faced Glasgow Rangers on the occasion of Sine Die suspension of Willie Woodburn. Ian's Captaincy is remembered as one of the most successful with a particularly happy social programme.

1984/85 – D. C. Abbot Dan Abbot is another retired banker. A Royal Bank of Scotland man. During his Captaincy the construction of the greenkeepers sheds was undertaken with careful safeguards for the members' interests agreed with the Estate.

1986/87 – D. P. Allan Duncan Allan is a member of the Lighthouse Service. With a beautiful slow graceful swing, Duncan is a low handicap golfer. Before and during his Captaincy he was a tireless worker on behalf of the Club taking personal responsibility for a large number of activities.

1989/90 – P. D. Lowe Peter is another excellent golfer. By contrast to his predecessor, Peter's swing is short and fast. A Customs and Excise man, Peter took over the Captaincy at a difficult time after the resignation of the previous Board in 1987. His sensible and even-handed approach did much to restore harmonious relationships. He is perhaps the only member of Longniddry Golf Club to have won the East Lothian Hope Medal. He followed this achievement by winning the summer foursomes competition in partnership with his father Douglas who won the Lothians Seniors' Competition all in the same year.

1990/91 – R. F. W. Fullard Ron Fullard is a Surveyor. He is a Newcastle man and was brought north to Longniddry about 1970 by his employers Scottish and Newcastle Breweries. He is a formidable golfer with a method all his own. Often played with the late lamented Ian Jackson.

1992/93 – J. A. M. Mackenzie Jim Mackenzie was, before his retirement, Roads Engineer for Scotland. He is an Inverness man. During Jim's Captaincy, important steps in relaxing the Club's dress regulations were taken. He also instigated the unpopular rule of regularly teeing up on the fairways during the winter which has had so much to do with the improvement in the quality of the course.

1994/95 – W. Thomson Bill Thomson who hails from Whitburn is another retired Royal Bank of Scotland Manager. His period of Captaincy was one of the most active and eventful. Significant improvements in the Clubhouse and on the course were achieved and a difficult rent review successfully completed.

1995/96 – G. Bonnington Like Alex Dudgeon before him, Gordon is a seedsman and cricketer. He has been for several years Captain of Haddington Cricket Club. As a previous Greens Convenor, he can take credit for the substantial improvement in the quality of the golf course. Teamed with John Gray who had not played competitive golf for a long time, he won the Scottish heat of the Volvo Pro Am at Gullane in 1996. Gordon conducted the Jubilee Year with a friendly courteous competence and encouraged an active and entertaining social programme.

APPENDIX IV
LADY CAPTAINS OF LONGNIDDRY GOLF CLUB

1923/25 –Mrs G. Jupp Ethel Jupp had not long moved with her family to Longniddry when she was elected first Lady Captain at the inaugural meeting of the Ladies Club. She had been a singer in her younger days - a member of the D'Oyley Carte Company and had appeared publicly in Iolanthe. She served as Captain for three years.

1926/27 – Mrs Banks Like Mrs Jupp, Madge Banks was a founder member of the Ladies Club. Her husband was a banker in Haddington. It was under Madge's Captaincy that the decision was taken that the Club should join the Scottish Ladies Golfing Association.

1928 – Miss K J Wishart Kathleen Wishart was another founder member. It was under her Captaincy that several of the regular competitions were decided upon; a monthly bogey competition during the winter on the second Tuesday; all competitions on Tuesdays in future; etc. She concluded her Captaincy by asking for a grant from the main Club of three shillings per lady member. It was refused.

1929/31 – Miss D Park A Curtis Cup player, Doris Park's golfing antecedents are given in full in the section on the Ladies Club. She won the Ladies Club Championship while she was Captain. This achievement was not repeated for 66 years.

1931/32 Mrs Snowdon Mary Snowdon lived in 'Westwood' beside the end of the first fairway. She took up the Captaincy in October 1931. During her Captaincy matches with seven other clubs including Goswick were arranged.

1933/34 Mrs Hilton 'Sibbi' Hilton lived with her husband Vernon in Gosford Road. Their house was called 'Divot'. It was later occupied by Secretary Wally Burt and his wife Mary. Nowadays its name is 'Sherwood'. 'Sibbi' is described as always wearing enormous drooping gold ear-rings

1935/36 – Mrs Rose Edith took some pleasure in achieving the Captaincy of the Ladies two years before her husband 'Tim' was elected Captain of the main Club. This in spite of the fact that she had refused an earlier offer of the Captaincy. Edith was an effective golfer according to her daughter Vice-President Kath, and she won the Ladies Club Championship in 1930.

1937/45 – Mrs J J Latta Annice Latta lived in 'Eldon' in Gosford Road. She was an excellent golfer winning the Club Championship in 1947. For many years she was Handicap Secretary to the Ladies Club. Annice remained Lady Captain throughout the war. She is commemorated by the Latta Cup and was elected Honorary Member of the Club in 1964.

1946/47 – Miss S M W Millar Sophie Millar was a particularly good golfer. She lived in Edinburgh. Upon her marriage she became Mrs G F Ford. She was a stalwart of the Scottish Ladies Golf Union and she was also a member of the Ladies Golf Union.

1948/49 – Miss A L Scott 'Nanny' Scott lives in Joppa. She contrived to be both a formidable golfer and a very generous person. She donated the Nanny Scott Salver to the Club. 'Nanny' was also a Convenor of the Ladies Club at Liberton and stalwart of the Scottish Ladies Golf Union.

1950/51 – Miss I M V Park Irene Park was a teacher by profession. She was another of the Park family of Musselburgh. She won the Ladies Club Championship in 1934.

1952/53 – Miss E S H McEwan Sophie McEwan lived in Edinburgh. She was a Mary Erskine former pupil. She was a PE teacher and is described as a great character. She was another firm supporter of the Ladies Golf Union. She is commemorated by the McEwan Quaich for competition by Senior Ladies.

1954/55 – Mrs P F Cadzow Betty Cadzow was originally from Carlisle. She was a very good golfer. Betty and her husband Peter were firm supporters of Longniddry Golf Club. They lived in Drem. For many years Betty was Honorary Treasurer of the Ladies Club. She holed her tee shot at the 6th in 1968.

1956/57 – Mrs Patrick Molly and Russel Patrick lived in 'Hilden', the house on the east side of Links Road which faces up Kings Road. After her husband's death Molly donated the Russel Patrick trophy to the Club for competition by the Junior Boys. Molly was elected an Honorary Member of the Club in 1967.

1958/59 – Mrs H Rodgers Mrs Rodgers (her Christian name is not recorded) and her husband owned the Golf Hotel in Gullane. It was Mrs Rogers who drew the Board's attention to John Kennedy when a new Clubmaster was required in the mid 60's.

1960/61 – Mrs W C Ritchie (Miss C M Park) Katie Park's golfing history was a most distinguished one like that of her cousin Doris. Details of it are given in the section on the Ladies Club. It seems that by chance both Katie's Club Championship (1954) and her Captaincy did not come until comparatively late in her career given that she had been playing very high-quality golf since the early 30's.

1962/63 – Doctor Donaldson Rose Donaldson came of a golfing family. Her brother Dr T E (Eric) Donaldson won the Eden Tournament in 1955. Rose was a chest specialist at East Fortune Hospital. With much coal mining in East Lothian at the time, she had a busy professional life. She was quite short in stature but very strong. In all, she won the Longniddry Ladies Championship ten times, nine of them consecutively from 1963-71. She is commemorated in the Club by the Donaldson Rose Bowl trophy.

1964/65 – Mrs I C P Thomson 'Babs' Thomson was born a McEwan. For many years she lived in the magnificent house 'Lincluden,' now 'Hestan', which looks over the bunkers of the first fairway. 'Babs' moved away from Longniddry, to North Berwick it was said, towards the end of the eighties.

1996/67 – Mrs D T Douglas Marjorie Douglas and her family lived for many years in

'Inchmaholme' beside the 16th tee. She donated the first lounge carpet to the Club during her Captaincy. Apart from her golf interests, she is also a senior figure in the Girl Guides County organisation.

1968 – Mrs D Rennie Dorothy is the daughter of Doctor Robarts who was personal physician to the 11th Earl of Wemyss . Like Mrs Douglas she has been involved with the Girl Guide movement at senior level. A good golfer in her day, she can still proudly display the blazer of her golfing blue for Edinburgh University on 1933-34.

1969 – Dr E M Campbell Joan Campbell has always been a most staunch supporter of the Ladies Club. She is an ophthalmologist by profession and a keen bridge player. Her golf is good too. She got a hole-in-one at the 6th in 1960. Like her predecessor, she served one year as Captain.

1970 – Mrs W S McEwan Mrs McEwan was the third Captain in succession to serve only one year in office. This arrangement was to continue until Mrs F Morgan in 1974. Mrs McEwan's husband Willie, was a physician and a founder member of the Golf Club.

1971 – Mrs P Stroyan Margaret Stroyan lived in Gosford Road when she was Captain of the Ladies Club. She frequently played with Maisie Walls who was of course her neighbour.

1972 – Mrs J C Morrison Jenny Morrison is a most popular member of the Ladies Club. She is described as 'always being in a hurry'. She lives at Longniddry Farm. She donated the Morrison Cup to the Club for competition by the Ladies.

1973 – Mrs T Porteous Bella Porteous has been associated with the Club since her youth. During holidays she sometimes served in the dining room. Bella has been both Secretary and Captain of the Lady Artisans. She continues to support Vice-President Tom in all his many activities associated with the Club.

1974/75 – Mrs F Morgan With Florence Morgan the two year duration of the Lady Captain's term was restored. Florence recalls that in 1973 the Ladies decided that the single year term was too short. In her spell as Captain, Florence saw the Ladies Home Internationals played at Longniddry for the first time. Although there was a 20 year break in the middle, Florence had a long playing career. In the Lifeboat Competition of 1992 she came second at the age of 80.

1976 – Mrs A D Sproul Dora Sproul has always taken a keen interest in the RNLI. She donated the Dora Sproul Cup which is contested annually in the Lifeboat Competition. Subsequently Dora presented the Dick Sproul Cup to the Club in memory of her husband Dick. Dora served for one year.

1977/78 – Mrs L A de Vries Lily is described as a great character and quite unpredictable. It is said that life under her Captaincy was never dull. Lily's sons Derek and Gordon donated a handsome seat in memory of their mother. It sits on the terrace of the Clubhouse.

1979/80 – Mrs J A Fisher Ella Fisher was a well-liked Captain, very highly thought of in the Club. It was established under Ella's Captaincy that prior to all ladies major competitions, the course would be closed 30 minutes before the ladies first tee-off time.

1980/81 – Mrs B C Cooper Barbara lives in Edinburgh and is particularly remembered for the way she zipped in and out of the Club in her natty wee sports car. She was also reckoned to be a pretty good golfer in her day.

1982/84 – Lady Kincraig Lady Kincraig served a longer than normal term as Lady Captain because Ethel Jack, her successor, was not available to take over the post. She was a very organised person and during her period of office she made sure that proceedings were conducted in a brisk and business-like fashion.

1985/86 – Mrs P C Jack Ethel is one of the Longniddry team which won the Granger Cup in 1975. This was a first for Longniddry. Ethel is a Scottish Internationalist and an influential figure with the LGU and the SLGU.

1987/88 – Mrs R Lawrie Netta lives in Selkirk. During the winter she made many journeys in unpleasant conditions to attend evening meetings at the Club. She is another member of the 1975 Granger Cup-winning team. Netta is the first lady to have chaired a full Directors' meeting of the main Club.

1989/90 – Mrs S W Laird Audrey hails from Musselburgh. About 1970 she had followed Elaine Osborne as Honorary Secretary of the Ladies Club. During her Vice-Captaincy she was very much involved as was her Captain Netta Lawrie in the Directors' deliberations leading up to and following the matter of 'the Starters' in 1987. Audrey also gave unstinting support to husband Stuart during his Captaincy of the Club in 1980-81.

1991/92 – Mrs T Reekie Terry Reekie is a good golfer with a very positive cheerful approach to the game. She now lives in Gullane with husband ex-Captain Billie. During Terry's Captaincy the need for a general refurbishment of the Ladies accommodation was highlighted and a start made.

1993/94 – Mrs S Hume Susan Hume is of course the wife of Jimmy Hume who began his golfing career at Longniddry Golf Course and is now Professional to the Gullane Golf Club. Upon taking up the Captaincy, Susan was very aware of two important and imminent ladies events to take place at Longniddry. The first was the East Lothian Ladies Championship in 1995 and the second was the Ladies Home Internationals in 1996. She addressed herself therefore to the condition of the ladies accommodation as a matter of urgency. During her tenure of the Captaincy, Susan took responsibility for the renovation of the ladies locker room whilst in the ladies lounge she organised new furniture and re-hanging of the curtains. Susan's foresight and application ensured that the ladies quarters were in excellent condition not only for the two visiting competitions mentioned, but also for the lady members' day to day enjoyment.

1995/96 – Miss S Bell Susan Bell is a mathematics teacher by profession. She is also a low handicap golfer and she won the Ladies Club Championship in the first year of her Captaincy. This was the first time that the double had been achieved since Doris Park 66 years before. Susan in her spell as Captain saw both the Ladies East Lothian Championship and the Ladies Home Internationals conducted successfully and harmoniously at Longniddry

APPENDIX V

SECRETARIES OF LONGNIDDRY GOLF CLUB

1921-36	G. A. Connor	1963-64	R. W. Burt	1977-81	S. W. Davis
1936-56	R. C. Cutter	1964-70	N. C. Osborne	1981-93	G. S. Dempster
1956-63	A. H.. Lawrence	1970-77	J. Gunn	1993-Present	N. R. Robertson

CLUBMASTERS OF LONGNIDDRY GOLF CLUB

1921 - 29	J. Shackleton	1956 – 1962	T. Robb
1929 - 52	A. Shearlaw	1962 – 1965	G. Morawisc
1952 - 56	Major Gill	1965 – present	J. G. Kennedy

PROFESSIONALS OF LONGNIDDRY GOLF CLUB

1923 - 30	G. Thomson	1957 - 77	G. Durward
1931 - 32	J. White	1977 - Present	J. Gray
1932 - 57	W. Morris		

HEAD GREENKEEPERS OF LONGNIDDRY GOLF CLUB

1921 - ?	A. Wright	1938 - ?	W. Wood	1961 - 94	D. Herd
? - 37	W. Brown	? - 59	T. Hogg	1994 - 95	C. Hildersley
1937 - 38	A. Samuel	1959 - 61	J. Campbell	1995 - Present	K. Anderson

APPENDIX VII

CHAMPIONS OF LONGNIDDRY GOLF CLUB

1931 – W B C Miller W B C Miller was also Club Champion of Duddingston in 1931 and 1932. He was Captain of Duddingston from 1950 to 1953 and President of the Lothians Golf Association 1960 to 1962. He is described as always being very smartly dressed and in the 30's as wearing 'co-respondent' shoes - i.e. one black and one white - which were for a time the very height of fashion. Two of his early gold medals are owned by the Club.

1932,34 & 37 – A F Simpson See Captains.

1933 & 38 – J H Martin Johnny Martin has been described as 'a great wee golfer'. He was a close friend of Gus McVey. A schoolteacher, he represented the Lothians and may have played for Caermount on occasions.

1935 – T G Dempster No relation to Gilbert Dempster. T G Dempster is said to have been a good golfer. He became Captain of North Berwick Golf Club, and was champion of several clubs besides Longniddry.

1936 – J McCredie See Captains.

1939 – W C Menzies An Edinburgh University Student when he won the Club Championship, W C Menzies had broken the course record by three shots with a 66 the previous year. He is thought to have moved to Carlisle about 1949.

1939 – 46 No competition

1947 – P Barr See Captains.

1948 – J D Amos Mr Amos was a banker. He played frequently for the bank in the Despatch Trophy. Longniddry was his second course. It is thought that Mr Amos' home course was Craiglockhart.

1949 – R E Muirhead No information.

1950 – G B Henderson Mr Henderson was a master baker and confectioner, owning several shops. Consequently he played on occasions for the Baxters. He won the championship of several clubs in the Lothians. It is thought that he was also a member of Dalmahoy.

1951,52 & 54 – J K Henderson Kello Henderson was a Bank Inspector in his professional role. He was extremely popular at Longniddry and seen as 'a real character'. Kello regularly played for the bank in the Despatch Trophy and he represented the Lothians. He retired to Troon.

1953,55 – S B Williamson Sandy Williamson is an honorary member of three golf clubs: Gullane, Longniddry and Royal Burgess. He has been Champion of all three more than once, but he never achieved all three titles simultaneously. His golfing career started with his victory in the British Boys Championship in 1939. He reached the final of the Lothians Championship three times, 1952, 53 and 55. On the first two occasions he was defeated by W C D Hare and on the third which was held at Longniddry, he lost to A M M Bucher. He was an internationalist 1947, 48, 49, 51 and 52 and Walker Cup Reserve 1949. He is currently scoring better than his age (75) at Gullane.

1956 – W D Smith Dick Smith's course is Selkirk, though he is originally from Troon. His other clubs are Prestwick, The Royal and Ancient, Royal Troon, Southerness and Gullane. He is a qualified Solicitor and is involved at high level in the Borders woollen industry. He was the leading amateur in the Open in 1957 and Scottish Amateur Champion in 1958. Abroad, he won the Indian Open Amateur Championship in 1945 and the Portuguese Open Amateur in 1967 and 70. Back home again he and his partner, Mrs B Singleton, won the Worplesdon Mixed Foursomes in 1957. Dick won the Royal and Ancient Medal in 1971 and played for Scotland in the Home Internationals six times. He played for Great Britain against Europe in 1958 and in the Walker Cup the following year when he met Jack Nicklaus. It is said that during their match they established a lasting friendship.

1957 – C R D Leeds Dr. Leeds was an eye specialist, a first class consultant and a very good golfer. He attended Professional Bill Morris when he collapsed on the first tee as he was about to referee the second 18 holes of the 1957 Championship.

1958 – H G Mackersy H G Mackersy lived in Portobello. Another banker and a good golfer, he used to compete in the President's Putter Competition at Deal. He was a Watsonian and won the Club Championship of Duddingston in 1936.

1959,60 – T G Gass See Captains.

1961 – G E Robertson Graham's father had been Communications Manager of the 'Scotsman' and a very keen member of Longniddry Golf Club. Graham himself is a Scottish Widows Executive. He is also a Dalmahoy member. In 1968 he reached the final of the Lothians Amateur Championship.

1962,65,68,73,78,83 – A Harvey Alex is one of two sons of John Harvey of Heart of Midlothian fame. Alex is a highly respected figure in Scottish Golf and in Longniddry Golf Club. He has been beaten only once in the final of the Club Championship which he has won six times. He has also been Vice-Captain of Longniddry Golf Club and it is greatly regretted that an unfortunate combination of circumstances deprived him of his opportunity to be Captain of the Club. He went to the last 16 of the British Amateur at Muirfield in the early 70's. In the course of this he defeated two formidable Americans and then Charlie Green himself. He regularly plays in Longniddry's Winter League Team.

1963 – D L Hayward. In 1949 David Hayward equalled the course record at Luffness with a 68. In the same year he played for Lothians. He was Musselburgh Golf Champion in 1951 and he broke the course record there also while still Club Champion with a 71. In 1955 he got to the final of the Scottish Amateur. David was a banker and played for what was then the National Bank of Scotland in the Evening Despatch Trophy.

1964,66 – P A Burt. Peter Burt is the son of R W ('Wally') Burt who was Secretary of Longniddry Golf Club in the early sixties. Peter is the only man to have beaten Alex Harvey in the final of a Longniddry Club Championship, though, as Peter points out, Alex got his revenge the following year. Among Peter's other successes were the Willie Park Putter at Musselburgh and the Haddington 36 Hole Open. Longniddry lost Peter when he went off to university in the USA. He is now a member of both Gullane and the Honourable Company and he is featured in

Norman Main's recent history of Muirfield. Peter A Burt is now Chief General Manager of the Bank of Scotland.

1967 – D Baillie David Baillie is a grandson of Richard Baillie the building contractor who constructed the older dwellings beside the 9th tee. He was a member of the first winning Longniddry Winter League Team in 1966/67 and also of the team which won the competition in 1970/71. David has now moved away from Longniddry but he is always sure of a warm welcome when he manages to return for a visit.

1969,71,75 – J W Montgomery John Montgomery's business interests on behalf of Lucas brought him for a time to Longniddry from the west. A County Class golfer, he was one of the members of the Longniddry team which won the Winter League in 1973/74. It was shortly after his last Club Championship win that his business took him south of the border.

1970 – L Reilly Lawrie Reilly is of course one of Scotland's most renowned centre forwards and the spearpoint of Hibernian's 'famous five' forward line. As a golfer, Lawrie is as fast as he was as a footballer, and for many years he would be out very early in the morning scorching round the course. He was dismissed from the Club Championship on two occasions when Alex Harvey beat him at the 9th extra hole. Lawrie Reilly was a member of the Longniddry team which won the County Cup in 1965 at Gullane and also of the teams which won the Winter League for the Club in 70/71 and 73/74.

1972 & 76 – F A Hall Fraser Hall was British Universities Champion in 1964. He beat Alan Murphy 5 and 4 in the final at the Southport and Ainsdale course. Fraser was a member of three of the Longniddry teams which won the Winter League namely: 1970/71, 73/74 and 77/78.

1974 – T Dickson Tommy Dickson from Port Seton is a comparatively small man with a powerful swing. Another 'great wee golfer'. Also a good footballer and was signed by Hibernian although he is not thought to have made the first team. Tommy is an Engineer and now lives in Australia. This is Tommy's second emigration. The story goes that he was partnering Billie Reekie in the summer foursomes. They had got through some early rounds when Tommy decided that he would emigrate to South Africa and suddenly did so. Billie got a phone call some days later. It was Tommy and it was a local call. "I didn't like South Africa", he said, "Are we still in the foursomes?" In fact they were, and Tommy and Billie played in the next round, Tommy having emigrated and then immigrated between ties.

1977 – J R Johnston Jim is also a member of Musselburgh Golf Club. He has been both Club Champion and Match-Play Champion there. Of average build Jim has a sweet smooth swing. He has reached the final of the Longniddry Club Championship four times in all, winning twice. Jim is a Civil Servant by profession.

1979,84,87 & 94 – P S Thomson Steven is one of a string of excellent players who have come up through the junior ranks of the Club. Steven's father Peter was a keen golfer and a well-liked member of the Club. Steven got an early introduction to the game therefore, and when the opportunity arises, pays tribute to Professional John Gray 's teaching abilities. Steven has a powerful swing which sends the ball away on a long drawing flight. His first introduction to the Championship finals was in 1976 when Fraser Hall played very well to beat him. Steven soon put this behind him and he is one of the most successful players in the Club Champions listing. He has reached the final on seven occasions and won four times.

1980,82 & 85 – K Cunningham Keith is another local man. By profession an Architect, he has a classic swing and is a particularly good long iron player. He was a member of Longniddry's winning team in the Winter League in both 1973/74 and 84/85.

1981 – B McPhie Bryan is a Perth and Kinross County Player. He is also a member at King James IV Island Course in Perth. He is powerfully built and has been described as a tigerish match player. With Wilma Gilmour, he has formed a very successful partnership for mixed competitions. By profession Bryan is a Contracts Engineer with British Gas.

1988 & 89 – N Davidson Another player from a Longniddry golfing family, Neil came up from the ranks of young golfers to win the Club Championship when he could not have been much older than 20. Neil was only the third player in the Club's history to defend the Club Championship title successfully. He is lightly built and has a very smooth economical swing. His profession when he first won the Championship was insurance, but he went back to university and recently graduated with a B Sc Honours in Business Studies. Neil is an all-round sportsman enjoying ski-ing and wind surfing.

1990 & 91 – A W Wilson Gus Wilson is a long time member of Glencorse Golf Club as well as Longniddry. He is a County Golfer and has been described as a very powerful hitter of the ball.

1992 & 96 – M S Stanton Michael's father is Peter Stanton, another long standing Longniddry member. Michael is an insurance man. He has a quite unassuming manner but he is a formidable match player. He was runner-up in the Lothian Boys Championship and a member of the Longniddry team which won the County Cup at Muirfield in 1976.

1993 – R W F Burge Dick Burge is a banker, a man of sharp wit and quick repartee. He was brought up in London and is a Tottenham Hotspur fan. His family also have local connections. He gained his Club Championship by defeating his good friend Steven Thomson in the final. He was a member of the Longniddry team which won the Winter League in 1984/85.

1995 – D G R Hunter Donald's father Stanley Hunter had won the Club's 'B' Championship four years before, the nearest there has been to father and son holding both Championships at the same time. Donald is a Customs man. He proved to be an excellent Champion supporting the Club on many occasions, including the County Cup victory at Muirfield in 1996. In the Winter League, Donald formed a most successful partnership with Raymond Russell .

Until 1996 only four players had successfully defended the title:

51/52 – J. K. (Kello) Henderson	88/89 – Neil Davidson
59/60 – T. G. (Gil) Gass	90/91 – A. W. Wilson

Gil Gass' defence of the title included a hole in one at the 6th in 1960.

Only four members have been both Captain and Champion. They are:
A F Simpson, J McCredie, P Barr, G Gass.

None have held both Offices at the same time.

Only Alex Harvey and Steven Thomson have won both the Club Championship and the Sawers Cup Handicap Competition in the same year. Alex achieved this twice 18 years apart in 1965 and 1983. Steven's double was in 1984.

CHAMPIONS OF LONGNIDDRY LADIES GOLF CLUB

1929, 36, 38, 46 – Miss D Park See Lady Captains.

1930 – Mrs J C Rose See Lady Captains.

1931 – Mrs Gore-Greenshields Unfortunately there is little recorded about Mrs Gore-Greenshields. All we have is that Mrs Gore-Greenshields took responsibility with Miss E H Sawers, Secretary of the Ladies Club, for the arrangements relating to the first RNLI Competition at Longniddry in September 1931.

1932 –- Miss S M W Millar See lady Captains.

1933 – Mrs A Cleland Irene lived in Musselburgh. She was an International Hockey Player and keen all-round sportswoman.

1934 – Miss I V M Park See lady Captains.

1935 – Miss N Sawers Nancy was the daughter of Bailie Tom Sawers who was to become Captain and later Vice-President of the Club. It must have been during the war that Nancy took seriously ill. The sun lounge on the west gable wall of 'Woodburn' at the bottom of Lyars Road was built for her convalescence. Nancy is now Mrs McLagen and lives in Perth.

1937 – Mrs Lockhart Cowan No information.

1939 – Miss M Nicol Mabel Nicol was a close friend of Nanny Scott and Betty Adam. She often wore a beret and was sometimes called Mabel with the beret. She was known to be a wonderful iron player and she used to chivvy her friends to compete, persuading for example, Betty Adam to enter the British Ladies Championship at Gullane.

1947 – Miss J J Latta See Lady Captains.

1948 – Miss E C McLarty Elizabeth is yet another good keen golfer. She is a County Player. She lives in Edinburgh and also plays at Musselburgh.

1949,50,53,58,60,62 – Mrs E C Beddows See Ladies Club.

1951 – Miss S M W Millar See Lady Captains.

1952 – Mrs G B Henderson Abbie was a good golfer like her husband who won the Men's Club Championship 1950, 53 and 55. Mrs Henderson was a very tough competitor particularly expert in match play contests.

1954,55,57,59 – Mrs W C Ritchie (Miss C M Park) See lady Captains.

1956 – Mrs H. Rogers See Lady Captains.

1961,63,64,65,66,67,68,69,70,71 – Dr. R Donaldson See Lady Captains.

1972 – Mrs R M Lees Louise is very much of a golfing family. Twenty years before she became Lady Champion, her husband Mr R M Lees of Liberton, broke the Longniddry course record with a 65. Louise's daughter, Patricia, went one better and has won the Longniddry Ladies Championship no less than eight times.

1973 – Miss K Rose Kath Rose is the daughter of two Club Captains and founder members: Edith of the Ladies Club and Tim of the Men's. She and her sister Elizabeth were brought up in 'Shalimar' at the edge of the 17th fairway. Only Kath's accelerated elevation to Vice-President prevented her from being elected Lady Captain in her turn.

1976,77, 84 – Miss S Macnamara (Mrs E A E Quinn) Shelagh Macnamara is one of the several excellent lady players who have come up through the junior ranks of the Club. Shelagh has been outstanding both as a junior and as an adult competitor. Her voice is now influential in Scottish Women's golf. She was convenor of the Scottish Ladies Golf Association in 1990 and bears responsibility for training within the Scottish Ladies Golf Union.

1978 – Mrs J R Beveridge   Joyce Beveridge is a Home Economics Teacher. A popular and cheerful character who can always be relied upon to play well. A pretty good golfer.

1979-81 & 1985-88 – Miss P J Lees   Patricia has won the Longniddry Ladies Championship on eight occasions, four of them consecutively. In 1984 she also won the Babe Zaharias Ladies Open at Longniddry with a net 73 in a field which included the American Curtis Cup Team. Patricia was East Lothian Ladies Champion in 1986 and she holds her Golfing Blue from Edinburgh University.

1989 & 92 – Miss J Hunnam   Joyce is a formidable golfer. A very straightforward and forthright person, she is dedicated to ladies' golf and to Longniddry Golf Club. Her many talents include an expertise in the mounting, annotating and presentation of publicity material and photographs. The framed photographs of Hilary Monaghan and Raymond Russell in the main lounge were prepared by Joyce.

1991 – Miss L McRaild   Lindsey is another excellent young lady golfer who has come up through the junior ranks of the Club. She was Junior Champion in 1987 and 88. She is now a school teacher, living near Lincoln, where she still plays golf and hockey as well.

1993 & 94 – Mrs J Denholm   Julia is a good all-round sports lady. A good tennis player as well as a good golfer. She is also a member of Dalmahoy Golf Club.

1995 – Miss S M Bell   See Lady Captains.

1996 – Miss V Kirkland   Vera is a remarkably good golfer. Her slight figure belies her hitting ability. She is one of the very few left-handed players in the Club.

LADIES AT 1996 HOME INTERNATIONAL RECEPTION

June Mc Ewan, Cristine Paxton, Jean Kennedy and Susan Bell

Shirley Black

Bunty Smith

221

APPENDIX IX

'B' CHAMPIONS OF LONGNIDDRY GOLF CLUB

(Dr. I. A. Forbes Trophy 1969)

1969	J. G. Morrison	1983	T. H. Fairlie
1970	P. A. Harkess	1984	D. Mackay
1971	J. G. Morrison	1985	R. M. Air
1972	D. Mackay	1986	J. McDougall
1973	B. Cox	1987	T. S. Miller
1974	N. A. M. Ritchie	1988	R. J. Johnston
1975	A. F. Harkes	1989	G. Bonnington
1976	N. Learmonth	1990	G. A. Falconer
1977	W. B. Laidlaw	1991	S. Hunter
1978	T. W. D. Bryson	1992	W. Gordon
1979	B. W. O'Connor	1993	G. A. Falconer
1980	R. Learmonth	1994	D. S. Wojtacha
1981	W. Watson	1995	R. R. Sharp
1982	A. G. Mackay	1996	W. Gordon

APPENDIX X

OPEN CHAMPIONS OF LONGNIDDRY GOLF CLUB

(Gordon Durward Trophy)

1967	B. Gallacher	1982	J. Huggan
1968	H. J. Fisher	1983	S. Morrison
1969	J. R. Inglis	1984	M. G. McLaren
1970	L. G. A. Morton	1985	J. R. Johnston
1971	C. L. Wood	1986	L. Gray
1972	A. Wight	1987	R. D. Ballantyne
1973	F. C. Black	1988	R. Russell
1974	F. C. Black	1989	B. Shields
1975	J. Hamilton	1990	M. Robson
1976	C. McLachlan	1991	G. Stangoe
1977	C. McLachlan	1992	B. Smith
1978	F. C. Black	1993	A. Turnbull
1979	J. B. Dunlop	1994	J. Noon
1980	J. McLean	1995	K. Nicholson
1981	S. Morrison	1996	C. Cuthbert

JUNIOR CHAMPIONS OF LONGNIDDRY GOLF CLUB

1982 M. G. McLaren	1987 R. Russell	1992 G. Ferguson
1983 C. Imlah	1988 P. Wardell	1993 M. Robinson
1984 M. G. McLaren	1989 D. Scott	1994 D. Christian
1985 E. Gray	1990 C. White	1995 J. Peacocke
1986 R. Russell	1991 R. McRaild	1996 J. Peacocke

GIRL CHAMPIONS OF LONGNIDDRY GOLF CLUB

1983 Caroline Mackay	1988 Lindsay McRaild	1993 Hilary Monaghan
1984 Caroline Mackay	1989 Hilary Monaghan	1994 Gwen Smith
1985 Anne Laird	1990 Hilary Monaghan	1995 Heather Robb
1986 Anne Laird	1991 Hilary Monaghan	1996 Heather Robb
1987 Lindsay McRaild	1992 Hilary Monaghan	

SYKES TROPHY *for Junior Open Annual Handicap Competition*

1969 C Strathearn	1979 S Edmiston	1989 A Campbell
1970 T D Forrest	1980 J G McKinley	1990 J Menzies
1971 G Gill	1981 M McLaren	1991 K Nicolson
1972 M Scoular	1982 D H Burns	1992 M Sneddon
1973 M Scoular	1983 W Main	1993 G McGuff
1974 J L Masterton	1984 G Tait	1994 C Hogg
1975 M Robson	1985 J Hawkins	1995 E Robertson
1976 M D Robson	1986 J Devlin	1996 G Thomson
1977 T W Sheppard	1987 A Oldcorn	
1978 A Morrison	1988 C Inglis	

THE RUSSEL PATRICK TROPHY *For Annual Junior Handicap Competition*

1959 M W Walls	1972 W Colvin	1985 Eric McKay
1960 A P Barr	1973 C Sked	1986 Elliot Gray
1961 M W Walls	1974 C Gass	1987 R McRaild
1962 C Passmore	1975 P O'Neill	1988 Alastair Rennie
1963 A P Barr	1976 P W Reid	1989 Simon Mees
1964 R I Porteous	1977 S Johnston	1990 Richard Stark
1965 C Passmore	1978 G A Pollock	1991 Graham Ferguson
1966 M C Douglas	1979 J G McKinley	1992 Stuart Letchford
1967 G M Fleming	1980 M Yuile	1993 Simon Mees
1968 C G Sked	1981 M Black	1994 E Gray
1969 P Hawkins	1982 D Edwards	1995 M G Lawrie
1970 C R Sked	1983 C Imlah	1996 A Skeldon
1971 C Sked	1984 Elliot Gray	

LONGNIDDRY AND THE EAST LOTHIAN COUNTY CUP

The East Lothian County Cup is thought to be the oldest golf team trophy in the world.

Its origins go back to 1867 when at a meeting in Aberlady on 10th October, golfers under the leadership of Mr Peter Brown, resolved to request Mr Hope of Luffness to permit the game of golf to be played over the Luffness Links. Mr Hope's permission was received within a fortnight. A Golf Club was then formed with Mr Hope as President, and all natives and residents of the County of East Lothian eligible for membership.

During the following year, 1868, Lord Wemyss offered to present a Trophy to the Club. This was gratefully accepted. The Club already had several prizes, so it was proposed that the annual custody of Lord Wemyss' cup should be offered for competition over the Luffness Links to representatives of other Golf Clubs in the County. This suggestion was endorsed with enthusiasm by Lord Wemyss himself and old Tom Morris who had been consulted. Acceptances of the contest were received from five Clubs: Dunbar, East Lothian, Haddington, Tantallon and Thorntree. Those together with Luffness took part in the first competition. Thorntree emerged as winners.

For thirty years the County Cup Contest was held over Luffness Links. Then in 1898 a new golf course was laid out at Craigielaw, and the name of the Club was altered to Kilspindie Golf Club. In the two years required for the new course to mature, the County Cup Competition was held at Muirfield. A little later in 1906 it was decided that three courses should host the event in rotation: namely North Berwick, Gullane and, of course, Kilspindie. The format of the competition has not changed since its inception: it is a straight draw among the entered Clubs. Hole and hole knock-out by double foursomes decides the winners.

In 1928 at the request of the Earl of Wemyss , Longniddry was added to the list of courses, and the Longniddry representatives celebrated the occasion by winning the Trophy.

Sixty-eight years later when Longniddry Golf Club was celebrating its 75th year of existence, its team won the trophy again - its 8th success in the event.

The winning Longniddry teams were as follows:

EAST LOTHIAN COUNTY CUP
LONGNIDDRY WINNERS

1928	A. F. Simpson, H. Pollock, G. C. Killey, W. B. C. Miller	at Longniddry
1934	R. B. Denholm, A. F. Simpson, C. H. Johnston, J. McCredie	at Gullane
1947	J. A. McVey, G. B. Henderson, C. H. Johnston, T. P. Gorrie	at Longniddry
1965	A. Harvey, L. Reilly, A. Barr, P. Burt	at Gullane
1974	T. F. Dickson, J. M. Montgomery, K. Cunningham, M. Scoular	at Dunbar
1986	P. S. Thomson , N. T. Elliot, D. G R. Hunter, A. Harvey	at Longniddry
1990	M. S. Robinson, P. S. Thomson, A. W. Wilson, N. Davidson	at Gullane
1996	D. Hunter, M. Stanton, P. Thomson , S. MacKay	at Muirfield

LONGNIDDRY AND THE WINTER LEAGUE

The Winter League was started in 1965.

Its chief architects were Gus McVey of Longniddry and Graham Proctor of Tantallon.

Five Clubs were involved originally: Bass Rock, Dirleton Castle, Dunbar, Tantallon and Longniddry.

There was only one rule to the observed. That was that the activities of the League should not interfere with the winter golf of ordinary Club members. This meant that the League matches were to be played only when the course concerned would be quiet.

The first secretary of the Winter League was Jacky Johnston from Tantallon and he was followed by Longniddry's Alex Harvey who did the job for many years.

A Longniddry member Mathew Black, JP, presented a handsome trophy for the event. Mathew is a banker and a well known after-dinner speaker, flourishing a cigar like George Burns. There are now 13 or 14 Clubs involved, which makes it difficult to accommodate all the necessary matches whilst still observing the declared single rule. Mathew is quoted as saying, "If I'd known that there were going to be so many Clubs involved, I'd have got a bigger trophy."

The basis of play is that teams of four play on the day with three scores counting. An individual prize is given for the best round on the last day.

Over the years, Longniddry has won the League 8 times. So far it is the only Club to have won the contest four times in succession.

The details are as follows:

Winter League Longniddry Winning Teams

1966/67 – D. Allan, T. G. Gass, R. Anderson, C. McCulloch, A. P. Barr, T. Porteous, D. Baillie, W. J. Weston, A. Harvey, L. Reilly, R. M. Johnston, J. McVey (N P Captain, D. Lowe

1970/71 – C. Passmore, M. H. Dunbar, H. M. McGilvray W. M. Reekie, J. W. Montgomery, F. A. Hall, D. Baillie, A. Harvey, L. Reilly, T. Porteous T. A. Gass

1971/72 – No team recorded

1972/73 – No team recorded

1973/74 – A. Harvey, J. W. Montgomery, W. A. Bell, J. A. McVey, F. A. Hall, W. M. Reekie, W. Weston, T. Porteous, I. B. Jackson, T. G. Gass, T. F. Dickson, L. Reilly, M. Scoular, J. B. Issott. K. Cunningham

1977/78 – W. J. Weston, I. B. Jackson, P. D. Lowe, H. M. McGilvray, J. B. Issott, A. Harvey, F. A. Hall, J. B. Johnston, R. G. Blaikie, W. A. Bell, M. Scoular

1978/79 – No team recorded

1984/85 – K. Cunningham, N. Elliot, M. S. Robinson, A. Harvey, C. McNeill, R. Burge, I. B. Jackson, W. J. Weston, J. A. McVey, P. S. Thomson, B. McPhie, K. Archibald, G. Sked, M. G. McLaren, E. R. Gray, D. G. Hunter.

INTERNATIONAL REPRESENTATION

1. Walker Cup Players	*Date*	*Home Club*	*Venue*
W. B. Torrance	1922	Duddingston	National Links Long Island, U.S.A.
W. D. Smith	1959	Selkirk	Muirfield
R. Russell	1993	Longniddry	Interlacken Edina,Minnesota

Although all three players were Longniddry Club members, Longniddry was Home Club to Raymond Russell only.

W. B. Torrance played for Great Britain in the first Walker Cup match in 1922. One of his opponents in the foursomes was R. J. (Bobby) Jones.

W. D. Smith's singles opponent in 1959 was Jack Nicklaus who won by 5 and 4. It is said that the two players formed a lasting friendship during the match.

Raymond Russell was just 21 when he played for Britain at Interlacken.

2. Curtis Cup Players, (G.B. vs U.S.A.)	*Date*	*Home Club*
Doris Park	1936	Longniddry and others
Mrs E. C. Beddows	1936	Longniddry and others

3. Vagliano Cup, (G.B. vs Europe)	*Date*	*Home Club*
Doris Park	1933	Longniddry and others

4.International Championships

1929	Miss Mary Wood	Ladies Open Championship of India
1945	W D Smith	Indian Open Amateur Championship
1967 & 70	W D Smith	Portuguese Open Amateur Championship
1953	Miss Nancy Jupp	Women's Amateur Championship of Norway
1936, 1950 & 1952	R. W. Burt	Open Championship of Uganda Tanganyika (Tanzania) Kenya

Of course, Jack White, professional at Longniddry 1931/32, was an Open Champion, but he won the trophy in 1904 long before he came to Longniddry Golf Club.

HONORARY MEMBERS

Unfortunately because of the loss of some of the Club's records, the following list of Honorary Members may be incomplete. For example, although no evidence survives, it is surely likely that Doris Park and her cousin 'Katie' were Honorary Members.

	Date of Election		*Date of Election*
The 11th Earl of Wemyss and March	Not recorded	Mr J A McVey	1972
		Mr P Barr	1975
The 12th Earl of Wemyss and March	Not recorded	Dr. R Donaldson	1977
Sir David Kinloch Baronet	Not recorded	Miss S McEwan	1982
George Mitchell	Not recorded	Miss N Scott	1982
Miss Nancy Jupp	Not recorded	Mr F Wood	1982
W S B Williamson	1939	Mr J Ogilvie	1983
Mr W Morris	1946	Mr T Porteous	1983
Mrs C Beddows	1950	Mrs G Durward	1984
Miss Emma Sawers	1950	Mrs M Walls	1984
Mr S Shearlaw	1953	Mrs D Rennie	1984
Mrs S Shearlaw	1953	Mrs A M Barr	1987
Mr R Himsworth	1953	Mr J B Segrott	1990
Mr T Hogg	1954	Mrs W A D Sproul	1990
Mr M F Yorke	Not recorded	Mr D G Herd	1993
Mr A H Lawrence	1964	Miss J J Smith	1994
Mr W H McNeill	1964	Mr G D Dempster	1994
Mrs J J Latta	1964	Mr R G Russell	1994
Mrs Russel Patrick	1967	Miss H Monaghan	1997
Mr T Waugh	1968	Mrs D C Rennie	Not recorded
Mr H M White	1968	Miss K Rose	Not recorded

LONGNIDDRY COURSE RECORDS

Max Faulkner

Kel Nagle

PW Harrison

C Hardin

J Noon

R Russell

Original Course Score Date

1. First reference
R B Denholm 67 before August 1932

2. W C Menzies

4 4 3 4 4 3 4 4 3	33
3 4 3 3 4 4 4 4 4	33

66 August 1938

New Course

3. J Brash (Professional) 75 April 1947
  T A Fairbairn (Amateur) 77 April 1947

4. Name not recorded 68 before June 1952

5. R M Lees (Amateur)

4 4 5 4 4 2 5 3 4	35
3 3 4 3 3 3 3 4 4	30

65 June 1952

6. T Haliburton (Professional) 64 August 1961
  B Hunt (Professional) 64 August 1961

7. M Faulkner (Professional) 64 July 1970

New Course First Extension (12th and 15th)

8. J Montgomery (Amateur) 65 1972

New Course Second Extension (4th and 6th, 19 extra yards)

9. K Nagle (Professional) 64 June 1975

10. C Hardin (Professional Sweden)

3 4 4 4 3 3 3 3 4	31
3 4 4 3 3 4 3 4 4	32

63 July 1987

11. P C Harrison (Professional)

4 3 4 3 3 3 4 4 4	32
3 4 3 3 4 3 4 3 4	31

63 July 1987

13. J Noon (Amateur)

4 4 4 2 4 3 3 4 3	31
4 4 5 2 4 4 2 4 3	32

63 3 September 1994

12. R Russell (Amateur)

4 4 4 3 3 3 5 3 3	32
4 3 4 2 3 4 3 4 4	31

63 10 September 1988

MEMBERS AS AT JUBILEE YEAR

Mr JA Abbie	Mr CG Baillie	Mr FRA Boyd	Mrs KA Clark	Mr GN Davidson
Mr DC Abbot	Mr K Baillie	Dr G Boyd	Mr L Clark	Mr JL Davidson
Mrs H Abernethy	Mr NW Baines	Mr RB Boyd	Mr W Clark	Mrs MC Davidson
Mr WD Abernethy	Mr R Baines	Mr J Boyle	Mr DAM Clarke	Mr N Davidson
Mrs EH Adam	Mr GD Baird	Mr JM Bremner	Mrs B Clarkson	Mr A Davis
Mr CI Aiken	Mr S Baldry	Mr R Bristow	Mr JG Clarkson	Mr AM Dawson
Mr NR Aiken	Mr AG Ballantyne	Mr JB Brotherstone	Mrs E Clegg	Mr N Deans
Mr PD Aiken	Mr GS Ballantyne	Mr JW Brotherstone	Mr GBR Clifford	Mrs A Delaney
Mrs SEM Aiken	Mr A Banks	Miss SE Brotherstone	Mr GS Clifford	Mrs EDN Dempster
Mr R Air	Mr J Banks	Mr A Brown	Mr A Cockburn	Mr GC Dempster
Miss A Aitchison	Mr A Banks Snr	Mrs DC Brown	Mrs NC Coldham	Mr C Denham
Mr AA Aitchison	Mrs CM Barber	Mr DMG Brown	Mr FD Collen	Mr R Denham
Mrs AB Aitchison	Mr J Barber	Mr GD Brown	Mr JA Colthart	Mrs J Denholm
Mr I Aitchison	Mr PA Barber	Mr GF Brown	Mr GS Conacher	Mr A Devlin
Miss LJ Aitchison	Mr SW Barber	Mr JNG Brown	Mr CW Coney	Mr JW Dickson
Miss SL Aitchison	Mrs MH Barclay	Mrs PA Brown	Mr HW Coney	Mrs MM Dickson
Mr A Aithie	Mr G Barnie	Dr D Bruce	Mr AF Conroy	Mr R Dickson
Mr CT Aitken	Mrs AM Barr	Mr DJ Bruce	Mr DS Conroy	Mrs SM Dickson
Mrs I Aitken	Mr VJ Barron	Mrs IB Bruce	Mrs BC Cooper	Mr EAP diMarco
Mr MD Aitken	Miss KE Baxter	Mr RD Bruce	Mr PF Cooper	Mrs J Doherty
Mr TW Aitken	Mr EO Beber	Mr SGA Bryce	Mr JAD Cormie	Mr DB Donaldson
Mr WD Aitken	Mr J Becker	Mr T Brylak	Mr JM Cornwall	Mr JA Donaldson
Mr AN Alcorn	Mrs I Begbie	Mr JS Buchan	Mr P Cornwall	Mr WA Donaldson
Mr DE Allan	Mr RDM Bell	Mr AC Buchanan	Mr B Cowan	Mr DP Douglas
Mr DS Allan	Miss SM Bell	Mr GW Buchanan	Mr RJ Cowan	Dr GH Draffan
Mr DWT Allan	Mr J Bellany	Mrs M Buchanan	Mr DL Cowie	Mrs JR Draffan
Mr JH Allan	Mr IJ Berry	Mr T Buchanan	Mrs RE Cowie	Mis LC Draffan
Mr K Allan	Mrs JR Beveridge	Mr FR Burge	Mrs EA Crawford	Mr BJ Drumm
Miss LJ Allan	Mr MM Bilsland	Mr RWF Burge	Mr JF Crawford	Mrs GB Dryden
Mr CH Anderson	Mr DM Bisset	Mr E Burton	Mr AE Crosbie	Mr J Duffy
Mrs DA Kinloch	Mr M Bisset	Mr PR Burton	Mrs EC Crosbie	Mrs AF Duncan
Anderson	Rev AG Black	Mr SP Burton	Mr JP Cummings	Mr J Duncan
Mr EH Anderson	Miss CM Black	Mr AA Butler	Miss LA Cummings	Mr JR Duncan
Mr HW Anderson	Mr RA Black	Mr DR Butterworth	Mr LJ Cummings	Mr A Duncanson
Miss JE Anderson	Mrs SE Black	Mrs JB Cadzow	Mr D Cunningham	Mrs ES Dundas
Mr K Anderson	Mr GR Blackie	Mr TP Cairns	Mr JB Cunningham	Mrs I Dunlop
Miss KE Anderson	Mr J Blackwood	Mr HS Calder	Mr K Cunningham	Miss AG Durham
Mrs M Anderson	Mr M Blackwood	Mr JR Calder	Mr RF Cunningham	Mr RG Dye
Mrs PE Anderson	Mr H Blaik	Mr N Callendar	Mrs J Cunnison	Mr C Earle
Mr PJ Anderson	Mr R Blaik	Mr R Callendar	Mr JH Cunnison	Mrs JS Earle
Mr RAM Anderson	Mr G Blain	Mrs MT Cameron	Mrs NMM Curran	Mr T Edmond
Mr RD Anderson	Miss HE Blair	Mr RH Cameron	Mr D Currie	Mr DR Edwards
Mr RH Anderson	Mr RJ Blair	Mr CM Campbell	Mr JM Currie	Mr RL Edwards
Mr SH Anderson	Mrs AE Blott	Dr EMJ Campbell	Mr MB Currie	Mrs M Elder
Mr K Anderson DFC	Mr A Blyth	Mrs M Campbell	Mrs MB Currie	Mrs KG Elliott
Mr G Arbuthnott	Mr A Blyth	Miss MD Campbell	Mrs IR Curzon	Mrs M Elliott
Mr AB Archibald	Mr G Bonnar	Mr MI Campbell	Mrs M Curzon	Mr NT Elliott
Mr I Archibald	Mr C Bonnington	Dr JS Cargill	Mrs RE Curzon	Mrs EJ Ellis
Mr J Archibald	Mr G Bonnington	Mr G Carmichael	Mr JH Cuthbert	Mr JDK Ellis
Mrs A Armstrong	Mr BJ Boucher	Mr W Carrol	Mr D Cuthbertson	Mr G Eunson
Mr G Armstrong	Mrs CAW Bowers	Mr WH Chapman	Mrs HE Cuthbertson	Mr TH Fairlie
Mr J Armstrong	Mr P Bowers	Mr RI Chatwin	Mr JR Cuthbertson	Mr BL Falconer
Mr G Arnott	Mr R Bowers	Mr GM Cheyne	MR RC Cuthbertson	Mr GA Falconer
Mr W Atherton	Mr C Bowsher	Mr W Chirnside	Mr BC Dalgleish	Miss J Falconer
Mr D Ayton	Mr Chris Bowsher	Mrs H Chuter	Mr AL Darling	Mrs JM Fallon
Mr AS Baillie	Mr JF Bowsher	Mr IH Chuter	Mrs D Davidson	Mrs MR Fenton

Mr WA Fenton
Mr AAH Ferguson
Mr AG Ferguson
Mrs CI Ferguson
Mr GJ Ferguson
Mr GM Ferguson
Mr GN Ferguson
Mrs J Fiddler
Mr JJ Fiddler
Mr SL Fiddler
Mr RF Finney
Mr T Finney
Mr AFM Fisher
Mr JN Fleming
Mr J Fletcher
Mr CEB Forbes
Mrs HV Forbes
Mr R Forbes
Mrs S Forbes
Mr DJ Ford
Mrs E Ford
Mr G Ford
Mr P Ford
Mr RJ Ford
Miss CL Forrest
Mrs EM Forrest
Mr J Forrest
Mr NR Forrest
Mr D Forrester
Mr DK Forrester
Mrs SE Fraser
Mr RW Fullard
Mr GW Fyfe
Mrs EM Galloway
Mr T Galloway
Mr TH Galloway
Mr J Gardner
Mr W Garrett
Mr TG Gass
Mrs EM Gauld
Mr MWJ Gauld
Mr DR Gemmell
Mrs J Gemmel
Mr A Gibson
Mrs GE Gibson
Mr DR Gillan
Mr DW Gillan
Mr GG Gillan
Mr DJ Gillies
Mrs ECD Gillies
Mr KR Gillies
Miss LM Gillies
Mrs SE Gillies
Mr A Gilmour
Mr DG Gilmour
Mr J Gilmour
Miss R Gilmour
Mr S Gilmour
Mrs W Gilmour
Mr W Gilmour
Mr A Glasgow
Mr E Glasgow
Mr RE Glasgow

Mr R Gledson
Mr J Glover
Mrs MM Glover
Mr BR Goldstraw
Mr AJ Good
Mr RR Goodwin
Mr CC Gordon
Mr DG Gordon
Mrs ME Gordon
Mr W Gordon
Mrs H Gorrie
Mr J Gorrie
Mr JS Gorrie
Mr NJ Gourlay
Mr WWT Gowans
Miss AH Gracie
Ms KJ Gracie
Mrs M Gracie
Mr CF Graham
Mr M Graham
Mr N Graham
Sir N Graham
Mr RM Graham
DR RY Graham
Mr D Grahamslaw
MR A Grandison
Mr K Grandison
Mrs CD Gray
Mrs D Gray
Mr JW Gray
Mrs AM Greig
Mr JA Greig
Mr WR Grieve
Mr DA Guild
Mr G Guiney
Mrs CF Guthrie
Mrs R Haig
Mr TCR Hall
Mr WJL Hall
Mrs Y Halliday
Dr AD Hally
Mrs MR Hally
Miss EL Hamilton
Mr P Hamilton
Mr RT Hamilton
Mr GAM Hammond
Mr AF Harkes
Mrs D Harkess
Mr G Harkess
Mr I Harkess
Mr P Harkess
Mr PA Harkess
Mr J Harkess
Mrs MM Harkness
Mr JRL Harman
Mr DW Harris
Mr F Harris
Mr G Harris
Mr SR Hart
Mr A Harvey
Mr JA Harvey
Mr RW Harvey
Mr CW Harvie

Mr GJ Hastie
Mr J Hastie
Mr RJ Hastie
Mr G Hawthorn
Mr R Hay
Mrs AMG Henderson
Mr GD Henderson
Miss JRHenderson
Mr DG Herd
Mr RJ Herkes
Dr C Hirchhauser
Mr CW Holmes
Mr PC Holmes
Mr A Honeysett
Miss GM Hope
Mr ST Hope
Mr WSC Hope
Mr JB Hopton
Mr D Hubbard
Dr D Hubner
Mrs S Hume
Mr TR Hume
Miss J Hunnam
Mr WJ Hunnam
Mr A Hunter
Mrs CE Hunter
Mr DGR Hunter
Mrs MH Hunter
Miss PJ Hunter
Mr S Hunter
Mr SF Hunter
Mr WB Hunter
Mr GH Hutchison
Mr SJ Hutchison
Mr J Inglis
Mr CB Innes
Mr KW Irons
Miss JM Irving
Mr MS Jack
Mr IB Jackson
Mr RK Jackson
Mr CR Jamieson
Mr G Jamieson
Mr MD Jamieson
Mr JC Jardine
Miss BA Jarron
Mrs NAC Jarron
Mr PH Jarron
Mr T Jarron
Mrs AL Jarvis
Mr BL Jarvis
Mr A Johnston
Mr AB Johnston
Mr B Johnston
Miss J Johnston
Mr JR Johnston
Mrs PJ Johnston
Miss RA Johnston
Mr RJ Johnston
Mr T Johnston
Mr FD Johnstone
Mr BPR Jones
Prof DR Jones

Mrs JA Jones
Mr PW Jones
Mr T Jones
Miss NCM Jupp
Mr EA Keiller
Mrs LI Kelly
Mr P Kelly
Mr AF Kemp
Mr CAM Kemp
Mr T Kemp
Mr J Kennedy
Miss K Kennedy
Mr JC Keppie
Miss Gillian Kerr
Mr J Kerr
Mr RJ Kerr
Mr S Kerr
Mr A King
Mr DT King
Mr D Kinghorn
Mrs AC Kinnear
Mr KW Kinnear
Miss V Kirkland
Mr RS Knight
Mr A Laidlaw
Mr RJ Laidlaw
Mr WB Laidlaw
Miss A Laird
Mrs AA Laird
Mr MSM Laird
Mr SW Laird
Mr G Lamond
Mrs C Lamont
Mr NJ Lang
Mr G Latham
Mr FG Latimer
Mrs JB Latimer
Mr D Lauder
Mr LP Lawns
Mrs EW Lawrie
Mr MG Lawrie
Mrs R Lawrie
Mr T Lawrie
Mr J Learmonth
Mr N Learmonth
Mr R Learmonth
Mr GCB Lees
Mr N Lees
Mrs RM Lees
Mr WB Lees
Mr TA Leigh
Mrs ELM Leitch
Mr G Leitch
Mr SJ Letchford
Mr J Lickrish
Miss ML Lim
Mr I Lindsay
Mr IJ Little
Mr J Little
Mr JD Little
Mr JM Little
Mr JM Little
Mr RJ Little

Mr W Little
Mrs A Livingstone
Mr A Livingstone
Mr MGM Lockhart
Mr RJ Long
Mr A Longmuir
Mr A Lothian
Mr J Low
Mr JD Low
Mr D Lowe
Mr PD Lowe
Mrs RP Lumsden
Mr AC Lyall
Mr A Lyle
Mr CF MacDonald
Mrs H MacFarlane
Mr C MacGregor
Mr A MacKay
Mr AG MacKay
Mr AG MacKay
Mr AS MacKay
Mrs DH MacKay
Mr EG MacKay
Mr SM MacKay
Mr AM Mackechnie
Mrs JW Mackechnie
Mr CJ Mackechnie
Mr JAM MacKenzie
Mrs PC MacKenzie
Mr J MacLean
Mrs M MacLean
Mr MA MacLean
Mr NJ MacLean
Mr AR MacPherson
Mrs E MacRaild
Mr J MacRaild
Miss L MacRaild
Mr RJ MacRaild
Mr JAC Macfarlane
Mr D Maciver
Mrs F Maciver
Mr KAI Mack
Mr AI Mackay
Mrs J Mackay
Mrs OAD Mackay
Mrs V Mackenzie
Mr F Malcolm
Mr IG Malcolm
Mr JP Malcolm
Mrs LI Malcolm
Mr WG Malcolm
Mrs DM Marsh
Mr GR Marshall
Mr J Marshall
Mr T Marshall
Mrs CM Martin
Miss JC Martin
Mr K Martin
Mr WW Martin
Mr F Mason
Mr James Mason
Mr John Mason
Mr KW Mason

Mr C Mather
Mr R Mathie
Mr R Matthews
Mr LS Matthews
Mr PG May
Mr WB McAinsh
Mr A McAlpine
Mr J McBride
Mrs M McClure
Mr SDJ McClure
Mr WL McClure
Mr AO McCran
Mrs LA McCusker
Mr WS McDade
Mr JA McDougall
Mr JD McDougall
Mr A McEwan
Mrs JC McEwan
Mr JA McEwan
Mr HM McGilvray
Mrs CA McGregor
Mr JD McGregor
Mrs JF McGregor
Mrs D McInroy
Mr GD McIntosh
Mrs MB McIntosh
Mr N McIntosh
Mr D McIntyre
Mrs AL McKay
Mr D McKay
Mr R McKay
Mr F McKenzie
Mr G McKenzie
Mr JJ McKenzie
Mr J McKimmie
Mr GJ McKinlay
Mr RG McKinlay
Mr DT McKinnon
Mr R McKirdy
Mr DG McKnight
Miss FE McKnight
Dr K McLean
Mr M McLean
Mr CHS McLennan
Mr A McLeod
Mr G McLeod
Mr N McLeod
Mr A McMurray
Mrs HS McNeil
Mr JB McNeil
Mr B McNeill
Mr C McNeill
Mr ERW McNeill
Mr JB McNeill
Mrs JD McNeill
Mr JR McNeill
Mr WH McNeill
Mrs L McNicoll
Mr B McPhee
Mr JG McPhee
Mr JJ McPhee
Mr MM McPhee
Mr R McRobbie

Mr S McRobbie
Miss C Medine
Mr S Mees
Mrs WH Mees
Mr AJ Meikle
Mrs M Mellor
Mr B Menzies
Mr AJ Merriman
Prof GHW Milburn
Mr HJ Milburn
Mrs JM Milburn
Mr RC Millar
Mr IJ Miller
Mr JT Miller
Mrs SM Miller
Mr TS Miller
Mr GR Milligan
Mr R Milligan
Miss E Milne
Mr TA Milne
Mr AD Mitchell
Mrs AM Mitchell
Mr JB Mitchell
Mr JR Mitchell
Mrs MJ Mitchell
Mr D Moffat
Mr MR Molan
Mrs E Monaghan
Miss H Monaghan
Mrs C Moodie
Mr PH Moodie
Mrs AM Morgan
Mrs CW Morgan
Mr GS Morgan
Miss J Morgan
Mr RT Morris
Mr DR Morrison
Mr JG Morrison
Mrs JR Morrison
Mrs P Morrison
Mr JT Morton
Mrs P Mould
Mr WC Mould
Mr A Muir
Mr B Muir
Mr C Muir
Mr D Mulholland
Mr A Munro
Mr J Murdoch
Mr GA Murphy
Mr AD Murray
Mr JW Murray
Mr SD Murray
Mr J Mutch CBE
Mr DJ Naughton
Mrs SI Naylor
Mr AQ Neil
Mr JM Neilands
Mr C Neill
Mr DA Nicholson
Mr RP Nicol
Mr AC Nicoll
Mrs EM Nicoll

Mrs H Nicoll
Mr MA Nicoll
Mr JD Nisbet
Mr R Nisbet
Mrs C Nixon
Mr JD Noble
Mr G O'Connor
Mrs S O'Connor
Mr PJR O'Malley
Mr A Ogg
Mr GR Paisley
Mrs PM Paisley
Mr G Palmer
Miss FSM Park
Mr GAS Park
Mr GL Parkinson
Mr CD Paterson
Miss CEM Paterson
Mr CG Paterson
Mrs CMM Paterson
Mr JM Paterson
Mr ERL Paton
Mr WG Patterson
Mr B Paxton
Mr J Peace
Mr J Peacocke
Mr PK Peacocke
Mr R Peacocke
Mr G Pearce
Mr CMcF Peebles
Mr RW Penman
Mrs E Pennykid
Mr KHC Pennykid
Mr GW Pettigrew
Mr RG Pettigrew
Mr DMR Phillips
Miss EC Phimister
Miss IG Phimister
Mrs MA Phin
Mr M Pisacane
Mr JE Pollington
Mr G Pollock
Mrs JM Pollock
Mr ED Poole
Mr DT Porteous
Mrs I Porteous
Mr T Porteous
Mr RW Potts
Mr RF Pow
Mr F Prain
Mrs JDM Prain
Mr WC Price
Mrs EAE Quinn
Mr WW Raeburn
Mr RK Rain
Mr D Ramage
Mr HD Ramage
Mr J Ramage
Mr SA Ramage
Mrs FDS Ramos
Mr BW Rawle
Mrs EM Rawle
Mr A Ray

Mrs AM Ray
Dr PJ Reading
Mrs T Reekie
Mr WM Reekie
Mr AN Reid
Mr GG Reid
Mr JL Reid
Mr PW Reid
Mr WJ Reid
Mr L Reilly
Mr LJ Reilly
Mrs A Rennie
Mr AB Rennie
Mrs DC Rennie
Mr DL Rennie
Mr GC Rennie
Mrs KS Renouf
Mr RW Renton
Mrs JG Reynolds
Miss LJ Reynolds
Mr SW Reynolds
Mr WS Reynolds
Mr AS Rhead
Mr A Richardson
Mr AP Richardson
Mrs R Richardson
Miss SM Richardson
Mr STR Riddell
Mr A Robb
Miss HL Robb
Mrs LM Robb
Mr A Roberts
Mr AP Robertson
Mrs C Robertson
Mr C Robertson
Mr CM Robertson
Mr DN Robertson
Miss FM Robertson
Mr HB Robertson
Mr I Robertson
Mr IA Robertson
Mr JIR Robertson
Mr LMR Robertson
Mrs MT Robertson
Miss TM Robertson
Mr MJ Robinson
Mr MS Robinson
Mr DI Robson
Mr IH Rolland
Mr D Rose
Dr E Rose
Miss K Rose
Miss SB Rose
Mrs AD Ross
Mr AD Ross
Mr JM Ross
Mr KD Ross
Mr MC Roynon-
Jones
Mr AH Russell
Mr K Russell
Mr RA Russell
Mr RG Russell

Mr S Russell
Mr RW Salter
Mr AM Sanders
Mrs JE Sanderson
Mr B Sandilands
Mr BA Sandilands
Mr CJ Scott
Mr D Scott
Mr DR Scott
Miss H Scott
Mr J Scott
Mr JR Scott
Mr JR Scott
Mr L Scott
Mrs M Scott
Dr MM Scott
Mr P Scott
Mr A Scoular
Mr JD Scoular
Mr R Scoular
Mr R Scoular Jnr
Mr J Seawright
Mr PA Seawright
Mr JD Shalliday
Mr DJ Shand
Mr D Sharp
Mrs JK Sharp
Mr RR Sharp
Mr DA Shearer
Ms MA Shearer
Mr JO Shedden
Mr JO Shedden
Mr GD Shepherd
Mr S Sherlock
Mr CH Simpson
Miss JF Simpson
Mr CW Sinclair
Mr GJ Sinclair
Mr M Sinclair
Mr IA Skeldon
Mr WA Skeldon
Mr J Slimon
Mr JH Small
Mr DE Smart
Mrs MS Smart
Mrs C Smillie
Mr JS Smillie
Mr A Smith
Mr AFB Smith
Mr AH Smith
Mr AJ Smith
Mr BH Smith
Mr C Smith
Mr C Smith
Mr D Smith
Mr DG Smith
Dr DM Smith
Mr DPG Smith
Mrs EJFD Smith
Mr F Smith
Mr G Smith
Mr GA Smith
Miss GJ Smith

Mr H Smith
Mr I Smith
Miss JS Smith
Miss JW Smith
Mr K Smith
Mr KD Smith
Mrs LSE Smith
Mr M Smith
Miss MS Smith
Mr RO Smith
Mr WB Smith
Mr WD Smith
Mr JD Sommerville
Mr M Souness
Mrs DS Sproul
Mr M Stanton
Mr PJ Stanton
Mr AM Stanway
Mr R Stark
Mr IM Steedman
Mr J Stein
Mrs P Stein
Mr P Stein
Mr R Stevenson
Mr WG Stevenson
Mr AL Stewart
Mrs E Stewart
Mr GM Stewart
Mr George M Stewart
Mr JF Stewart
Mrs R Stewart
Mr DA Stirling
Mr EA Stirling
Mr ST Storrie
Mr WJ Stovin
Mr A Strachan
Mr AA Strachan
Mr AG Strachan
Mrs P Strachan
Mr P Strachan
Mr J Stretton
Mr GWJ Studholme
Mr S Sullivan
Mr GN Summers

Mr N Summers
Mrs A Sutherland
Mr JD Sutherland
Mr JDG Sutherland
Mrs JE Sutherland
Mr JR Sutherland
Mr MJ Sutherland
Mr WM Swan
Mr AJ Sword
Mr IP Sword
Mr BA Szifris
Mr I Tait
Mr AR Tapp
Mr A Taylor
Mrs EA Taylor
Mr G Taylor
Mr DCA Thain
Mr L Thain
Mr E Thayne
Mr R Thomas
Mr TG Thomas
Mr PK Thompson
Mr A Thomson
Mr AJ Thomson
Mr AM Thomson
Mr Angus Thomson
Mr C Thomson
Miss CJM Thomson
Mrs EG Thomson
Mr IDF Thomson
Mr JC Thomson
Mr JW Thomson
Mr James Thomson
Mr K Thomson
Mr L Thomson
Mrs M Thomson
Mrs PS Thomson
Mr R Thomson
Mr RG Thomson
Mr T Thomson
Mr W Thomson
Mrs WI Thomson
Mr WJ Thomson
Mr AG Thorburn

Mr G Thorburn
Mr G Thorburn
Mr RB Thorburn
Mr WS Tiffney
Miss CR Toland
Miss AH Torbet
Mr FSJ Trotter
Mr CTB Tulloch
Mr EH Turnbull
Mr GC Turner
Mr GG Turner
Mr S Turner
Mr AC Tweedie
Mr WA Tweedie
Mr B Tyson
Mr GN Urquhart
Mr KW Waitt
Mr WT Waitt
Mrs JM Wake
Mr P Walker
Mr TM Walker
Mrs A Wallace
Mr GT Wallace
Mr HW Wallace
Mrs M Walls
Mr J Walshe
Mr D Wardell
Mr JPH Wardlaw
Mr AJ Ware
Miss HA Warne
Mr MS Wason
Mr A Watson
Mr B Watson
Mr J Watson
Mr RI Watson
Mr W Watson
Mr GN Watt
Mr IA Watt
Mr JB Watt
Mr MB Waugh
Mr MG Waugh
Mr F Webb
Dr RWJ Webster
Lord Wemyss

Mr GW Weston
Mr WJ Weston
Mrs LD Whillans
Mr CK White
Mrs MM White
Mrs SM White
Mr AAG Whitelaw
Mr GT Whitelaw
Mrs JS Whitelaw
Mr K Whitson
Mrs H Whittington
Prof HW Whittington
Mr RH Whitworth
Mr AC Wilkie
Mr J Williams
Mr SB Williamson
Mr AW Wilson
Mr J Wilson
Mr MR Wilson
Mrs SM Wilson
Mr SH Winter
Mr C Wiseman
Mrs R Wiseman
Mr JG Wishart
Mr DS Wojtacha
Mr AM Wood
Mr C Wood
Mr FC Wood
Mr IJ Wood
Miss LK Wood
Mr MM Wood
Dr P Wood
Miss SJ Wood
Mr TJ Woolley
Mr J Wybar
Mr DR Wyllie
Mr AG Young
Mr DA Young
Mr DM Young
Mr HG Young
Mr R Young
Mr AEJ Youngs
Mr RD Yule
Mr SM Yule

SUPPLEMENTARY LIST

Mrs CM Abbot
Mr RH Abernethy
Miss LJ Aitchison
Mr GS Anderson
Miss GS Binnie
Mr K Bonnington
Mr EK Brechin
Mrs J Clark
Mr SP Conroy
Mr MJ Devine
Mr MW Devlin
Mr DJ Dickson
Mr Moray Gauld
Mr A Hall
Mr Dale W Harris
Mr AJ Holliman
Mr SJM Holmes
Mr A McEwan
Miss LM MacKay
Mr JG MacKenzie
Mrs DA McLeod
Miss M McNeill
Mr B Marchbank
Mr AM Masson
Mr GM Medine
Mr RAJ Muir
Miss RE O'Connor
Mr K Pettigrew
Mr AB Purves
Mr DA Roberts
Mr PL Ruthven
Mrs M Scoular
Mr GF Stewart
Ms VS Strachan
Mr JF Welch
Ms C White
M BJ Whittington
Miss L Wiseman